Franciscan Leadership in Ministry

Spirit and Life: A Journal of Contemporary Franciscanism serves as a vehicle for the publication of papers presented at various conferences, symposia, and/or workshops that seek to bring Franciscan tradition into creative dialogue with contemporary theology, philosophy, psychology, and history. The journal is an occasional publication. During the fiftieth anniversary year of The Franciscan Institute (1991), the publication of this journal was a refounding of an earlier Franciscan Institute Series entitled *Spirit and Life* established in 1948 by the Reverend Philotheus Boehner, O.F.M., one of the co-founders and first director of The Franciscan Institute.

As is explained in greater detail in the Foreword, the papers contained in this volume arose from the Franciscan Leadership Seminar, a project of corporate renewal organized by the Holy Name Province of the Order of Friars Minor.

This book was designed and typeset by Robert Lunsford and printed by Professional Graphics Printing Co., Laurel, Maryland.

ISBN 1-57659-132-8

Address all correspondence to:
    The Franciscan Institute
    St. Bonaventure Universiy
    St. Bonaventure, NY 14778

Spirit and Life

A Journal of Contemporary Franciscanism

Volume 7   *1997*

Franciscan Leadership in Ministry

Foundations in History, Theology, and Spirituality

Edited by
Anthony Carrozzo, O.F.M.
Vincent Cushing, O.F.M.
Kenneth Himes, O.F.M.

Contents

Abbreviations v

Foreword vi

A Note on the Authors viii

1   Introduction: The Contexts for Pastoral Leadership, ... 1
     by Anthony Carrozzo, O.F.M., Vincent Cushing, O.F.M.,
     and Kenneth Himes, O.F.M

2   Franciscan Tradition as a Wisdom Tradition, ... 27
     by Zachary Hayes, O.F.M.

3   Christology—Cosmology, by Zachary Hayes, O.F.M. 41

4   Human Dignity in the Theology of St. Bonaventure, ... 59
     by Thomas A. Shannon

5   Ministry, Sacramentality, and Symbolism, ... 79
     by John Burkhard, O.F.M. Conv.

6   Fraternity and Sorority in Franciscan Leadership, ... 97
     by Helen Rolfson, O.S.F.

7   Contemporary Ecclesiology and the Franciscan Tradition, ... 113
        by William McConville, O.F.M.

8   Hermitage or Marketplace? 125
        The Search for an Authentic Franciscan Locus in the World,
        by Michael F. Cusato, O.F.M.

9   Contemplation and Compassion: 149
        A Franciscan Ministerial Spirituality,
        by Michael W. Blastic, O.F.M. Conv.

10 "Blessed Are They Who Mourn": 179
        Tears, Compunction, and Forgiveness,
        by Elizabeth A. Dreyer

11 Conflict and Power: 205
        The Retrieval of Franciscan Spirituality
        for the Contemporary Pastoral Leader,
        by Joseph P. Chinnici, O.F.M

12 The Franciscan Tradition: 227
        Strangers and Pilgrims,
        by Mary Meany

Abbreviations
Franciscan Sources Cited in this Volume

Writings of Saint Francis

Adm	*Admonitions*
EpFidI	*First Version of Letter to the Faithful*
EpFidII	*Second Version of Letter to the Faithful*
EpLeo	*Letter to Brother Leo*
EpMin	*Letter to a Minister*
EpOrd	*Letter to the Entire Order*
EpRect	*Letter to the Rulers of the Peoples*
FormViv	*Form of Life for St. Clare*
RegB	*Later Rule*
RegNB	*Earlier Rule*
SalVirt	*Salutation of the Virtues*
Test	*Testament of Francis*

Other Early Franciscan Sources

1Cel	*First Life of St. Francis by Thomas of Celano*
2Cel	*Second Life of St. Francis by Thomas of Celano*
3Cel	*Treatise on the Miracles by Thomas of Celano*
Fior	*Fioretti*
LegCl	*Legend of Clare*
LP	*Legend of Perugia*
L3S	*Legend of the Three Companions*
Proc	*Acts of the Process of Canonization of St. Clare*
RegCl	*Rule of Clare*
SP	*Mirror of Perfection*
TestCl	*Testament of Clare*
3EpAg	*Clare's Third Letter to Agnes*
4EpAg	*Clare's Fourth Letter to Agnes*

Works of Bonaventure

DM	*The Disciple and the Master: Sermons on St. Francis,* translated by Eric Doyle
LM	*Major Life of St. Francis*
RF	*Rooted in Faith: Homilies to a Contemporary World,* translated by Marigwen Schumacher
Sent	*Commentaries on the Sentences of Peter Lombard*
SJ	*The Soul's Journey into God*

Foreword

This collection of essays has been long in the making. In March 1993 a group of scholars came together to discuss pastoral leadership within the Franciscan tradition. The gathering was convoked under the auspices of the provincial administration of Holy Name Province of the Order of Friars Minor and funded by a grant from the Mae Bonfils Foundation of Denver, Colorado. Holy Name Province, through the direction of Anthony Carrozzo, O.F.M., then minister provincial, had begun a program of corporate renewal under the heading of "Refounding Through Ministry." Vincent Cushing, O.F.M., and Kenneth Himes, O.F.M, served on the provincial council at the time the renewal process was begun. The administration of the province thought it would be important to reflect upon the intellectual foundations for "refounding" and the idea of the Denver meeting was born.

As the reader of this volume will see, it was a diverse group of individuals who first met in Denver in 1993. Each person came with his or her own reading of the Franciscan tradition and a distinctive understanding of the role of the Franciscan movement within the broader Christian tradition. The participants represented a range of theological competencies: systematic theology, ecclesiology, sacramental theology, moral theology, church history, spirituality, Franciscan studies. What united the diverse group was the excellence of their work and their interest in reflecting seriously upon how the Franciscan tradition might serve as a resource for the ongoing renewal of gospel life in our time.

At the initial meeting, the participants, in what came to be called the "Franciscan Leadership Seminar," analyzed what they thought were crucial areas of concern for developing an approach to leadership with a Franciscan spirit. Each member then decided upon a topic for a paper to be written that would examine one of the areas of concern. One year later, in March 1994, after a first draft of each text had been distributed, the principals reconvened in Denver to discuss the paper and suggest possible revisions to one another's work.

In March 1995 the seminar members met a third and final time. They were joined by a group of twenty Franciscan friars of Holy Name Province, including the entire provincial administration, in a weekend of lively exchange on the material of the papers. As a result of the three-year-long seminar the authors were afforded a deliberate and interactive process that permitted writing and rewriting after spirited and thoughtful conversation. The papers contained in this volume are the end result of the process. We believe each paper can be read with profit on its own and that the sum total of the contributions makes for a wide-ranging and richly informative study of a theology and spirituality for Franciscan pastoral leadership.

All that remains for us is to thank those who made the seminar and this volume possible. First, our gratitude goes to the contributors for their participation in the seminar project. Second, we are grateful to Nancy Steckel, whose organizational skill made the smooth running of the seminar possible. Third, we wish to acknowledge publicly the generosity of the Mae Bonfils Trust. Finally, for the completion of this volume in its present form we are indebted to William R. MacKaye for his editing skills and to Edward Coughlin, O.F.M., for his patience in awaiting the completion of this volume and his kindness in publishing it under the auspices of The Franciscan Institute of St. Bonaventure University.

Anthony Carrozzo, O.F.M.
Vincent Cushing, O.F.M.
Kenneth Himes, O.F.M.

A Note on the Authors

Father Michael Blastic, O.F.M. Conv., earned his doctorate at St. Louis University. Formerly on the faculty of the Washington Theological Union, he now teaches on the faculty of the Franciscan Institute at St. Bonaventure University. A popular lecturer, Father Blastic has research interests in the early origins of the Franciscan Order as well as in the implications of the Franciscan tradition for contemporary issues of justice, peace, and the environment.

Father John Burkhard, O.F.M. Conv., teaches at the Washington Theological Union. He has interests in foundational theology, ecclesiology, ministry, and ecumenical and interreligious dialogue. He completed graduate studies at the Collegium Canisianum, Innsbruck, Austria, receiving an S.T.L., and earned his Ph.D at the University of Strasbourg, France. Father Burkhard taught at St. Anthony-on-Hudson Seminary in Rensselaer, New York, where he served as academic dean and later as president.

Father Joseph Chinnici, O.F.M., earned his D.Phil. in ecclesiastical history from Oxford University. Author of numerous articles and books, he has taught on the faculty of the Franciscan School of Theology at the Graduate Theological Union in Berkeley, California. Formerly provincial minister of the Province of Santa Barbara of the Order of Friars Minor, Father Chinnici has also taught on the faculty of the Franciscan Institute at St. Bonaventure University.

Father Michael Cusato, O.F.M., currently serves as a member of the provincial council of Sacred Heart Province of the Order of Friars Minor. Formerly on the faculty of Siena College, Father Cusato holds a doctorate in history from the University of Paris IV-Sorbonne. At present he teaches at the divinity school of the University of St. Thomas in St. Paul, Minnesota. As a specialist in medieval religious history he has particular expertise in the history of the Franciscan Order. Author of several articles in scholarly journals, he is preparing for publication a book on the renunciation of power as a major theme of thirteenth-century Franciscan history.

Dr. Elizabeth Dreyer is a well-known author and lecturer on spirituality. Her writings have examined the theology of grace, medieval women mystics, lay spirituality, and the role of affectivity in Bonaventure. She holds a doctorate from Marquette University and has served on the faculties of several institutions including the Catholic University of America and the Washington Theological Union. She and her husband live in Hamden, Connecticut.

Father Zachary Hayes, O.F.M., is professor of systematic theology at the Catholic Theological Union in Chicago, Illinois. He is a member of Sacred Heart Province of the Order of Friars Minor. A noted Bonaventure scholar, Father Hayes is a past recipient of the John Courtney Murray Award of the Catholic Theological Society of America. He earned his doctorate at the University of Bonn, Germany.

Father William McConville, O.F.M., is on the faculty of Siena College in Loudonville, New York. A member of Holy Name Province of the Order of Friars Minor, he received his doctorate from Vanderbilt University. Father McConville served on the faculties of St. Bonaventure University and the Washington Theological Union before becoming president of Siena College. Upon leaving Siena's presidency, he returned to full-time teaching. His interests focus on ecclesiology, mission studies, and foundational theology.

Dr. Mary Meany is associate professor and former chair of the Department of Religious Studies at Siena College. With a Ph.D. from Fordham University, she initiated a popular course on the Franciscan tradition at Siena. Dr. Meany is an active participant in the American Academy of Religion and the International Congress on Medieval Studies. She and her family live in Clifton Park, New York.

Sister Helen Rolfson, O.S.F., is a Rochester (Minnesota) Franciscan, currently serving as associate professor of theology at St. John's University, Collegeville, Minnesota. She is a student of liturgy, spirituality, and monasticism, and has translated a number of medieval Flemish spiritual texts. For more than a decade she has been a member of the international ecumenical dialogue between the Roman Catholic Church and the classic Pentecostals.

Dr. Thomas Shannon is professor in the Department of Humanities at Worcester Polytechnic Institute in Worcester, Massachusetts. Professor Shannon, who received his doctorate from Boston University, is an active participant in many of the ethical debates surrounding health care and biological research. His extensive writings include two books and several articles that examine the ethical theory of John Duns Scotus. Professor Shannon lives with his wife and children in Worcester, Massachusetts.

Father Anthony Carrozzo, O.F.M., Father Vincent Cushing, O.F.M., and Father Kenneth Himes, O.F.M., the conveners of the Refounding Seminar and chief editors of this volume, are all members of Holy Name Province of the Order of Friars Minor, which sponsored the seminar. Father Carrozzo, who has a D.Min. from the Jesuit School of Theology at Berkeley, California, is director of the Franciscan Institute at St. Bonaventure University and vice president of the university. Father Cushing, president of the Washington Theological Union, was the first Catholic president of the Association of Theological Schools in the United States and Canada. His S.T.D. was awarded by the Catholic University of America. Father Himes, who earned his Ph.D. at Duke University, is professor of moral theology at the Washington Theological Union. He served on the board of directors of the Catholic Theological Society of America and has been a visiting faculty member at the University of Virginia, Notre Dame University, Howard University Divinity School, and Boston College.

1

Introduction:
The Contexts for Pastoral Leadership

Anthony Carrozzo, O.F.M.
Vincent Cushing, O.F.M.
Kenneth Himes, O.F.M.

Theories of ministry can be generic, that is, there can be essays on the theology of ministry that stay at a fairly broad level of generalization without delving into the particulars of ministry in a given time and place. But the practice of ministry must be context-specific, that is, ministry can only be done in a given locale, with and for a particular people, addressing a certain set of obstacles and opportunities. At the heart of Franciscan ministry is the call to evangelization (*General Constitutions of the Order of Friars Minor*, Nos. 83-85). And the work of evangelization must penetrate not only human hearts but the cultures within which human persons live (Paul VI, "Evangelii Nuntiandi," No. 20). That requires attention to the signs of the times according to the Second Vatican Council ("Gaudium et Spes," No. 4). As John Paul II reminds us in "Centesimus Annus," No. 3, it is the duty of pastors "to give careful consideration to current events in order to discern the new requirements of evangelization." We can only preach and witness to the gospel if we understand the environment in which we are living. Otherwise our words and actions, while well-meaning, may appear unresponsive to the hopes and fears of the people we serve. It is necessary, then, for our later reflections to examine, at the outset, the context of our ministry. We need to situate ourselves in a specific historical setting as we undertake the task of discussing pastoral leadership in the Franciscan tradition.

There are three angles of vision on our context to be examined: 1) a reflection on the present situation within the United States of religious life in general and Franciscan life in particular, with reference to our own internal reform (Anthony Carrozzo); 2) an assessment of the vocation of the Franciscan movement in the contemporary situation of the Catholic church (Vincent Cushing); and 3) a broad sketch of the ministerial setting provided by the culture of American society (Kenneth Himes).

I. Religious Life in the United States
Anthony Carrozzo, O.F.M.

In perusing "Perfectae Caritatis," I hardly recognize it as the radical document that once uprooted religious life. Its emphasis on the charism of the founder, the relational role of authority, and the gifts and talents of the individual are now commonly accepted. The document has provided endless insights, some refreshing, some frightening. Among the refreshments are new appreciation for the founding charism, renewed interest in the gospel, and reemphasis on caring for the world; yet these themes, especially the return to roots, resulted in a paradoxical rootlessness. On the negative side is our frightfully obvious failure to recruit new vocations to replace the present aging membership; the rampant individualism often putting members at odds with leaders; and frequent leadership burn-out. Such post-Vatican II developments are carefully traced in studies like the report by David Nygren and Miriam Ukeritis; the spiritual and theological dimensions are revealed in commentaries like Leddy's, Arbuckle's, and Schneider's.[1]

Current trends in religious life are certainly evident among contemporary Franciscans. Our present problem is to evaluate the trends, not in the light of the founding years alone but illuminated by the entire tradition, which is rich in unique and potentially energizing perspectives. Through seven-plus centuries we have experienced countless paradigm shifts created, whether consciously or not, by Franciscan renewalists and refounders. Their experiences, situated in diverse times and cultures, were not unlike our own. Their debates about world and institutions, about personhood and rela-

---

[1] David Nygren, C.M., and Miriam Ukeritis, C.S.J., "The Future of Religious Orders in the United States," Origins 24 (September 1992); Gerald A. Arbuckle, S.M., *Out of Chaos* (New York: Paulist Press, 1988); Mary Jo Leddy, *Reweaving Religious Life: Beyond the Liberal Model* (Mystic, Connecticut: Twenty-Third Publications, 1990); Sandra Schneiders, I.H.M., *New Wineskins: Re-imaging Religious Life Today* (New York: Paulist Press, 1986).

tionships (mystical or human), though linguistically different, were also like ours. And they are still valuable to today's renewalists and refounders, who continue looking for help with the same ageless questions.

Before looking at how these traditional and contemporary issues overlap, we must delve into the question: What is the difference between renewal and refounding? Renewal points to restoring the best of the past in present circumstances, while refounding searches out new paradigms to help dreamers create a new vision of Franciscan life. Renewalists, then, are the tradition's storytellers while refounders are its dreamers. The tradition needs both: if we have only storytellers we will live in the past; if we have only dreamers we will be founding a new religious order instead of refounding Franciscan life. So both concepts merit attention.

Renewal began with the call of Vatican II to return to the charism of our founders. Though Pius XI had made the same call years before, a call that went unheeded, this time Franciscans responded almost immediately. We returned to our sources (lugging around everywhere the tome of Franciscana known simply as the *Omnibus*), studied our various strains and traditions, and worked hard to recapture a spark of the pristine zeal and enthusiasm. After some years of this, we came to realize two overriding facts: first, that Clare was just as significant to our founding experience as Francis, and second, that the founding experience did not complete the picture of Franciscan life (even though some still argue that practically everything degenerated after Francis and Clare).

Despite that, Franciscans are fortunate to possess a priceless written heritage encasing its traditions. It is a remarkable series of personal stories told from various perspectives by real men and women who actually lived the mendicant experience and still share with us their visions. Sometimes they reveal more of themselves than of the charism, so the sum of the parts does not add up to anything approaching a how-to-be-a-Franciscan manual. Nonetheless, the stories are a magnificent historical treasure of great usefulness to Franciscan self-awareness. But they also contain an inherent danger to which most of us eventually succumbed when we hitched on to our favorite accounts, retold them in our own language, and argued as if they alone gave the perspective for renewal. Old battles raged as if never fought before. Giles and Bonaventure, Leo and Elias lived again! Some of us looked to renewal as a means of restoring the old order; others, as a means of founding something new. But each seemed intent on his or her individual viewpoint.

Perhaps that was the most telling aspect of Franciscan renewal: the individual, the premise being that individual conversion would lead to renewal of Franciscan life. This emphasis was quite justified by the sources. What other founder said it more explicitly than Francis to Leo?: "In whatever way it seems best to you to please the Lord God and to follow his footsteps and his poverty, do this with the blessing of God and my obedience."[2]

The Dilemma of American Franciscans

Today's American Franciscans grew up in a secular society where individual human rights are a top priority. Entering religious life, we brought with us this reverence for the individual and factored it into our commitment to the gospel life, christening it "the Franciscan creed of individualism." The challenge to return to our roots may have produced an unworthy byproduct: Franciscanized individualism.

But as we battled American, Franciscanized individualism, we may have lost a Franciscan sense of the intrinsic worth of the individual. Respect for the individual is evident in Francis's care for each member, in Bonaventure's journey into God, and particularly in the theological spirituality of John Duns Scotus. Duns Scotus provides us with a most positive notion of the individual, suggesting that, in all species, it is the individual who is chosen by God. He writes: "It is the individual that is primarily intended by God."[3] Certainly this insight gains momentum in his notion of *haecceitas*, which he defines as that "element that makes this individual be this particular individual and no other."[4] It is, then, the "thisness" rendering a thing unique.

Bonaventure, on the other hand, places more emphasis on the person, teaching that the person is a word of God who speaks of God. He writes: "'Person' is something additional to the individual, since the individual, determined by matter, possesses too little perfection."[5]

---

[2] *EpLeo.*
[3] Shannon, 1994
[4] Shannon, 1994.
[5] *II Sent*, d. 3, art. 2, q. 3; see also ibid., q. 2.

Avoiding this intriguing scholastic debate, it may be best in these individualistic days to accept the insights of Thomas Merton, that Franciscan-influenced and influencing prophet of contemporary religious life, who said that the true self is discovered in the person while the false self is discovered through the individual. He thus prodded us to rescue the person from the individual, for the individual craves self-fulfillment while the person searches for evangelical self-forgetfulness.[6]

Francis of Osuna, a fifteenth-century Spanish friar, expressed this distinction like this: "Entering into yourself is the beginning of rising above yourself."[7] In other words, by remaining within ourselves we succumb to individualism; by rising above ourselves from the experience of entering into ourselves, we become persons in Christ. In this sense, our Franciscan tradition does not glorify individualism but rather honors the dignity of the person. It is the person who gains so much freedom from the Rule of 1223. It is Leo-the-person whom Francis loves and supports and encourages to make the gospel-way into a freedom-walk. It is Duns Scotus's "thisness" that respects and honors each person's uniqueness and dignity.

"Perfectae Caritatis" addressed personal dignity within the context of authority, but our societal values easily translated the document's intent into a form of individualism that now and again invaded religious life, to the serious detriment of relationships within the community. What an anomaly! We need only recall the many affiliative candidates who came to community life in a self-defeating search for fulfillment of individualistic needs rather than motivated to become a Christ-centered person who enters into relationships as the only way "to subsist in love."[8]

As individualism rather than personhood permeates religious life, renewal becomes more and more narcissistic, since it escalates fraternal relationships as a primary affiliative value while downgrading the sense of mission and ministry. Here again, the Franciscan heritage seems to make us particularly prone to this error of opting for fraternity over ministry. However, the two are not at odds. Rather they are a wonderful example of Bonaventure's "coincidences of opposites": seemingly opposed on the surface, they coincide when viewed through the lens of contemplation.

---

[6] Merton, 1972: passim.
[7] Osuna, 1981: p. 266.
[8] Merton, 1972: p. 53.

Francis's genius as a founder can be conceptualized in a fraternity-ministry spiral grounded in the brotherly relationship between Jesus and himself. With Christ as the axis, the spiral curves outward to gather into itself all creatures great and small, as expressed in Francis's mystical masterpiece the "Canticle of Creation." All taken together form a creational system of brotherhood and sisterhood, since the fraternal bond, the source of our true identity, arises from relationship to Christ, marking our fraternity as fundamentally Christological rather than simply anthropological. The ultimate Franciscan question is: "Who are you, O Lord, and who am I?" When Francis asked the half-question "Who am I?" he concluded dismally that he was "a useless person and an unworthy creature." But when he asked the question, "Who are you, O Lord?" he learned that he was the troubadour of the Great King, a singer of his praises.

The spiral of fraternal and ministerial experience developed gradually from Francis's solitary encounter with the leper; it expanded further with his power of attracting others to his evangelical brother-sister experience; and later still, it assumed more permanent form and substance with his "return" to the townspeople of Assisi, not as a lord upon his horse but as a brother, a lesser brother at that. His openness to all people, evidenced in his frequent journeys and his letters to the faithful, led to entirely new kinds of ministerial relationships. His fraternity, founded on personal relationships, developed its own distinctive ministerial style whose very nature was to be relational and collaborative. Francis offered the medieval world a new way of relating: less by power and hierarchy, more by humility and solidarity, all of which can be symbolized by the spiral recreating itself throughout history in the lives of Franciscans who transform individualism into personhood-in-Christ.

This transformation takes place in solitude within fraternity— again a coincidence of opposites. Merton indicates this truth when he writes that solitude tends only to unity. For him, as for the Franciscan, the shallow "I" of individualism is converted into the deep "I" of the spirit through contemplative living. Only then is solidarity truly possible, for its *fundamentum in re* is a gathering of persons rather than a conglomerate of individuals. Merton beautifully portrays this when he writes:

> In Louisville, at the corner of Fourth and Walnut, in the center of the shopping district, I was suddenly overwhelmed with the realization that I loved all those people, that they were mine and I was

theirs, that we could not be alien to one another even though we were total strangers. It was like waking from a dream of separateness, of spurious self-isolation in a special world.[9]

Converting the Order and the Church

But even if all Franciscans experienced this transformation, something more remains to be done: the conversion of the institution, since the church and the Franciscan Order are corporate realities visibly structured in an institutional pattern. A person lasts a life span, whereas the institution perdures through all historical ups-and-downs and all the fluctuations of changing membership. It is not enough then, that persons be transformed; institutions need to be converted as well. This is the purpose of refounding: the structural transformation of the church and religious life.

An institution, like a person, can be a means and sign of grace dispensed through fraternal relationships, certainly, but also through corporate relationships: relationships "of the body." The church, as an institutional body, has many and diverse parts, members, activities—all functioning in concert for the wellness of the whole. Bodily members must not fail to function lest the whole be threatened, sometimes to the point of disintegration. This Pauline reality must be a conscious part of our conversion experience. And here again, Merton is right on target by insisting that the institution act "on behalf of the person." In other words, the function of the members, singly or collectively, is to promote the person—no easy task unless corporate structures become radically redirected. Such fraternal and ministerial transformations are not helped by promoting New Age spirituality over the spiritual experiences of structured religion. Even some Franciscans, ignoring our incarnational roots, join them in preaching the mystical as opposed to the institutional, forgetting that Francis, impelled by Greccio and ever concerned with heretical exaggeration, lived the mystical life within the institution, at the same time that he was witnessing its dilapidation and dedicating himself to rebuilding it.

Franciscan life today, like American life in general and religious life in particular, is "unbalanced." Seemingly either one is a person or an individual; an activist or a contemplative; a renewalist or a

---

[9] Merton, 1966, p. 140.

refounder; a brother or a minister. These opposites must contemplatively coincide into an institutional balance. Meanwhile, the struggle to make it happen continues to work itself out in the locales where we live and minister. Inattention to the cited dichotomies is possible only by ignoring the social setting of today's Franciscan pastoral activities. And if we do try to dodge the issue, how can we hope to provide pastoral leadership in the contemporary religious environment? In other words, how do we heal wounds? unite what has fallen apart? bring home the lost?[10]

We will do it, I believe, by striving to become more a person than an individual; by living and working contemplatively; by watering our roots while also trimming the tree of Franciscan life and ministry so that new branches may sprout; and by ministering as brothers and sisters. The success of renewal depends on the success of the companion piece, refounding our ministering brother/sisterhoods.

REFERENCES

Merton, Thomas, *Conjectures of a Guilty Bystander*. New York: Doubleday, 1966.

──────, *New Seeds of Contemplation*. New York: New Directions, 1972.

Osuna, Francisco de, *The Third Spiritual Alphabet*. Translated and introduced by Mary Giles. New York: Paulist Press, 1981.

Shannon, Thomas, "Cloning, Uniqueness, and Individuality," *pro manuscripto*, 1994.

II. Franciscan Pastoral Ministry in the Catholic Church
Vincent Cushing, O.F.M.

Can elements of the Franciscan tradition provide a context for contemporary pastoral ministry in the American Catholic community? Does the Franciscan tradition help in thinking about the pastoral mission of the church? New issues of pastoral ministry in regard to world peace, ecumenism, immigration, human sexuality, world population, the beginning and end of human existence raise serious and freshly minted questions for our time and church.

---

[10] L3S 58.

Challenging questions about church ministry leave the church itself unclear about what direction its pastoral ministry should take. We are clearly torn between those who wholeheartedly embrace the teaching of Vatican II and the thirty years of development that followed it and those who wish to revise it into preconciliar categories. Fortunately, despite the turmoil of the age no one downplays the role and value of pastoral ministry, but it highlights the confusion about the theological foundation for pastoral ministry and how it should be practiced.

Toward a Franciscan Ecclesiology

The term "Franciscan ecclesiology" brings together the Franciscan tradition and the demands of pastoral ministry. One can legitimately think of a Franciscan ecclesiology if one is willing to appreciate the theological note of the catholicity of the church. By "catholicity" I mean that characteristic of the church that we confess in the creed that describes the church's ability to relate to and situate itself well within the varied cultures and times of our world. Moreover, it affirms that the church does that while both preserving the apostolic, doctrinal heritage of the church in a way that yet fosters and develops the apostolic tradition in new and imaginative expressions. When we speak of a Franciscan ecclesiology we are talking about the symbiotic relationship between the apostolic tradition and the insights and doctrinal inflections that the Franciscan experience brings to that apostolic tradition. In such a manner we can fashion a Franciscan theology of church and pastoral ministry.

It is also legitimate to speak of an "American Catholic Church." One can describe its characteristics, its needs, its potential. This appellation is inflammatory to some, but unduly so. American values of democracy, broad participation, teamwork, religious tolerance, human equality, and concrete achievement are clearly present in the collective consciousness of the Catholic Church of North America. The challenge is for the church to reflect critically on those elements to see how we incorporate them into our theology of church rather than to presume their exclusion. Joining the American experience of Catholicism with the Franciscan tradition can yield both a nutritive and vibrant relationship. The Franciscan tradition exists across so broad a sweep of human history, peoples, and ages, that distinctive elements stand out over time as particularly apt in the development of pastoral practice.

Francis's life and ministry offer thematic elements for a contemporary pastoral ecclesiology. Using Raoul Manselli's recent life of St. Francis[1] as a guide to correlate the Franciscan heritage with contemporary pastoral ministry of the church in the U.S., we hear eight "calls" within the Franciscan tradition that recommend themselves for contemporary pastoral ministry:

- The call to ministry based on the needs of the faithful.
- The call to penance as the foundation for an ecclesiology of discipleship.
- The call to popular preaching and teaching.
- The call to build the local church.
- The call to a ministry of solidarity with the oppressed.
- The call to an ecology of the human spirit.
- The call to create a church of lay disciples.
- The call to a united church.

The Call to Ministry Based on the Needs of the Faithful

In our age we have seen a remarkable development in contemporary theology growing from the acceptance of human experience as an appropriate theological *locus*. This is exemplified both in Vatican II's "Pastoral Constitution on the Church in the Modern World" and in the "turn to the subject" prevalent in Christian anthropology. Early Franciscan ministry intuitively realized that the needs of the faithful were a call to ministry when they preached in response to those needs. Clearly those needs derived from a hunger for spiritual nourishment in everyday life.[2] Today the authorization for ministry is issued by church authority. Current church practice should not overshadow the natural and grace-filled origin of the call to ministry—human need. Indeed, the recognition of such need in today's world has led to new and creative ministries within the contemporary church, exemplified by such ministries as Project Renew, CFM, charismatic ministry, AIDS ministry, and the development of liberation and feminist theologies.

The task for the Franciscan movement is to ask how it will serve in the contemporary church. How do we join the Franciscan spirit

---

[1] Manselli, 1988.
[2] Lesnick, 1989.

and tradition with the need for creative responses to pastoral ministry today? The issues are not really theological issues, but rather strategic design of effective ministries and ways of knowing the genuine pastoral needs of people. This prompts us, then, to ask, What are the characteristics of Franciscan ministry?

The Life of Discipleship and the Call to Penance

The Franciscan experience begins with penance and conversion under the grace of God. The goal of penance is conversion. The goal of Franciscan ministry is personal and societal conversion, a turning away from the evil and destructive pathways of life and the society in which we live. In turn, this experience of conversion brings discipleship. Franciscan ministry should enable a person to become a believing and practicing disciple. This presumes the Franciscan minister is also a fellow traveler on the way, a practicing disciple who walks with people pastorally and enables them to learn the way of Christian discipleship. This involves a sharing of one's life and values, a holistic, kinetic ministering that enables a person into a way of living so he or she can walk the way of the Lord. This aims at mature discipleship in which the disciple in turn becomes a "discipler." He or she will be able to unpack and replicate personal experience by story, devotion, and life experience for other people on the way.

This call to conversion is a hallmark of Franciscan life. We see it both in Francis's life, in the establishing of the three branches of the order, and in the setting up of confraternities close to churches associated with the order.[3] These churches were not local parishes in our sense of the term, but urban centers that served as pastoral and lay ministerial hubs for all within their sphere. From each center people went out to minister to the city and society. The friars served the people by preaching, sacramental celebrations, and formation in the charism of Francis, in a way that helped them, in turn, to care for the sick, reach out to the poor, and comfort the bereaved.

This approach to "discipling" involves deep, human reflection, hard work, and daily practice on the meaning of becoming a "convert" and the spiritual growth of the contemporary Christian. Moreover, conversion is authentic when it is long-term. To speak of

---

[3] Holmes, 1986.

communities of conversion presupposes a Franciscan community of *fratres et sorores conversi*, one of the ancient Latin appellations for members of religious institutes. It is, by its nature, a call to perseverance in religious life and ministry.

The Call to Popular Preaching and Teaching

The Christian church appreciates anew the meaning of the gospel for our world. The Catholic Church's openness to scripture, now joined to the grace-filled insight of our Protestant colleagues about the centrality of the word, continues to bring new life and insight into our world and church. To preach and teach the gospel is a mandate to communicate in depth to all strata of society. This brings with it a basic task: to understand the hunger of our Christian people and the hunger of the world in which we live. This is faithful to the method of Vatican II's "Pastoral Constitution on the Church in the Modern World" in asking what are the hopes and needs of the human family. This suggests the need for a methodology of social analysis and theological reflection central to effective pastoral ministry. Unless we understand the values, change mechanisms, social agents, and catalysts for change in society, we risk preaching an irrelevant gospel.

This describes the educational goal of pastoral ministry. Its aim is to introduce the disciple into the mystery of Christ. In turn, this calls for effective and affective approaches to preaching and teaching. Lectures, CCD classes, and pulpit oratory are not enough. Holistic and humanistic adult education is especially important in a time of cultural change like this when the architectonic plates underlying our universe of meaning have begun to shift. Ministers need a working understanding of the cognitive pathways of contemporary society, and they need to realize that unless we are working those channels we miss communicating the gospel.

This suggests a contemporary Catholic evangelical movement that would entail gospel preaching and gospel living, a way of teaching that is simple and popular, and ongoing Bible study as characteristic of lay and religious Catholic life. In our day people are rightly fearful of fundamentalism either in scripture or church. Such fear, however, should not put people into paralysis about new ways to incarnate the gospel message in church and world. An openness to new ways of thinking and living the age-old gospel can invigorate the church and bear witness to the life-giving message of the gospel to the world.

The Call to a Ministry of Solidarity with the Oppressed

The gospel witnesses to the radical equality of all, and to the special right of the poor and oppressed to justice and a human life. This call echoes the finest elements of our Franciscan tradition. Here social analysis and the correlation of scripture to life take place. Prophetic witness is a call to unearth systemic sin, structural oppression, and societal sins of omission. The need to design systems of justice, charters of human rights, and structures of freedom and support, and to do this with the poor, the oppressed, the minority, and the alienated is an evangelical imperative in our age. Solidarity in a way that touches their lives, brings dignity, and resonates with the gospel's deepest values remains a challenge for Franciscan ministry. The risk, of course, is to be either messianic in proclaiming deliverance or patronizing in struggling to unity with others. The values of sisterhood and brotherhood, a way of walking with people on their journey, deep and reflective understanding of the experience of poverty and oppression remain as grace-filled calls to the Franciscan minister. Ministry and discipleship will be shaped by such experience to be earthy, human, supportive, and sacramental. Only when it can appreciate the life of the other from inside, can it walk their way with understanding and respect. Such ministry carries an interior asceticism and personal conversion for the Franciscan minister that is hammered out, shaped, and refined in being with the oppressed.

The Call to Build the Local Church

Grace is local, tangible in the human experience, an instance of the church happening before our eyes. The action of grace in the human person is an experience of church that witnesses to the truth of the ancient Orthodox maxim that the church comes to be when the human spirit and the Holy Spirit intersect and interact. The transforming grace of God changes the local, human setting. The specificity of the sacramental tradition resonates strongly with Duns Scotus's thought on the uniqueness of the individual. The Franciscan approach to the specific and the transcendence of grace affirms that the local church is the church we experience and wherein we are nourished. Franciscan ministry that is prophetic and nutritive will appreciate and critique the cultural setting of life lived in the contemporary world. If that life is inhumane, oppressive of the human spirit, derogatory of lived values, shorn of meaning, wretched in experience, then the church, precisely as Franciscan and local, needs to challenge the inhumanity and the evacuation of meaning. A ministry of exorcism as well as a ministry of discernment will address what is going on in history locally. It will take seriously the individual in society and the role society plays in human nurture. Evil will be seen to be such. The good, wherever it is in life—the arts, literature, nature—will be celebrated as both graceful and as a vestige of God in creation.

The Call to an Ecology of the Human Spirit

Through global communication, advances in space exploration, and the catalytic role of science (as well as through a string of industrial crimes and ecological disasters), we now realize the beauty and vulnerability of the universe. We see it as created gift, entrusted to us to be enjoyed and cared for. In this age, in which conflicting ideologies propose either to destroy nature or idolize it, we need retrieval and critical reflection on how the created world and the spiritual life interrelate. The issue is not simply one of an appreciation of creation; it also carries import for what it means to be disciple and church in the twentieth and twenty-first centuries. Moreover, our concern extends from the physical universe to our cultural environment. The arts, popular entertainment, the media—all convey values that either nurture or demean the *humanum*. In such sites the struggle of the human spirit goes on. When one reflects on the humanism of the "Canticle of Creation" or thinks of the primacy of Christ as extending to the entire universe, then the possibilities for an ecology of the Spirit stand forth. This yields a spirituality of stewardship of the human and the created, calling forth a reverential approach to the broad dimensions of both. It also directs us to a deeply sacramental appreciation of the symbolic as nutritive of the spirit.

The Call of the Laity to the Church of Tomorrow

In its beginning, the Franciscan movement was clearly a lay movement in the church. The people could grasp it. Preaching a popular piety, calling to discipleship, ministering in the cities and towns, it looked neither for clerical privilege nor the separation of monastic life. The Franciscan movement exemplified its concern for the laity by founding, developing and forming laity into both the Third Order and confraternities. Although the First Order eventually became clerical, concern for the laity persisted, transformed into the devising of numerous popular devotions that accepted where people were spiritually as the place to begin the spiritual journey.

Vatican II spelled out the outlines of a systematic theology of the laity. Since then both church and world have insisted on a renewed approach to lay theology and ministry. How will we foster this development so that the role of the laity can take root? As ordained church leadership shrinks in numbers, we need to ask where lay theologians, pastoral experts, religious sociologists, community organizers, catechists, and Bible teachers will come from and how they shall be educated. This presents an unparalleled opportunity for the Franciscan movement both to join and support lay colleagues as they assume positions of servant leadership in church and world.

When we consider the complexity of American society and its increased secularization, we need to ask what the lay vocation is in every aspect of the Christian life. Two negative elements in the life of the church prevent us from taking up this task effectively: clericalism and the alienation experienced when the official church exercises its teaching authority in arrogant ways. The First Order is still struggling to free itself from a clericalism that stifles its charism. Those efforts must continue until the movement can articulate how it will live in the church as a nonclerical group. The *magisterium's* pronouncements on the ordination of women exemplify graphically the destructive way the church engages its teaching task. Not only is such an approach simply no longer effective; it engenders in its train a host of related problems in pastoral ministry.

The Call to a United Church

Francis had vision breathtaking in its boldness and simplicity to the sultan. Francis's elegant sensibility and courtesy enabled him to speak as brother to a fellow worshiper of God. We live in a time when the Christian churches lack credibility because of division. Within the Catholic Church we have witnessed the drying up of the movement towards Christian unity. What service can an evangelical and Franciscan movement bring to our world to bear witness once more to the evangelical imperative of Christian unity? This calls for both a theological grounding and a pastoral strategy. A basic insight of Vatican II acknowledged the churchly reality of other Christian bodies and simultaneously refused to equate the Roman Catholic Church with the one true church of Christ. This church teaching has been effectively ignored by the official *magisterium*, and we see a return to a neotriumphalism in the church's self-understanding.

We are dealing with power, a clericalized ministry, and the renewed attempt to uphold the Catholic structure of the Counter Reformation. Key issues for the reform of the church will be lost if the basic insights of the ecumenical movement continue to be jettisoned by the official church. The meaning of the ecumenical movement has been barely appreciated by Catholics. Sadly, the Franciscan movement is equally inactive and ineffective. Despite the heroic efforts of such groups as the friars and sisters of the Society of the Atonement, the larger body of Franciscans remain uninterested or, in some cases, deeply inimical to the movement towards Christian unity.

Conclusion

A pastoral and ecclesial context for the Franciscan movement in the church envisions a church with a sense of destiny: to create and nourish disciples of Christ, so that they, in turn, might heal a broken world. This experience of Christ in the Spirit is communicated by personal contact within a community of disciples. That community of Christ is nourished by the life with other disciples, by a rich sacramental life, and by informed, pastoral teaching and preaching of the word of God. The life of the community of Christ, in this approach, is characterized by mature discipleship and effective work of justice and mercy.

Moreover, the church looks to the quality of life of the world in all its dimensions and reaches out to form a bond of unity and cooperation to all touched by the Spirit of God. These points call for a vigorous, engaged, wide-ranging intellectual and faith-based conversation with the worlds in which we live. We need both a ritual of exorcism and an enlightened conversation to challenge pernicious ideologies both within and without the church to foster the presence of grace in our world.

As the Franciscan movement spread through Europe it engaged the issues of its time. We ask what a vibrant sense of the coming of

Christ says to today's world. An understanding of Christian destiny can serve to energize the people of God because it can communicate to us that we are heading towards fulfillment in Christ. This will describe our goals on earth today and tomorrow. A destiny we believe in, a sense that one is on the way—all serve to energize people in everyday life. They stem from the evocative calls of the Franciscan movement to serve the people of the church.

REFERENCES

Holmes, George, *Florence, Rome, and the Origins of the Renaissance.* Oxford: Clarendon Press, 1986.

Lesnick, Daniel, *Preaching in Medieval Florence: The Social World of Dominican and Franciscan Spirituality.* Athens, Georgia: University of Georgia Press, 1989.

Manselli, Raoul, *Life of St. Francis of Assisi.* Chicago: Franciscan Herald Press, 1988.

III. Ministry in the Culture of the United States
Kenneth Himes, O.F.M.

Generalizations about a culture as diverse and panoramic as that of the United States will always be risky. It is not difficult to cite trends which run counter to almost any description of American life. Still, it is possible to delineate certain dominant themes that reflect the experience of most people living in the United States today. Some of the themes are obvious and much commented upon by religious authors, while others may not have had as direct and immediately apparent influence on people's religious experience. In what follows I have selected a few salient aspects of American culture and examined them for their impact upon the environment in which Franciscans live and minister.

Privatization

The term "privatization" has been coined to name the phenomenon in which religious faith persists as an element of people's lives as the public impact of religious beliefs, actions, and institutions declines. Privatization can be distinguished from both secularism and secularization. The former is an ideology that denies the reality of transcendence in human life. It limits reality to the material world. To use the image of the religious sociologist Peter Berger, secularism holds for a "world without windows." Secularization describes the sociological process through which elements of social life have been removed from the hegemony of religious control. Today the arts, education, business, and the professions, as well as other areas, have been freed from the decisive influence of religious institutions, even though they are generally open to participation by religious persons and groups. This liberation has often benefitted not only society but the church as well.

Privatization is what occurs when the opportunities for participation in public life are not acted upon by people in a reflexively religious way, e.g., the elimination of any reference to religious values from discussions within the business world about goals or strategies for economic life. This can occur even though business women and men may be personally devout, for privatization does not imply a lack of faith but an absence of faith that is publicly significant. In short, privatization reduces faith to purely personal or existentialist categories.

Faced with ministering in such a climate, the challenge to Franciscan ministers is to avoid the temptation to present the gospel in a way that permits privatization to remain unchallenged. Adopting an overly therapeutic model of ministry permits believers to see faith as essentially a private quest for meaning and support. The prophetic aspects of Christian life can be given short shrift if the community is not called upon to wrestle with the gospel's message for the marketplace or public square. By keeping faith private the Christian believer loses the ability to integrate human experience. Rather than the overarching meaning system that brings cohesiveness and coherence to all aspects of life, discipleship can be transformed into one identity alongside other identities, e.g. spouse, worker, parent, friend, citizen, consumer, etc. Thus, religion simply becomes one more activity among many in a person's life rather than the integrating element that invigorates and shapes all human activity.

At the same time, faced with such fragmentation, and living in nonintegrated worlds of private and public life, many Americans are looking for ways that a more holistic vision can be developed. This creates an openness to the power of the gospel and to the rich resources of the church's teaching, spirituality, and sacramental rituals as vehicles for transmitting a faith that transforms public as well as personal life. It is in this way that Franciscans may find a point of entry for promoting justice and peace concerns among American Catholics who are not poor. If the church's social mission can be understood as a call to people to bring the values of the gospel into the everyday aspects of people's lives, it may receive a better hearing than if it is promoted as a partisan political-economic ideology. Allying the social teaching of the church with the sacramental and spiritual elements of Catholic life can be a way of assisting people to develop an adequate moral and spiritual understanding of their everyday world.

Individualism

Few elements of American life are more noted than the persistent and pervasive individualism that marks the culture. Here are three aspects of individualism that have significant impact upon ministry today.

First is the moral individualism of our culture, which engenders the subjectivism recently lamented by John Paul II in "Veritatis Splendor." By subjectivism is meant the temptation to so exalt the individual's perspective and experience that no other dimension of moral experience counts against it. Judgments about right and wrong always are resolved in favor of one's own viewpoint; one's viewpoint is counted as the most telling factor because nothing outside the self is taken seriously. Within the subjectivist framework, all that can be asked is that the individual act sincerely.

Related to such a stance is relativism, which acknowledges that since the individual is the referent for deciding right and wrong no one can judge another's actions. Because one person concludes that a particular action is incorrect is no reason to presume others should conclude similarly. Instead, moral standards vary according to the perception of the moral agent.

Confronted with such popular and unreflective ideas, Franciscans must challenge people to accept the importance of communities of tradition for shaping and forming moral character. If ministers are to unleash the power of the gospel to call people to accept a truth larger than themselves, they must be sensitive to the present climate and possess the interior strength to resist the conventional wisdom premised on individualism. Helping people to see the importance of human rights and values that transcend personal preference and cultural expression is a needed corrective to the failures of moral individualism.

The second aspect I note is the religious impact of individualism. Today, many people are religious seekers who do not participate in the life of religious communities. Individualism undercuts the role of communities of tradition as bearers of religious truth. In their place we see the tendency to "shop around" or browse among a variety of religious traditions, picking up an element here or another over there. This movement toward religious eclecticism suggests a profound challenge to the Franciscan understanding. For us the gospel is not something that is adapted to suit one's life style and tastes; the gospel is the norm to which we seek to conform our lives. That understanding of religion seems in direct conflict with the stance of many religious seekers in our nation.

Helping people to see that adherence to a tradition deepens and enriches their personal journey will be a challenge for Franciscans to meet. The various ways in which traditional religious communities have suffered from the failures of their institutional practices and structures provides a major obstacle to presenting organized religion in an appealing light. Religious men and women have themselves allowed the necessary institutionalization of the gospel tradition to become confused with time-bound and quite reformable practices and structures of community life. To combat religious individualism it will be necessary both to demonstrate the importance of participation in "communities of memory" and to distinguish between the useful and dispensable elements of organized church life.

Third, one must note that individualism has led to a disenchantment with institutions that extends beyond religion to much of political and social life as well. A number of studies demonstrate the widespread alienation that Americans feel when considering the institutions of public life. Many today see engagement in the processes of open democratic society as something to be avoided. It is within the realm of the private, in the intimate confines of family and friendship, that Americans seek fulfillment. The classical republican ideal of the active citizen finding a measure of satisfaction in the public square has almost disappeared for a large segment of the American populace.

The excesses of interest-group liberalism contribute to this alienation since much of the work of government appears to entail little more than distributing funds and privilege to various groups pursuing their private gain. In addition, the bureaucratic nature of large organizations seems an inhospitable setting for ordinary persons. The modern corporation, in this sense, is no less alienating than the modern state; neither appears responsive or useful to people. As a result the distrust of organized society grows and the withdrawal into private life continues.

Perhaps Franciscans can work with others to develop approaches to implement subsidiarity in public life. The search for more "people-sized" institutions may take various shapes—grassroots organizations pressing for improvements in common life, parish-based community organizing projects, institutions of higher education that maintain a sense of community amidst academic work, health care delivery networks that avoid impersonal medical care—but the effort to revitalize America's local communities becomes important if the church is to avoid speaking a language of community that finds no resonance in the concrete experience of people.

Economy

No society's culture can be understood without heeding the economic life of the people. In an economy as large, productive, and diverse as that of the United States, there are any number of comments that might be made. I raise just a few points.

One of the most obvious facts about the United States is its material abundance: it is rich in capital, natural and human resources, boasts a large consumer base, and enjoys a plenitude of goods and services. The American economic system promises the experience of a life beyond scarcity. One need only recall how unusual that is within the history of the human race to appreciate the achievement of the U.S. economy. At the same time, the material abundance of our nation does not erase the sense that the distribution of the goods produced by the economy can be considerably less than what standards of equity and social justice require. Some Americans experience a level of material well-being that can only be described as lavish while others undergo the daily suffering of lacking basic shelter, nutrition, health care, and opportunity for improvement. The gap between rich and poor has expanded as the nation moves toward larger groups of rich and poor extremes while the middle class shrinks. This trend has suggested to some the image of an "hourglass" economy. Maintaining a productive economy while also developing a fair distribution of economic rewards remains an ongoing challenge, especially as the American economy undergoes significant change.

This change is the transition from an industrial/manufacturing to a service/information economy. The development has led to a number of structural alterations, not the least of which is the diminishing number of high-wage jobs for skilled and semi-skilled blue-collar workers. As the economy changes we are seeing a growing gap between the wages of workers who are college-educated and those who are not. While once there were good paying jobs with a large measure of job security available to high school graduates, shifts in the national economy have significantly reduced the number of such posts.

The emergence of a class of workers described by former Secretary of Labor Robert Reich as "symbolic analysts" reflects the information-based nature of our present economy. People who manipulate, transmit, produce, and assess information have emerged as a significant segment of the affluent middle and upper classes. Knowledge increasingly plays the role that property once played in an earlier era. Access to valued information is generally more available to those with good educations, and today it is specialized skills in working with information that is prized, e.g. lawyers, accountants, brokers, bankers, nurses, teachers or other such roles. Without such skills it is difficult for less educated workers to move into high-wage jobs.

Apparent in this transition in American economic life are a couple of things: 1) the central role of education for economic advancement and 2) the widening gulf between well-paid elites who provide important information or services in a post-industrial society and the economically limited laborers competing for a decreasing number of skilled manufacturing positions. At the same time, all is not well with many of those lucky enough to hold good jobs. One of the effects of the shakeup of American business in the 1980s has been a decline in job security. Companies which once were thought of as offering chances for life-long career advancement have found themselves forced to merge, reconfigure, and alter long-standing practices of personnel management. This has led to a rise in early retirements, midcareer job losses, and an increased reliance on part-time and temporary workers. As a result workers no longer feel the same sense of loyalty towards a company which is regularly forced to "streamline" personnel commitments.

Consequently, the American workplace today is filled with anxiety. People may feel dissatisfied with their jobs but due to the precarious nature of business they are hesitant either to voice complaints or risk leaving to seek new employment. There is a feeling of being "hemmed in" as economic growth slows and new job opportunities seem inadequate to meet the expectations of those presuming an ever-rising standard of living. As many observers have reported, the present generation of young Americans are the first who do not believe they will have it better than their parents. The end of such hopes casts an unexamined shadow over the social fabric of the nation. The traditional optimism and "can-do" sensibility of Americans may be sorely tested in the coming years.

Helping people come to terms with diminished expectations, sustaining a sense of caring for others amidst personal worries, assisting in the search for meaning and accomplishment in areas outside the workplace, these are but a few of the challenges facing church ministers. Owing to the linkage of education and economic opportunity, Franciscans serving in institutions that offer a good education to poor and lower-middle-class families now find themselves involved in a ministry of growing importance for helping the poor.

Pluralism

It is impossible to walk the streets of a major American city, scan the channels on cable television, or glance over the magazine and newspaper racks of a large newsstand without realizing that the United States is a pluralistic society. Alternative lifestyle advocates, ethnic pride celebrations, educational curriculum debates, arguments over political and economic ideologies, interreligious dialogues—all these express the profoundly diverse nature of modern American life. It has become unfashionable to speak of the U.S. as the great melting pot that blends homogeneously, and more correct to suggest a rich social mosaic with individual parts that maintain their unique color and shape. In many places and ways the banner of multiculturalism is unfurled.

While American society has never been quite as uniform as some recent critics have suggested, the vocal insistence on pluralism as a good does mark something of a new age in public life. At the same time the celebration of pluralism can ignore issues that have not gone away. First, perhaps, is the feasibility of achieving a truly multicultural society. History offers few examples of successful societies where different cultures continued to be held in equal esteem with equal vitality and social force. In truth, history appears to suggest that in every society there will be a dominant culture even if subcultures coexist as well.

The more realistic aim may be to work for a dominant culture open to receiving new energy from different cultures and appropriating elements of subcultures in such a way that the dominant culture is reshaped. Attaining a culture capable of integrating other cultures, not simply dominating them, is a worthy social goal. But this will not occur if we fail to understand that there is a dominant culture that must be made receptive. A simple refusal to come to terms with society's dominant culture, or denial that it exists, may only mean that members strongly attached to a subculture are permanently marginalized politically, economically, and socially.

One of the reactions to the reality of pluralism in our society is a return on the part of many educators, pundits, public officials, and civic leaders to the quest for establishment of common values amidst diversity. An example of this is the interest among political philosophers in reinvigorating the idea of a common good and the rise of various spokespersons for a communitarian critique of the individualism inherent in Anglo-American liberalism. In many schools there is renewed interest in developing an understanding of the narratives, values, and ideals that undergird political democracy and economic freedom. Parents who once distanced themselves from religious practice now seek assistance in transmitting a moral framework to their children, and look to churches, synagogues, mosques, and temples as sources of formative moral traditions. American pluralism has not led to a disparaging of all tradition; instead it is revitalizing the interest of many to find within our diverse cultural traditions a set of coherent values and practices that can establish the conditions for a fruitful common life.

A church that is universal and a religious community that is globally aware can be major helps in the task of developing a pluralism that respects otherness even as it fosters a spirit of communion. The Franciscan movement has, as part of its heritage, a sense of hospitality that can welcome the stranger into our midst. The welcome in turns can lead to a dialogue whose goal is not assimilation or conversion but understanding and cooperation. As part of a movement that has had experience in being both part of a dominant culture and being a marginalized subculture, Franciscans can bring special gifts to ministries with immigrants, ethnic and racial subcommunities, and those offering a different voice and perspective on the American experiment.

Freedom

Central to Americans' understanding of themselves and their national life is the quality of freedom. Ours is a culture which prizes freedom and few words conjure up stronger emotional resonance in the hearts of U.S. citizens. Two dimensions of freedom of special import for the context of ministry are freedom as self-determination and freedom of association.

Emphasis on self-determination is a primary theme in the American narrative. The selection and pursuit of one's own life plan is seen by most Americans as a right. There is strong resistance to any institution or group that is perceived as infringing upon that freedom to choose for oneself how one shall live. Appeals by leaders, be they religious or secular, must be presented in a manner that is persuasive rather than coercive. Political self-determination is an ideal for which America has been prepared to wage war, and economic self-determination is an aspiration that continues to attract millions to U.S. shores. Despite its dubious standing as a practical norm the slogan "Everyone should have a say in the decisions that affect them" has a power and appeal to most Americans.

There is much that is admirable in the ideal of self-determination. Taking responsibility for one's life and decisions is a positive thing. Developing a personal identity and character is an impossible task apart from the ability to exercise a measure of freedom. We fashion a self through the history of our free choices and accepting that call to freedom is a sign of human maturity. Self-determination is closely bound to our sense of ourselves as human persons and expanding the scope of free self-determination can be an important project for any culture that promotes the dignity of the person.

But there is no clear-cut guide for determining a self in our society. Securing the conditions for the exercise of self-determination is not the same as providing assistance for the wise exercise of such freedom. As a formal concept self-determination is undoubtedly a good, but as a lived reality the achievement of an authentic self is often frustrated by a lack of wisdom and insight concerning the choices available to the person. Finding communities of wisdom that can mentor the self in developing and pursuing a life plan is a vital complement to self-determination. In our society, the search for wisdom communities is possible but perilous owing to the expansive freedom of association afforded Americans. Possible because our culture permits a broad range of action by communities to influence both public life and individual persons. Perilous because our open society permits the dissemination and promotion of many false narratives as well as the unregulated establishment of many communities of folly rather than wisdom.

Communities founded upon the gospel can find the freedom of association afforded us in this culture to be of great assistance in helping Americans in the exercise of their self-determination. Required is the ability to present the truth of the Catholic tradition in a way that is accessible and convincing. But undoubtedly, speech will be insufficient in this regard when people find themselves faced with the cacophony of voices vying for a hearing in our society. Needed most will be communities who witness to the truth by the quality of the lives of their membership. If Franciscans can build communities of faith capable of a genuine public witness to the gospel, then the freedom of association that marks American culture will permit those communities to flourish and attain wide influence.

As with the other elements characteristic of American life the implications of freedom are neither inevitably positive nor negative. There is darkness and light in the culture of the United States. Ministry today needs the skill and courage to work with those elements of our culture that reflect something of the truly human as well as the willingness to withstand those aspects of our culture that undercut the truth of the gospel to which Franciscan men and women are devoted.

2

Franciscan Tradition as a Wisdom Tradition

Zachary Hayes, O.F.M.

T
o anyone who looks carefully at the history of religions and religious movements, it is obvious that religion is capable of remarkable good. But it is likewise capable of horrible atrocities. What appears to be serious religion to one person may seem to be nonsense to another. People have wreaked havoc on one another in the name of God and for the sake of God. They have killed each other on battlefields of holy wars and crusades waged in God's name. They have offered each other to the gods in bloody sacrifices on stone altars and in sacrificial fires. They continue to murder others in the name of life and for reputedly religious motivations.

It is simply not enough to "mean well" when it comes to religion. It is not enough to think that any program which claims to spring from religious motivation is by that fact alone worthy of serious commitment. We must learn to distinguish between genuine religious motivation that can make authentic ethical claims on us and blind, unthinking fanaticism. This can be difficult to do. It is particularly difficult in the context of our highly secularized culture, with our current awareness of the wide diversity of cultures and religious traditions. "Whose God? Which religion?" we might wish to ask. And each serious believer is convinced that he or she is somehow concerned with the true God. But how is it possible that the true God can reveal such diverse and contradictory messages to people who presumably mean well?

By what criteria are we to judge right and wrong, true and false? In view of the weighty problems that are so widespread in our culture and our time, pastoral leadership that is morally responsible must face these issues at some point. Difficult as it may be, it is nonetheless critical for responsible religious leadership that we learn to think carefully and critically about the implications of what we believe. Somehow we need to move beyond the tendency to isolate religious concerns from hard, critical thinking. One of the "heresies" of our time is the tendency to isolate and highlight the present moment as *the* moment of insight and truth. Yet when we look at the daily papers or watch the evening news, we must wonder at the signs of moral confusion and existential desperation. With such signs on every side, we are well advised to look for wisdom wherever we might find it. Only wisdom will guide us through the perils of modernity and post-modernity. The accumulation of data and knowledge so popular in this age of "infomania" is not sufficient to meet the questions and problems of the present.[1] A mere accumulation of data does not tell us what to do with the data. And all the information in the world does not assure us that human life has meaning and is of ethical significance in the long run. When all the information is in, one still must ask about a possible framework of values within which to assess the information and make it beneficial to human life.

It is with these problems in mind that I approach the Franciscan tradition, one of the great historical wisdom traditions. I do this from several perspectives that I find helpful in sorting out the significance of this tradition for the development of ministerial leadership today. First, I shall discuss the relation between the spiritual tradition and the intellectual tradition in the origins of Franciscanism. Second, I shall turn to the nature of the Franciscan intellectual tradition as a wisdom tradition. Finally, I shall suggest some implications of this approach for ministerial formation and leadership in the church today.

A Spiritual Tradition and an Intellectual Tradition

In the aftermath of the Second Vatican Council, it has become a commonplace for religious orders to speak of the renewal of their communities. Such renewal typically has involved an appeal to the charism of the order's founder or foundress as the central guide. Informed and illuminated by the light of that founding experience, one attempts to redefine the meaning and purpose of the community in the context of the contemporary world. I offer no suggestions as to what this might mean for other communities. I wish to speak only of what it might mean for Franciscans.

---

[1] Heim, 1993: pp. 41-42

For communities who take their inspiration from the life and example of Francis of Assisi, a simple, direct appeal to the vision of the founder is virtually impossible. Joseph Ratzinger, now Cardinal Ratzinger, explained why years ago in his early *Habilitationsschrift* on the theology of history in Bonaventure.[2] Ratzinger noted the tendency of all the early *legendae* dealing with the life of Francis to provide not a simple, neutral, objective account of the life of the saint, but rather to lay out elaborate theological interpretations of his work. Usually these interpretations were intended to provide an image of Francis appropriate to a particular ideological position about the meaning of the order. Such interpretations make it difficult for the modern reader to discern where the "Francis of history" ends and the "Francis of interpretation" begins.

The significance of this become clearer if one compares the question of the *legendae* to the question of the New Testament. It is an exegetical and theological commonplace that the Christian Scriptures do not present a pure, straightforward account of the history of Jesus and of his teaching. We are always confronted with faith-inspired interpretations of that history from the perspective of the post-Easter community. The beginnings of Christianity are found not solely in the work of the historical Jesus but in that work *together* with the impact which it had on others, especially on the early disciples. Similarly, if the problem of the *legendae* is taken seriously, the original documents of the Franciscan movement take us back not simply to Francis in his historical individuality, but to Francis and his impact on others. We know that impact was diverse. The many *legendae* suggest differing views as to what is most important about Francis, and how one might most appropriately be true to his inspiration.

The impact was shaped in part by the growth of an intellectual tradition that, from the earliest years of the Franciscan movement, interacted with the spiritual tradition and was the source of an important dynamic in the life of the community. It is in this combination of a spiritual tradition and an intellectual tradition that Franciscans will best find the meaning of their origins.

---

[2] Ratzinger, 1971: pp. 39ff.

a) The Defense of the Spiritual Tradition

For most of us who live seven centuries after Francis, what Francis seemed to be about appears solid and self-evident. For Francis himself, and for his contemporaries, however, this may not have been the case at all. If anything can be said about Francis with confidence, it is that he was a man of profound, even radical religious experience. But not everyone trusted that experience. The experience, a puzzle at first to Francis himself, was never given adequate institutional expression among Francis's followers. Then and now, it was an experience that was potentially incendiary. If there is any truth to Plato's pronouncement that the unexamined life is not worth living, this experience of Francis deserved serious examination. Now as then it challenges our ordinary understanding of the gospel. Taken as an authentic religious experience, it places pressing ethical demands on those who take it seriously. Perhaps Francis's greatest bequest to later generations is a vision of human life and an insight into the meaning of the gospel that demands and deserves serious reflective thought.

Within his own lifetime, the Order of Friars Minor was torn internally by debates about fundamental issues, debates that eventually reached to the highest levels of the Roman church. The presence of Franciscans in centers of higher studies provoked the well-known poverty controversies within a few years of Francis's death. Thus, the early history of the friars shows an order that, within a few years of its founder's death, was riven within and threatened without by conflicts over issues that seemed to be precious to the spirituality of Francis. The controversies revolved precisely around the nature of the following of Christ and the nature of the apostolic life.

Basic in these controversies was a particular image of Jesus. The "poor Jesus" was the exemplar of the radical poverty that seemed to be so much a part of the Franciscan inspiration.[3] We need not debate here the objections brought against the radical mendicancy represented by the Franciscans, merely indicate that people of the stature of Bonaventure came to the public defense of the spirituality of the mendicants early in the order's history. Bonaventure himself did this twice, once while still a student at Paris, in his well-known *Disputed Questions on Evangelical Perfection,* and again during his years as min-

---

[3] Burr, 1989: pp. 1-37.

ister general in his *Defense of the Mendicants*. Both of these works provide a sustained argument based on Scripture and the fathers of the church to legitimate the claim that the mendicancy represented by the Franciscans was an authentic Christian phenomenon.

We might suggest that the intellectual tradition, exemplified in this instance by Bonaventure and later by such men as Peter Olivi, provided a way of legitimating the spirituality of Francis and of the order, and of relating it to a larger historical context of spiritualities. It did this at a time when the meaning of the Franciscan movement was far from self-evident.

b) The Theological Underpinnings of the Spiritual Tradition

Around 1209 there were only twelve Franciscans. By 1250 there were 30,000. This was not simply a remarkable growth in numbers. Early on the order of Francis began to attract members from a more educated level of the population. The entrance of Alexander of Hales into the order signals the changing composition in the membership. The followers of the *simplex et idiota* of Assisi soon found themselves in the universities at Paris, Oxford, Bologna, and elsewhere. And an order whose ministry at first involved a simple, moralizing form of popular preaching now found its members engaged in forms of public ministry that called for more sophisticated training than Francis ever envisioned for his followers. The order of Francis had quickly become an order of studies.

With this, something new took place. The situation of the friars in the universities placed the spirituality and values of the Franciscan spiritual tradition in the mainstream of Western Christian culture. It significantly widened the outreach of the order. In this situation, the friars reflected on the meaning of their founder's spirituality in two ways. First, they reflected theologically about the meaning of Francis's spiritual journey. This sort of reflection we have already noted in the tradition of the *legendae*. Then the friars in the universities began to translate fundamental concerns of Francis's spirituality into what would become characteristically Franciscan theological and even philosophical doctrines. We might say they drew out the presuppositions and implications of the spirituality of Francis and gave them explicit formulations.

Here I have in mind Franciscan theology's distinctive emphasis on the nature of God as the supreme Good; its great sense of love, respect, and responsibility for the world of God's creation; and the way in which the Christocentric spirituality of Francis was eventually developed into the metaphysical and cosmological visions of the theologians of the order. In moving from spirituality to systematic theology, these friars took on in a critical way some of the major claims of the leading philosophy of the time. They thus engaged major cultural categories of their time in a critical, creative way. Within the world of medieval theology, the way in which Franciscan thought differs from that of Aquinas is evidence of a genuine theological pluralism.

In all of this, the early theologians were inspired by the spirituality of Francis. In that spirituality they sensed implications that far transcend the pedestrian assessments of most of us even today. They presented a vision of a Christian humanism inspired by the saint of Assisi. This is something unique. I know of no other case in which the religious experience of a founder of a religious order provided the basis for specific doctrinal positions in systematic theology. Neither Albert the Great nor Thomas Aquinas did this with the experience of Dominic, nor does it seem to have happened with Benedict or with other founders of religious orders.

The Intellectual Tradition as a Pursuit of Wisdom

The attitude of Francis toward studies, like most matters in Franciscan history, is a matter of debate.[4] Without going through the different viewpoints, we might summarize Francis's view toward studies in the following way. While he never seemed enthusiastic about education, he conceded the need of studies at least for some friars. Such studies were to be integrated into the ongoing personal transformation of the spiritual life of the friars involved. Friars involved in studies should act in the light of what they have come to know. And studies would commonly be related to forms of ministry.

Having said this, we must also state that Francis was concerned with the danger of pride and self-esteem involved in studies.

---

[4] Iriarte, 1974: p. 121; Manselli, 1988: p. 123.

Perhaps the major issue here is not learning as such, but rather the way in which a Franciscan relates to learning. How does one transcend the pretensions of the academic world and cultivate humility in one's learning? The poverty and humility of Francis ought to mean that those who engage in studies learn to avoid taking even knowledge as their personal possession. Moreover, as is true of any work, studies should not be allowed to extinguish the spirit of prayer and devotion.[5]

These reflections about Francis and the question of studies set the stage for the next reflections on the shape of the early Franciscan tradition as a wisdom tradition that embraces both a profound spirituality and a level of critical, reflective theology. First, though, some observations about the historical background for wisdom theology with its roots in Augustine and its chief exemplification in the world of monasticism. This style of theology would eventually have a significant impact on the early school of the Franciscan friars at Paris and, through this school, on the greatest of the Franciscan wisdom theologians, Bonaventure.

a) Augustine, the Master of Wisdom

In Western Christianity, the wisdom tradition of theology is greatly indebted to the work of Augustine. Indeed, his style dominated the theological scene in the West until well into the High Middle Ages.[6] The Augustinian approach is emphatically concerned with integrating many levels of human and religious meaning into a unified vision of the whole of reality. It reflects a conviction that a deep knowledge of oneself leads to a deeper knowledge of God, for of all the reflections of God in the cosmos, the human being is preeminently the "image" of God. And it is in a better understanding of the inner cosmos of human consciousness that we come to a more appropriate knowledge of that divine mystery of which we are the image. In Augustine's terms, "I wish to know God and my soul. Nothing else? Nothing whatever."[7]

This knowledge is not simply a neutral, theoretical knowledge of God. It roots itself in the wonder of contemplative awareness of

---

[5] Esser, 1958: p. 201ff.
[6] Leclercq, 1961: pp. 11-17.
[7] *Soliloquium* I.2.7.

the divine. Augustine holds that one desires to know better the one whom one loves. In this sense, the move toward deeper contemplative wonder begins with an initial love of God who is the ultimate object of human love. Reflection upon the myriad ways in which the mystery of God is reflected in the created universe, and particularly in the human person, leads to a deeper knowledge of the mystery of God and hence to a deeper love of God.

The Augustinian wisdom tradition is *practical*, pointing the individual toward a richer experience of the deepest mystery of human life and its relation to God. Wisdom theology gives a priority to devotion, but understands the intellectual dimension as important though subordinate.

Given this basic orientation, it is easy to understand that the wisdom tradition tends to concentrate on the spiritual journey. The journey is a helpful metaphor that portrays life as a movement through a personal history to a goal that is never fully attained so long as the history is incomplete. Therefore, wisdom theology is concerned with stages of maturation along the journey. The space between initiation and full maturity is filled by certain rhythms and patterns of spiritual growth.

b) The Wisdom Tradition and the Challenge of Aristotle

The wisdom tradition maintained its dominance in the Christian West for centuries until the appearance of the fuller corpus of Aristotle's writings in the university setting of the High Middle Ages. Aristotelianism challenged the older word "wisdom" (*sapientia*) with the ideal of "knowledge" (*scientia*). The shaping of theology in relation to this new world view led, as in the case of Aquinas, to a new model that saw theology as clear and certain knowledge—*scientia*. The shift vested theology with a distinctly intellectual character that distinguished it from the affective, voluntaristic qualities of the Augustinian wisdom style.[8]

c) Bonaventure and the Wisdom Tradition

Whether and to what extent the Christian believer might court the pagan Aristotle was not at all clear, though there were various

---

[8] Aquinas, *Summa* I, 1, q.1.

attempts to deal with the obvious areas of tension. Aquinas made one, Bonaventure another. In Bonaventure's view, Aquinas went too far in courting Aristotle. On the other hand, Bonaventure was well acquainted with Aristotle and, as his great scholastic writings indicate, was enormously skilled in the logic and general methodology of the university that was Aristotelian in style. It would not be accurate to say he was either anti-Aristotelian or anti-intellectual. Yet, there is a stronger retrospective tone in his way of dealing with the new challenge.

Bonaventure's approach to theology in a sense retrieved the richness of the wisdom tradition in a new context. It represents what today we might call a more "holistic" vision of spirituality and theology. Aware of the claims of the new and challenging Aristotelian views, and capable of employing the philosophical principles and techniques for the development of theological positions, Bonaventure sees all of this to be instrumental in realizing the only final goal of human life—the goal known not through philosophy but through the revelation of God in Jesus Christ. One does not reject the claims of reason in principle, but one attempts to integrate them into the broader vision of the journey of humanity and creation to a final, mystical union with God.

For Bonaventure, theology in its intellectual dimensions is an important discipline, but it cannot be allowed to be limited to this level. The theological endeavor as intellectual must lead the human person beyond the neutrality of mere cognition of the true to affective-contemplative delight in the good and the beautiful. In Bonaventure's work, the affairs of the heart and those of the head are kept in a remarkable, living relation to each other.

The outstanding Bonaventurean expression of the wisdom model is found in the *Journey of the Mind into God*. One might well see this work not as a theoretical statement, but as an account of Bonaventure's own spiritual journey through which he came to inform the life of scholarship with the Franciscan ideal of the imitation of Christ. Perhaps nowhere else in his writings do we find such a compact statement of his integral vision of reality and of its Christ-centered focus. The spiritual life is a journey into this unified reality. The initiate with the appropriate motivation enters on the way. The way is found above all in the person, history, and destiny of Jesus Christ. The journey can be described as an *imitatio Christi* through which the individual's relation to self, to other people, to the whole of creation, and to God is shaped primarily by the paradigmatic values of the life of Christ. The journey moves through all levels of external reality (nature mysticism) to the many levels of the interior world of human consciousness (mysticism of the soul), to the mystery of God as triune mystery of life-giving love (metaphysical mysticism). The goal of the journey is the experience of loving union with God in this life in the form of mystical experience; and in the next life, in the form of beatific vision. If we take the vision of this miniature masterpiece together with the vision of the *De reductione artium ad theologiam* we find the charter for a Christian humanism that is immensely rich. It draws all levels of reality and all the disciplines, arts, and sciences through which human beings organize their knowledge of reality into the context of the spiritual journey. All aspects of creation are fair game for the study of the friars. All can be and ought to be drawn into the spiritual journey to God. We might suggest that this vision is rooted in the spiritual vision of Francis of Assisi, who perceived a fraternal relation among all the creatures of God.

Theology, in such a context, is not knowledge for the sake of knowledge. It is, rather, knowledge for the sake of deepening love. Theological wisdom is, for Bonaventure, principally a wisdom of the will including both intellectual knowledge and affect. More specifically, it is a *habitus affectivus* that lies in the middle between that which is purely speculative and that which is purely practical or ethical, embracing both of these and partaking in both.[9] In this framework, at least ideally, knowledge is integrated into a process of human transformation, and oriented specifically to the deepening of human love for the good, and above all for God, the ultimate Good.[10]

In Bonaventure's own words, we study theology principally *"ut boni fiamus."*[11] Thus, theology is not practical in the sense of contemporary pragmatism. It is practical, rather, in the sense that it contributes to the intellectual, moral, and spiritual transformation of the human being. Obviously, if that transformation is authentic, it will flow into a transformed style of life.

---

[9] I *Sent*. prooem. q.3.
[10] Quinn, 1973: p. 683.
[11] I *Sent*. prooem. q.3.

I would suggest that this orientation as it is found among the early friars with clear roots in the Augustinian tradition reflects the concerns of Francis that theological knowledge should not be allowed to become mere ideas or words, but should move to some appropriate form of action, since "action speaks louder than words." Without genuine spiritual depth, action can be mere formalism. Without appropriate action, knowledge can be pure speculation. Theological wisdom as described by Bonaventure embraces both the speculative and the practical. Theology, viewed in this way, can be seen as a reflection on the experience of discipleship, both at the personal level and at the ministerial level, and then on the cognitive structures through which this experience is expressed.

Implications for Today

At least part of the reason for the rise of studies in the Order of Friars Minor may be found in the role that the order came to play in the public life of the medieval church, particularly in new forms of preaching, confessional work, teaching and disputation, and dealing with a variety of heresies. In pursuing their role, the followers of the *simplex et idiota* of Assisi found themselves operating at many levels within the church and in society in ways that demanded considerable intellectual skills.

There is a sense in which we may see the relation between Francis and the theologians of the order such as Bonaventure as a relationship between intense, personal, religious experience on the one hand, and serious, sustained, critical reflection on the other. When we look at the roots of the Franciscan tradition from this perspective, we are challenged not simply to retrieve the experience of Francis: we are challenged as well to retrieve the spirit of critical, constructive reflection on that experience. The roots of the Franciscan tradition are both spiritual and intellectual, both experiential and critical. These stand as creative polarities in the tradition. In this light, the following implications about ministerial leadership suggest themselves:

1. Ministry and formation for ministry pursued from the basis of this tradition would highlight the importance of the religious dimension in human experience at the personal level and at the larger social levels. At the personal level, the place of God in a per-

son's life is the most fundamental issue, for this shapes the person's relationship to everything else. What we name as God is that which effectively motivates us in life. What we name as God, therefore, is crucial. Can that reality, whatever it is, bear the weight of ultimacy for us? Religion is a way of dealing with the "big questions" about human destiny. Whence, whither, how, why? A ministerial preparation that fails to awaken the minister to these questions and to significant ways of dealing with them is a failure in relation to the needs of the church today.

2. In the spirit of the great Christian humanism of the past, training pursued from this tradition would investigate the relation of religion to other dimensions of human experience. How has religion interacted with the social and political areas? How has it interacted with the arts and the sciences? What are some of the positive and some of the negative factors that an educated person ought to be aware of? How are we to understand and deal with the religious factor in the shaping of society and culture? And particularly today, how are we to listen to the wisdom of other religious traditions and allow that wisdom to engage us as Christians?

3. A critical attitude would involve a number of important and difficult issues. People commonly take religious faith to involve some sort of knowledge, that is, they make cognitive claims in the name of religion. Or they claim to have special revelations from God. These claims are commonly understood to reflect God's will for the believer, and often this understanding goes on to shape the believer's expectations of those who do not share his or her belief. But not all religious believers seem to receive the same communications from God.

In view of this, a responsible religious leader must have some sense as to how one ought to assess such claims to knowledge together with their implications. What is the basis for making such claims? If we truly "know something" through religion, how is this form of knowledge related to other areas of human knowledge and experience? What sort of limitations must be put on these knowledge claims? Both with respect to ourselves, and with respect to others?

A model of ministry and ministerial training moving from this tradition would be suspicious of any uncritical religious claims. Clearly we need knowledgeable friars in all our ministries. How can we best respond to the often narrow movements within the church and in our society from a genuine spiritual richness? How can we avoid the all too frequent quick fix that is so prevalent in our age, and is often more destructive than helpful? In dealing with complex issues, simple goodwill is not enough. Nor are slogans. One needs to be able to think critically.

Specifically, we should be suspicious of fundamentalism in all its forms, whether it be scriptural fundamentalism or dogmatic fundamentalism (or scientific fundamentalism). The human mind is a gift of God and is to be accepted and used as such in the area of religion as in other areas of our life. God's word is addressed to creatures whom the Creator has endowed with the gift of intelligence, together with other gifts. Only if we are willing to engage in serious reflection will we be able to distinguish deep, authentic religious conviction from mindless fanaticism. This is particularly difficult, because religious claims cannot be tested in the same way as the claims of the positive sciences. They operate at a very different level. Yet they have a profound influence on human self-understanding and on human behavior, and it is important that they be tested.

4. Finally, an understanding of religious, ministerial leadership laying claim to the Franciscan tradition would give pride of place to the wisdom tradition that played such an important role in early Franciscan history. Knowledge itself is not yet wisdom, but it is a step in the direction of wisdom—and if anything is needed in today's world, it is wisdom. Such an understanding would attempt to engage serious religious convictions in a critical dialogue with the questions and values operative in our culture. It would be concerned with this not simply in a theoretical way, but in the hope of shaping a healthy style of life and learning to make wise and responsible judgments.

It would aim at communicating a sense of synthesis or unity. For this reason, it would be concerned with the relation between the various dimensions of human experience. It would hope to communicate significant insight into the human situation and to develop some sort of usable road map of reality. Inspired by the experience of Francis, Bonaventure created such a map that was intelligible for his own time and place. This might be an appropriate way to understand the task of ministerial preparation today. But this task must be carried out in circumstances that are fundamentally different from those of the past. While the major arteries of today's road map may look the same or at least very similar, the details will be considerably different. It will be a road map made for us people of the latter part of the twentieth century, understandable to us, and a guide to help us make our way through the complexity of our human experience of the world with a sense of meaning and purpose.

REFERENCES

Burr, David, *Olivi and Franciscan Poverty: The Origins of the Usus Pauper Controversy.* Philadelphia: University of Pennsylvania Press, 1989.

Esser, Kajetan, "Melius Catholice Observemus," *The Marrow of the Gospel,* Ignatius Brady, editor. Chicago: Franciscan Herald Press, 1958.

Heim, Michael, *The Metaphysics of Virtual Reality.* New York: Oxford University Press, 1993.

Iriarte de Aspruz, Lazaro, *The Franciscan Calling.* Chicago: Franciscan Herald Press, 1974.

Leclercq, Jean, *The Love of Learning and the Desire for God.* New York: Fordham University Press, 1961.

Manselli, Raoul, *St. Francis of Assisi.* Chicago: Franciscan Herald Press, 1988.

Quinn, John F., *The Historical Constitution of St. Bonaventure's Philosophy.* Toronto: Pontifical Institute of Medieval Studies, 1973.

Ratzinger, Joseph Cardinal, *The Theology of History in St. Bonaventure,* translated by Zachary Hayes. Chicago: Franciscan Herald Press, 1971.

3

Christology—Cosmology

Zachary Hayes, O.F.M.

A reading of representative publications dealing with environmental issues reveals that there are striking differences among those who are convinced that there is a serious problem in the way human beings relate to the world of nature. Some are convinced that the solution to the problem lies in the area of religion whereas others are convinced that it is precisely religion, and specifically the biblically based Christian tradition, that is the fundamental source of the problem. It is with this latter position that I would like to begin our reflections on the Christology of the Franciscan tradition and its possible relation to the environmental issues.

Our concern is to single out three major elements of this critique to provide a context for our discussion. First is the persistent criticism of the alleged anthropocentrism of the biblical tradition. In general terms, it is often argued that in this tradition, the chemical world, the world of plants, and the world of animals have no intrinsic meaning or value. They exist only for the sake of human beings— for whatever use humans may choose to put them to. It is felt that as long as we see things in this way, there is little chance that we will be able to deal with the environmental issues that seem to flow from this fundamental conviction.

One persistent reaction to this anthropocentrism is the call to a sort of egalitarian perspective. This usually involves the rejection of any sort of hierarchical thought that would place humanity at the top of the created order and the recognition of a fundamental equality among all creatures. The question this raises for us is: Is it possible to recognize a distinctive role for humanity with respect to the world of nature and still see real value and meaning in other creatures? Some elements in the Franciscan tradition might help us deal with such a question.

Second is the critics' contention that the other-worldly orientation of the Christian tradition inevitably brings with it a sense of
alienation from the cosmos in which we now make our home. For
here we are "aliens and exiles" (1 Peter 2:11). And, "here we have no
lasting city, but we are looking for the city that is to come" (Hebrews
13:14).

This is a problem long associated with the Marxist critique of
Christianity. Now, a similar critique arises from an environmental
perspective. If Christianity is a religion of salvation, and if salvation
is located not in this world but another, then much of Christian spirituality is concerned not with the quality of life here, but with the
process of becoming liberated from this world and moving to that
genuine "homeland" that awaits us in the other world. We have, in
fact, customarily referred to this world as a "vale of tears" and have
tended to see our time here as a time of "moral testing" after which,
if we make the grade, we will enter into our heavenly reward. We
have, in fact, prayed in at least one of the prayers of the Roman liturgy that we may learn "to despise the things of this world and rejoice
in the things of heaven."

For one who thinks this way, environmental issues are issues of
"this world." Is it not easy to conclude that such matters are not
genuinely religious issues? Christians might be interested in them
for a variety of humanistic reasons, but there is no clear religious
motivation for such concern. If our vision is fixed on eternity, why
should we be concerned with the fleeting, passing world of material
realities?

It is my conviction that religious people ought to hear this critique and take it seriously. I would like to indicate at least some elements in our Franciscan tradition that might suggest a different
approach to the question of salvation and hence to the question of
the Christian's relation to the world of nature.

This relates to a larger issue which is the third of our major concerns. Christian theology, for the most part, no longer has an effective cosmology that enables believers to relate to the world in its
physical character in a way that is consistent with their religious
symbols. Consequently, part of the process of reshaping our religious understanding of the world involves the formulation of such a
cosmology. This, in turn, would mean that faith must engage the best
insights of science concerning the nature of the physical world.

Science and Theology

A careful reading of the theological tradition prior to the modern era indicates that before the so-called Copernican revolution in our understanding of the physical universe, there existed a religious cosmology that involved not only the insights of faith but the physical understanding of the cosmos as it was known at that time. We might suggest the significance of such a cosmology very directly. A cosmology that relates religious convictions to a physical vision of the cosmos allows the believer to come to an understanding of the world in which he or she exists and of the believer's place in that world. It allows the believer to deal with the symbols of religious faith in the context of the physical world as understood at a particular point in time. The breakdown of such a cosmology by the shift from a geocentric model to a heliocentric model led eventually to the isolation of theology from the development of modern science.

For those educated in the Western world in the twentieth century, the physical vision of the cosmos has changed drastically. But our religious language, shaped at least in part by what is now seen to be an archaic physics, has remained largely unchanged in theology and liturgy. As contemporary believers, we live in two worlds. In our everyday experience, we live in a culture deeply conditioned by the insights and theories of modern science. But in the context of the church, its theology, and its liturgy, we live in a premodern world.

Responses to this situation have been diverse, and I don't intend to discuss them here. I merely wish to suggest that if we intend to formulate an effective cosmology for people of the latter part of the twentieth century, we should found it on some sort of conversation between our faith concerns and the insights and theories of science. The views of Pope John Paul II concerning the relation between science and theology are helpful in this regard.

The holy father avoids looking to the sciences for any sort of apologetic purpose. We should not fall into the trap of thinking that science should or can provide a basis for religion. This is a dead-end street. Nor should we look to science for some sort of apologetic proof for the truth of specific theological positions. This also is unnecessary and unwise. Yet the holy father speaks of the relation between science and theology as "crucial for the contemporary world." The pope envisions not a fusion of science and theology into a single discipline, but an ongoing dialogue between the two disciplines. Religion is not based on science, nor is science an extension of religion. The dialogue must recognize the autonomy of each. But both must be seen in relation to their potential contribution to the good of humanity. "We must ask ourselves whether both science and religion will contribute to the integration of human culture or to its fragmentation," notes the holy father. In his words, "It is a single choice and it confronts us all.... Simple neutrality is no longer acceptable."[1]

Scientific Cosmology

This is not intended to be a course in contemporary physics. I want only to highlight some of the qualities of the cosmos as it is perceived in contemporary science. We need be concerned only with the broader features of the scientific vision and with those insights that are more firmly established. We are not concerned here with the more speculative matters of science, nor with specific theories concerning the origin of the universe or the origin of life. For example, while the so-called Big Bang theory is currently the most widely accepted model dealing with the question of cosmic origins, it is not the only one. There are, however, other more basic insights that I propose to examine, whether they are accounted for by means of the Big Bang theory or some other.

The most fundamental shift in our understanding of the cosmos is the move from the vision of a universe launched essentially in its present form by the hand of the Creator at the beginning of time to a vision of the cosmos as a dynamic, unfolding chemical process, immensely large in both time and space. This process, which is still going on, has a long history of emergent novelty. It is characterized, to a great extent, by chance and by what seems to be some form of law. The cosmos as viewed in classical terms was relatively small both in space and in time. The contemporary perception sees a cosmos almost unimaginably large, and growing larger with the passage of time. The cosmic process is a highly unified process in which there is a remarkable degree of interdependence among all the elements involved. In such a vision, from a scientific perspective, life emerges out of the chemistry of the universe, at least on this planet. So also does conscious, intelligent life. But all forms of life, including

---

[1] John Paul II, 1989: pp. 1-9.

human life, are deeply embedded in the chemical processes that are operative throughout the cosmos.

The whole of this cosmic process, according to much scientific literature, is to be understood as a fact with no meaning or purpose discernible. This makes the whole, together with individual elements within it, highly ambiguous. Human life seems to stand out in this cosmic process in a qualitative sense; but when the human phenomenon is viewed in the broader context of cosmic history, the human race seems, to some scientists, to be a mere transitory episode in a much larger cosmic history. As a consequence, human values and human individuals rank as relatively insignificant. To many, the human race poses a particular sort of problem within the whole of the process.

On the other hand, the anthropic principle, in its various forms, suggests to some scientists that the initial conditions at the beginning of cosmic history were remarkably fine-tuned to bring forth intelligent life. This in turn seems to suggest that "mind" or intelligent life is fundamental to the universe and not an accidental intrusion or a foreign visitor to a universe otherwise devoid of intelligence.

Such a vision of the cosmos, elements of which are commonly communicated in the science courses offered in our schools and in educational television as well as in popular television programs, is at least implicitly a part of the mental makeup of many twentieth-century people. If such a vision is taken seriously at all, it will modify our way of thinking of God and of God's relation to the world. It will likewise modify our understanding of humanity's relation to the physical cosmos and to God. This, in turn, will affect our attitude toward nature and will have practical implications for an environmental ethics.[2]

Historical Distortions

It seems clear that if we read our tradition in its great, creative moments, it can be seen as a religious tradition with a keen sense of the religious significance of the material universe. It seems equally clear that for most Christians today, this dimension of the Christian tradition has been lost. Because it is lost, many Christians do not see

---

[2] Barbour, 1989: p. 26.

the relation of humanity to the cosmos as a specifically religious issue.

Some of the problems felt today with the biblical tradition derive less from the religious insights native to that tradition than from the engagement of the tradition with a variety of cultural systems in the course of the centuries. A few examples help to clarify this for our purposes.

1. It is well-known that a major philosophical tradition with which Christians engaged in serious discussion was that of Platonism and Neo-Platonism. An element of the Platonic tradition is its tendency to think of material reality in rather negative terms. Its primary focus is on the realm of ideal forms that transcend the material beings of our empirical world. As this philosophical outlook entered the context of Christian spirituality and theology, it became difficult for Christian Neo-Platonists to come to terms with the earthier biblical sense of materiality as an element of God's creation. Generations of Christians have been formed with this unresolved tension. Even today many Christians are left with a sense that religion is about the soul rather than about the body. They seem to have clearer ideas about the salvation of their souls than they do about the destiny of their bodies.

2. Western Enlightenment philosophy has fostered an anthropology that understands humanity as essentially above and independent of nature, and therefore as lord and ruler of nature. It is arguable that this is an appropriate understanding of the biblical tradition. Regardless of the outcome of that debate, when this sort of Enlightenment anthropology is taken as the proper interpretation of the text of Genesis 1:28, a particularly problematic situation arises. The conjunction readily gives the believer the impression that in enacting the Enlightenment understanding of humanity's relation to the world of nature through technological manipulation and control, we are but fulfilling the divine will with respect to the world. That is, our cultural project with all its philosophical and technological dimensions is given a form of religious legitimation. In consequence, it is easy to see why the depredation of the world of nature can be seen by many to be rooted in the biblical vision.

3. The understanding of the universe cast by Newtonian physics engenders another dilemma. When the cosmos is seen as a mechanical system of material things operating with mathematical consistency on the basis of immutable laws, two things happen. First, the

human spirit stands out as foreign to the cosmos. Thus, the anthropology just described is reinforced from another direction. Second, such a universe has no need of God except as the creator who sets up the universe in the beginning. Indeed, this seems to have been the understanding of many deists. The religious world of revelation, miracles, and so on is foreign territory to such a world view. The religious sense of divine immanence is lost in the face of the God of modern deism, or eventually of atheism.

With these problems in mind, I would like to offer some reflections on the nature of the Christian, and specifically the Franciscan, tradition. Some of the elements of that tradition might well join in conversation with the scientific image of the cosmos described above. By engaging the insights of science with those of faith, we may be able to communicate a new cosmology that would put a more personal face on what otherwise seems to be a purely chemical process uninterested in humanity. If we can do that, we will be able to communicate a stronger sense of the ethical significance of human consciousness that this cosmic process has brought forth. Finally, we will be able to mediate a sense of meaning and hope in what otherwise seems for many to invite a sense of cosmic terror. Simply put, this immense, dynamic, organic, chemical process that today's science describes is, from a Christian perspective, the home in which a loving Creator has placed us, and it is the object of God's creative and salvific love.

Cosmic Christology in the Franciscan Tradition

Franciscans have a strong tradition of cosmic Christology that they have almost forgotten. In recent generations we have allowed our Christology to revolve exclusively around the salvific significance of the crucifixion of Jesus as a sacrifice for our sins. I do not question the validity of that concern. I want only to suggest that, in the light of the broader and older tradition, this is only one dimension of the meaning of the Christ-mystery. Already in the work of Alexander of Hales, the intimate relation between creation and incarnation is obvious. This theme would be developed emphatically by Bonaventure. And certainly as far back as Bonaventure, and clearly in such writers as Matthew of Aquasparta, William of Ware, and John Duns Scotus, Franciscan authors refused to limit the meaning of the Christ-mystery to that of being a remedy for sin.

These Franciscan masters were all convinced, in one way or another, that what happened between the world and God in the mystery of Christ could not have been an afterthought on God's part. God intended it from the very first moment of creation. The Christ-mystery must be thought of in terms of the fundamental aim of God in creating the cosmos. We might say that, for this tradition, the mystery of Christ pertains to the very nature of the cosmos as God intended it. I would like to single out particular elements of this tradition and ask about their possible relation to the image of the cosmos given us by science.

Elements of the Christological Tradition

1. *Predestination of Christ.* Probably the best-known position of the Franciscan masters is the Scotistic theory of the absolute predestination of Christ. For the English-speaking world, the work of Allan Wolter, O.F.M., has done much to recall and reformulate this theory of John Duns Scotus. As Wolter points out, from a negative perspective Duns Scotus rejects the idea that the redemption of the human race is the fundamental reason for the coming of Christ. From a positive perspective, Duns Scotus holds that what God first intended in creating was the mystery of Christ as king and center of the universe.[3]

In the context of medieval theology, this amounts to a rejection of the idea that God first created a world that had no relation to the figure of Christ. Only after the fall of the human race did a "second decree" of God direct itself to the figure of a savior in the form of Christ. This, of course, is the theory communicated by most Roman Catholic catechesis and preaching at least until quite recently. To those who are completely convinced that this widely held theory is the only form that Christology can take, Duns Scotus's approach may have a dangerous edge. It is important to realize, therefore, that in the Middle Ages the Scotistic theory was a perfectly acceptable alternative to what eventually became the mainline position. One then situates the meaning of the cross within the context of a broader cosmic vision.

The Scotistic position has been rejuvenated in recent times not only in the context of historical studies but also by the writings of

---

[3] Wolter, 1980: p. 140.

Karl Rahner, who appeals to it explicitly in his attempt to discuss the relation of Christology to evolutionary thought patterns.[4] In Rahner's terms, what God intends first in creating is the reality of Christ. That Christ might be possible, there must be a human race. That the human race might be possible, there must be a world in which human beings can live. However one looks at this, it implies an intimate relation between the cosmos and the Christ-mystery.

While Bonaventure never formulated the issue in precisely the terms that Duns Scotus used, there can be little doubt that for him also the mystery of Christ was the key to the meaning both of the human race and of the entire cosmos. It might be helpful to single out a few elements of Bonaventure's vision.

2. *Matter and Spirit.* Here I would like to highlight the way in which Bonaventure describes the relation of matter to spirit in the cosmos and of both of these to the Word of God. The pertinent text is found in his *De reductione artium ad theologiam.* Bonaventure speaks here of an active orientation or an "appetite" in matter for union with the rational soul. Only in their relation to each other do they find their perfection. Now, in a similar way, the "highest and noblest perfection can exist in this world" only when a nature that brings together both created matter and created spirit is united in the unity of one person with the eternal Word of God. And this "was done in the incarnation of the Son of God."[5] This is clearly a statement about the significance of the incarnation as the summit of the creative work of God. In this particular instance, nothing is said of the relation of the incarnation to sin.

3. *Christ and Human Nature.* With regard to the relation of Christology to human nature, the text of Bonaventure's *Sermon II on the Nativity of the Lord* is important. The biblical text for the sermon is taken from the prologue of the Gospel According to John: "The Word became flesh" (John 1:14). The first section of the sermon consists of a profound meditation on the mystery of the divine Word as the principle of all God's creative and revelatory action. It points to the essential unity of the mystery of creation and salvation by its emphasis on the fact that both of these divine works are effected through one and the same divine Word. In the first instance, we are

---

[4] Rahner, 1966: pp. 157ff.
[5] Bonaventure, *De reductione,* n. 20.

dealing with the eternal, uncreated Word as the principle through which God creates. In the second instance, we are dealing with the same uncreated Word, but now as incarnate in history in the form of Jesus of Nazareth, through whom a fallen world is restored to its life-giving relation with God.

Even more emphatic is the final paragraph of the sermon. Here Bonaventure describes the mystery of the incarnation in the following way. The deepest, most noble potential of human nature is its potential to be united in a unity of person with the divine. It is this potential that is brought to act in the mystery of the incarnation. And insofar as this has taken place in Jesus, "the perfection of the entire created order is realized, for in that one being the unity of all reality is brought to consummation."[6]

What strikes one in this passage is, first, the way in which human potential for the divine is embedded in the order of creation; and second, the way in which the significance of the incarnation is related not to the "forgiveness of sin" but to the completion of the work of creation. As we know from other works of Bonaventure, the redemptive significance of Jesus does in fact relate to the issue of sin. But the incarnation is not decreed by God because of sin, nor is the overcoming of sin the total significance of the Christ-mystery. As seems obvious in this sermon, the incarnation is clearly given a broader, cosmic significance. We could express this in contemporary language as follows. Insofar as Christ is the unity of the divine reality with the created spirit and with bodily nature, Christ appears as the "cosmic person."[7]

Finally, for the Franciscan tradition, the cosmic Christ is not a sort of impersonal, abstract principle, nor a mathematical formula. Rather, the cosmic significance of Christ is always related to the way in which the awareness of this principle has emerged in human experience; namely, through the history of Jesus, the preeminent, historical embodiment of the eternal, creative, and revelatory Word of God.

4. *Logos-Christology.* Related to the above concern is the tendency to develop a strong form of Logos-Christology. This can be seen in the first section of the sermon by Bonaventure just mentioned. It

---

[6] Hayes, 1974: p. 74.
[7] Cousins, 1992: p. 189.

is perhaps more emphatic in Bonaventure's *Commentary on the Gospel According to St. John*. There, in his treatment of the prologue, Bonaventure sketches the core of a powerful theology of the Word. It is, in essence, a rich theology of revelation.[8] The points that stand out as relevant to our topic are these: The Logos is the divine principle through which all of God's operations *ad extra* are effected. It is through the Logos that God creates. The relation of the Logos to the cosmic order is unmistakable in this vision. It is this very same Logos, operative through the whole of history, that becomes enfleshed in the history of Jesus Christ.

Looking at this from the side of creation, one must conclude that the cosmos itself is the first and primal revelation of God through the divine Word. But the same Word is the principle through which God enlightens all who come into the world. With this Bonaventure moves to the history of revelation in the biblical tradition and to its embodiment in the person of Jesus Christ. While the cosmic revelation leads to an awareness of God as good and loving creator, the historical revelation intensifies that sense of the divine and leads further to an awareness of the same God precisely as the source of salvation and completion. That is, the God who creates is the God who saves. And the object of salvation is the world that God creates. Clearly for Bonaventure, the salvation of the cosmos is mediated through the salvation of humanity. And one can sense the struggle of the medieval theologian to find a way of expressing how it is that the world of God's creation is finally brought to fulfillment in the fulfillment of humanity. But the struggle itself is significant in that it highlights two factors: 1) humanity plays a distinct role in the salvation of the world; and 2) salvation is larger than humanity alone.[9]

What this orientation suggests is the need to be much more aware of the cosmic dimension of the Christian vision communicated through such a Logos-Christology. This might incline us to think of salvation as the process by which God brings to completion (= salvation) the world which God creates. With that in mind, we will be more inclined to develop an understanding of salvation that embraces nature as well as human beings.

---

[8] Hayes, 1974: p. 125.
[9] Hayes, 1994: pp. 110-114.

5. *Christ as Paradigm of Human Life.* A strong theme in the Franciscan tradition is the central role of Christ both in spirituality and in the cosmic vision just described above. This can be treated in two points. First, Christ in his destiny with God embodies the final destiny of the human race, and ultimately of the created order as a whole. Second, Christ, in his historical life and ministry, embodies the way to that destiny.

The first issue is the question of the final outcome of Jesus's life. This is expressed traditionally in terms of the resurrection. Jesus is not annihilated on the cross, but lives in a radically transformed mode in the presence of God in eternity. In biblical terms as well as in medieval terms, what happens in Jesus is the anticipation of the future of humanity and of the cosmos. We do not look forward to the annihilation of creation, but to its radical transformation through the power of God's life-giving, fulfilling Spirit.

This positive outcome of life is related to the way in which human life is lived in history. How should human life be lived? The answer to this lies at the core of the life and ministry of Jesus. It is the question of an agapistic ethics. If God is as Jesus suggested through his preaching and the actions of his ministry, then how ought we respond to such a God? If God is *agape*, as St. John summarizes the message of Jesus, and if all of creation and all of humanity exists only in the creative love of God, we must ask: What is an appropriate response? The decisive value that must lie at the heart of human life and human relations is that of *agape*. For us today, this must be reflected on in the context of a cosmos in which principles other than *agape* are at work, both in the world of nature and in the world of human culture. What does it mean to respond to situations in a loving way in a world marked by so much physical violence and moral insensitivity?

6. *The Role of Humanity.* The biblical tradition has long been convinced that the destiny of humanity is intertwined with that of the cosmos. This has been a significant part of the Franciscan tradition as well. Humanity has a distinct role to play in the destiny of the cosmos. In the Franciscan tradition, at least three things can be said about this. First, looking at humanity in terms of its relation to the created cosmos, the tradition sees humanity as that point at which the created order finds a personal consciousness and a personal voice with which to give conscious praise to God. This is important in defining the way in which humanity is "above" the rest of cre-

ation, as well as the way in which creation best "serves" humanity. In Bonaventure's words, the entire cosmos serves humanity principally by leading human beings to a conscious love for and praise of the Creator. This is a long way from a relation of human domination and control over nature.[10]

Second, looking at humanity in terms of our relation to God, human nature is best understood at its deepest level as a potential for receiving a personal self-communication of God. It is in such a personal self-communication that the fullest potential of creation as embodied in humanity is brought to act.

Third, in looking for an appropriate way to delineate the relation between humanity and the world of nature, we might be well advised to look to the sort of "familial" metaphor suggested by St. Francis's language of "brother" and "sister" in relation to a common, universal "Parent." Such a metaphor might place our efforts somewhere between the extreme of "domination and control" and the opposite extreme of total equality among all creatures.

Implications

1. Science tends to see the existence of the universe as a given datum. Its existence is a fact with no particular reason. It may be seen as a necessary fact, or it may be seen as a purely contingent fact. But basically, from a scientific perspective, it is a fact the meaning of which eludes the sciences. Our religious tradition sees the universe not as necessary but as contingent. But it sees this contingence as pointing to a deeper mystery of creative freedom. The existence of the universe, which does not have to exist but, in fact, does exist is grounded in the free, creative love of God. God calls forth, and sustains, and brings the world to completion by creative love. The world exists "for" something. And that purpose is expressed by Bonaventure in two Latin terms: *manifestare* and *participare.* The cosmos manifests the mystery of God in the nondivine. And creation is called into being so as to participate in ever deeper levels in the mystery of the divine life.

2. As we suggested earlier, the universe seen from the perspective of science is ambiguous. Einstein once put the issue in the form

---

[10] Hayes, 1994: p. 68.

of a question: Is the universe friendly or unfriendly?[11] As perceived in the Christian and Franciscan tradition, the universe is seen as remarkably congenial to humanity. This seems to be consonant with the anthropic vision of cosmology. The anonymous, almost fatalistic vision of cosmic reality in some areas of contemporary physics can begin to take on a friendlier character.

The issue for believers is not whether they can see the cosmos through the categories of science and still believe in God. Rather, the issue is what kind of God they believe in. Certainly, we need to move beyond the deistic-sounding God who is so utterly removed from us that the world is seen as alien to God. Theology will give more emphasis to the presence of God and the divine immanence to the world in its historical unfolding.

Precisely because the Christian tradition sees the world as grounded in the divine, creative love, it understands the world to be an apt receptacle of the divine. I take this to be the implication of the Christological dogma of Chalcedon, which is radicalized in the Franciscan tradition as we have seen above. The world receives the self-gift of God into its inner depth. And this mysterious gift of God does not destroy creation but perfects it and brings it to completion. In this, the deepest and life-giving relation between creation and God, lies the future not only of humanity but of the whole of God's creation. And because of this, we can live our life with a deep sense of meaning and purpose that cannot be derived from the insights of science alone.

3. This tradition communicates a strong sacramental sense. We are invited to give much greater emphasis to the sacred character of the universe. This does not mean that we identify the universe with God, but that we learn to see it as an appropriate means of manifesting and communicating the divine to the human.

Seen in this way, nature-mysticism need not become a divinization of the cosmos itself. Rather, it is a reading of the deeper meaning of the cosmos. The cosmos is a symbol system in which something of the mystery of the divine is communicated to those capable of reading the symbols. To recognize the sacredness of the cosmos in this way is different from the tendency among many religious environmentalists to replace the reality of God with the earth itself, or with some form of totally immanent principle.

---

[11] Haught, 1993 (1): p. 147.

This sense of the sacramental is radicalized in the Christian perception of Christ. The human reality of Jesus is the most focused statement of what God is about with the world more generally. Jesus is the preeminent instance of the sacramentality of the cosmos.

This sacramental sense of the whole of creation is brought to its completion in the understanding of the resurrection of Christ. For this mystery is but the anticipation in the individual Jesus of what God intends for all of humanity and, through humanity, for the cosmos. It is from this basis that Christians come to believe that the created cosmos is destined not for annihilation, but for a fulfillment brought about by the final, life-giving relation between God and creation. If Karl Rahner can speak of the eternal significance of the humanity of Christ,[12] it is quite possible to extend that to the cosmos as a whole.

4. This reading of the tradition suggests a sense of the closer relation between material reality and affairs of the spirit. The biblical tradition is a religious tradition for which material reality is not an evil but a good. What we look forward to is not an escape from materiality but the radical transformation through which matter and spirit will be brought to their final, life giving relationship in the presence of God. This sense of the importance of material reality is radicalized in the Christian understanding of the Christ-mystery. Therefore, spirituality should deal with bodily reality not only in negative terms but in positive terms as well. The negative terms have to do with the human tendency to place an undue importance on the bodily. The positive terms have to do with the fact that grace does not destroy nature but brings it to fulfillment.

5. If our earlier remarks suggested some problem with the spirituality communicated through the Neo-Platonic tradition, current readings of biblical and other sources suggest a different possibility for understanding spirituality. One might speak today of a spirituality of inclusion. This idea is suggested by John Haught[13] and seems to capture crucial elements of the Scriptures.

First, we recall that Christ reveals the agapistic way as the human way in the world. As Alfred North Whitehead pointed out,

---

[12] Rahner, 1967: pp. 35-46.
[13] Haught, 1993 (2): p. 140.

the history from which Christianity takes its origin suggests the importance of the "tender moment."[14] When we think about this in the context of the dynamics of the universe as perceived by science, it seems clear that this ethics is situated in the context of an eco-system which operates on a variety of other principles such as conflict, competition, etc.

What this agapistic vision meant for Jesus may be seen in the inclusive style of life he lived. He is presented in the gospels as one who constantly reached out to those who were not included by the social-religious structures of the time. Haught suggests that this life style of Jesus stands as the sacrament of what God is like, and therefore of what a God-like life would be like among humans with respect to each other and to the world in which they live. This points to the meaning of *agape*.

This might be seen as a possible corrective to the Neo-Platonic tradition mentioned earlier. We do not have to leave the world behind in order to find God. Rather, we bring the world with us into our relation with God. This seems to be coherent with what we have said about the sacramental character of the world. We might think of spirituality, then, in terms of entering into ever richer relations with people and things in the world, and thus into a richer relation with God.

6. This brings us to our final point: ecological ethics and religious motivation. Is there a way in which we can say that we are concerned with environmental issues not despite our religious convictions, but precisely because of them?

I think there clearly is. Precisely because of creation-theology in our tradition, and because of its radicalization in the Christian understanding of Christ, the cosmos is seen as the object of God's salvific, fulfilling love. Earlier I gave two texts from Scripture that suggest a feeling of "homelessness" as the spiritual condition of Christians living in this world. I have suggested that this fuels the fire of the critique which claims that precisely the biblical tradition is a major source of Christian indifference to environmental issues.

There is, in fact, a kind of homelessness involved in the Christian sensitivity. But it need not be seen as the homelessness of humanity yearning to escape this world for a more permanent world. It may

---

[14] Whitehead, 1933: p. 167.

well be seen as the homelessness of the world itself which has not yet arrived at its God-intended fulfillment. This cosmic reality is what comes to conscious awareness in human religious consciousness. In the form of human consciousness, this is the consciousness of an incomplete world yearning for its completion with God. What that fulfillment might look like we discover by reflecting on the mystery of the resurrection of Christ.

The spiritual journey of humanity, then, is not a journey out of this world. It is rather a spiritual journey that is deeply embedded in the journey of the cosmos itself. The universe is not at home until it comes to its end with and in God. Hence, the issue of spirituality is not to get out of the world, but to align oneself with the journey of the universe into God in the light of the ethics Jesus has made known to us as the appropriate way of relating to the world and to God.

If this is true, it means that human agency is involved in bringing the divine aim for creation to effective realization. And human beings are best thought of as created co-creators, called to enact an agapistic ethics that transcends the mechanisms of survival and pure biological necessity in the direction of altruism. It is finally in this direction that the kingdom of God lies.

If this is accurate, it suggests the place in our religious vision where a sense of ecological ethics can begin to take root. Our cultural tendency to define human relations to the world of nature in purely instrumental terms needs to be modified in the light of our religious tradition to make room for other sorts of relations. I think here of Michael Polanyi's concern for the esthetic dimensions in our experience of the world; or of Duns Scotus's sense of the importance of each individual creature in terms of what he called *haecceitas* ("thisness"), and what we today might call an intrinsic value. Simply put, human use and possible market value are not the only issues that ought to enter into our relation to the world of nature. They may not even be the most basic issues.

This is a way of saying that a respect and healthy concern for the world of nature should not be allowed to be turned into a passing fad. It may well be seen as an intrinsic element of the biblical and Christian tradition. It is also a profound expression of the Franciscan tradition.

REFERENCES

Barbour, Ian, *Religion in an Age of Science: The Gifford Lectures,* Volume I. San Francisco: Harper, 1989-91.

Cousins, Ewert, *Christ of the 21st Century.* Rockport, Massachusetts: Element, 1992.

Haught, John, *Mystery and Promise: A Theology of Revelation.* Collegeville, Minnesota: Liturgical Press, 1993(1).

————, *The Promise of Nature: Ecology and Cosmic Purpose.* New York: Paulist Press, 1993(2).

Hayes, Zachary, *What Manner of Man? Sermons on Christ by St. Bonaventure.* Chicago: Franciscan Herald Press, 1974.

————, "Bonaventure: The Mystery of the Triune God," *The History of the Franciscan Theology.* Edited by Kenan B. Osborne. St. Bonaventure, New York: Franciscan Institute, 1994.

John Paul II, "God and Nature," The Pope Speaks, Volume 34, No. 1. Huntington, Indiana: Our Sunday Visitor Press, 1989.

Rahner, Karl, "Christology Within an Evolutionary View of the World, *Theological Investigations* , Volume 5, pp.157-192. London: Darton, Longman & Todd, 1966.

————, "The Eternal Significance of Jesus for our Relationship with God," *Theological Investigations* , Volume 3, pp. 35-46. London: Darton, Longman & Todd, 1967.

Whitehead, Alfred North, *Adventures of Ideas.* New York: Macmillan, 1933.

Wolter, Allan, "John Duns Scotus," *Franciscan Christology.* Edited by D. McElrath. St. Bonaventure, New York: Franciscan Institute, 1980.

4

Human Dignity in the Theology of St. Bonaventure

Thomas A. Shannon

1. Introduction

"God had a bad day when he made a cab driver, sir,"[1] said Tony Cichielo, a retired bell captain at the Algonquin Hotel, to express his dismay about cabbies who no longer helped bellhops unload suitcases from the trunk of the cab. While directed to a particular group, the comment is one that many would think appropriate to generalize to most of the human race. Such pessimism is generated and documented by the daily media reports of murders, violence, and mayhem. Such reports are not limited to the reporting of crime, to which we have almost become numb. The dissolution of the Soviet Union released ethnic tensions that had been on hold since the Russian Revolution and expansion of the Soviet Union. Ethnic hatred has led to unspeakable horrors. We are experiencing the largest number of refugees since World War I and the response has been a virulent xenophobia in both Europe and America. Even the restrained optimism generated by the signing of the peace accord between Israel and the Palestinians has been tempered by those dedicated to continuing the hatred.

In another area—modern, high-tech medicine—an analogous problem touching on human values has arisen. Ironically, it is engendered by the very success of modern medicine. On the one hand, the combination of improved nutrition and public sanitation and the development of a variety of vaccines together with inoculation programs has helped expand the number of people who will live longer lives. In fact, the average life expectancy in the United States has almost doubled since 1900. On the other hand, the elderly are expe-

---

[1] "Bellhop." The New Yorker. Vol. LXIX (20 September 1993): p. 46.

riencing higher levels of chronic disease and physical debilitation that cannot be cured. The response frequently has been to employ so-called "half-way" technologies. These only compensate for a disabled function; they don't cure its impairment. A ventilator, for example, assists in breathing, but cannot repair damaged lungs. A dialysis machine can purify the blood, but it cannot cure end-stage renal disease.

The patient who does not recover for other reasons is now caught in a terrible double bind: remain on the technology for the rest of his or her life or remove the support knowing that death will follow.

Some feel that removing life supports is improper because death follows. Others feel that they do not have the authority to make such a decision. Still others would remove the therapy but fear that if they do a lawsuit will be initiated. And so families simply cannot come to any agreement. Additionally, the dominant ethic in medicine is to treat as aggressively for as long as possible. This ethic sees death as the enemy that must be held off as long as possible. Additionally some physicians see disease as a professional challenge and bring all resources possible to the bedside to defeat it.

The combination of overtreatment, the use of half-way technologies, and the lack of a cure for a disease all too often leads to the maintenance of a person if the technology supports it even though little or nothing curative can be done. The result is a kind of technological entrapment that in some cases can be and is prolonged for years.

What suffers significantly in such situations is human dignity: the dignity of a patient who becomes simply an object, sometimes comatose or in a persistent vegetative state, to be maintained; the dignity of health-care providers who, while acting out of compassion and providing what they consider the best care possible, become numbed by the futility of the situation and begin viewing the patient as an object.

Modern medicine is truly a gift to our world, and we would have a terrible setback were we to lose the gains we have made in recent decades. Yet the person stands in danger of being lost in the marvels that we have developed. Preventing such objectification of the patient is a particular challenge to health-care providers but preventing technological entrapment insofar as possible is a responsibility for all of us.

Finally, consider the cultural phenomenon that has been a major force in setting a context for how we think of ourselves and others.

This is the phenomenon of individualism examined in *Habits of the Heart*. The argument of Robert Bellah and his colleagues is that the American emphasis on individualism might "isolate Americans one from another and thereby undermine the conditions of freedom."[2] The focus of their book is on two kinds of individualism: expressive individualism, which looks to the fulfillment of one's life, and utilitarian individualism, which focuses one's attention exclusively on a specific goal. Such orientations can lead to a society that leaves little room for "love, human feeling, and a deeper expression of the self."[3]

The concern of Bellah and his co-authors is that these forms of individualism pull people from their communities and associations into isolation. This can lead to the realization of a fear identified more than a century ago by Alexis de Tocqueville: fear of "the mass society of mutually antagonistic individuals, easy prey to despotism."[4]

What we have in our American society are substantial threats to dignity and the value of the individual. These come from the individual and the social level, from politics and economics, from religion and philosophy. This essay looks to the Franciscan tradition to seek a vision that might help reorient ourselves, our parishes, and our communities to the reality of our human dignity. Specifically, I will present St. Bonaventure's vision of human dignity as a way of grounding our discussion. Bonaventure offers a richness of thought and imagery that may rekindle the smoldering embers in our heart and culture.

2. Bonaventure's Theological Vision

The richness of Bonaventure's vision, and more importantly, the synthesis of his vision make it impossible simply to pull an idea out of his writings and discuss it. I will present first an overview of themes and key terms in his conceptual framework. Then I will develop his vision of human dignity and from this draw several conclusions.

---

[2] Bellah et al., 1985: p. viii.
[3] Bellah et al., 1985, p. 33.
[4] Bellah et al., 1985, p. 38.

An Overview of the Conceptual Framework of Bonaventure

1. Exemplarity

An exemplar is "an original model in whose likeness all things have been shaped."[5] This template constitutes ultimate reality, and creation stands in its shadow and participates in the reality of the original. The significance of the doctrine of exemplarism in Bonaventure is that it is a way of showing the relatedness of creation to God and explaining the order and structure of creation.

The significance of exemplarity for both the structure of reality and for our salvation is stated directly by Bonaventure: "for any person who is unable to consider how things originate, how they are led back to their end, and how God shines forth in them, is incapable of achieving true understanding."[6]

2. Circularity

Bonaventure used the image of the circle to set out the great cosmic and spiritual journey: "grace, salvation, and eschatalogical fulfillment constitute the articulation of the successful completion of the journey."[7] Additionally, the image of the circle has its Christological dimension:

> Finally it is in this Word that we discover the perfection of that greatness of heart which brings all reality to its consummation and completion, since the figure of the circle attests to the perfection of bodies both in the macrocosm and in the microcosm. In the macrocosm, the greater bodies such as the heavens, the sun, and the moon are round in shape. So also in man, who is a microcosm, the more noble members such as the head, the heart, and the eye are round in form. But this figure is not complete in the universe. Now, if this figure is to be as perfect as possible, the line of the universe must be curved into a circle. Indeed God is simply the First. And the last among the works of the world is man. Therefore, when God became man, the works of God were brought to perfection. This is why Christ, the God-man, is called the Alpha and the Omega, the beginning and the end.[8]

---

[5] Hayes, 1994: p. 72.
[6] *Collationes in Hexameron*, III, 2; quoted in Hayes, 1994: p. 51.
[7] Hayes, 1994: p. 62.
[8] Bonaventure, *Sermon II*, pp. 73-74.

3. Goodness is Diffusive of Itself

The phrase *"Bonum est diffusivum sui"* is for Bonaventure a key concept. It is the sign by which goodness is manifested and recognized. A critical locus of God's self-diffusion is the human being, a composite being

> whose spiritual soul communicates its life and activities to a material body in such an intimate way that, together, they form a substantial union. Man thus stands in the center of creation as that creature in which the self-diffusing goodness of the Creator is most clearly and perfectly manifested.[9]

4. Plurality of Forms and Seminal Reasons

In keeping with the medieval tradition, Bonaventure held that reality was composed of matter and form. Form "has indeed the bestowing of a perfection as its chief function, but it does this by preparing the substance which it informs for other substantial perfections which it cannot itself confer on them."[10] What this allows Bonaventure to argue is that the human, containing all elements of the corporeal world, is the highest of an ascending series of forms and therefore is "the center of creation to which all other creatures point and in which the entire universe is contained."[11]

5. Order

Because the universe is the fruit of the creative power of God and an expression of the Word, it reflects the order proper to this origin. This order is twofold: creatures ordered with respect to each other and all of created reality ordered to its proper end.[12] This order is also hierarchical by nature because creatures are neither infinite nor perfect. Their very finitude, therefore, mandates an order within nature. And this order—or gradation of dissimilar beings—is both a source of beauty and a manifestation of the power and wisdom of God. Bonaventure's concept of a perfect order is one that has three terms:

---

[9] Schaeffer, 1960: p. 310.
[10] Schaeffer, 1961, p. 319.
[11] Schaeffer, 1961: p. 320.
[12] Hayes, 1994: p. 67.

the highest, the lowest, and an intermediary. A universe composed along these lines most perfectly fulfills the attributes of the Creator:

> The spiritual and the material realm of creation, which are the most distant from each other and manifest already in themselves the greatness of the Creator, are marvelously joined together in man, who thus represents the most perfect manifestation of God's power, wisdom, and goodness.[13]

6. Christocentrism

Following the religious experience and insight of his spiritual mentor St. Francis, Bonaventure developed a rich and vibrant Christology. This vision was also influenced by his understanding of perfect order as the middle between two extremes.

For Bonaventure, Christ is the center. Within the Trinity, the Word or Son "lives at the center of the Trinity. In this central person lives the fundamental structural law of all that is other than the Father. That person is found in the modality of a love which is both receptive and responsive."[14] Thus the Word is the center which mediates and unites. External to the Trinity, "all of God's communication *ad extra* takes place through the mystery of the divine Logos, which is the immanent self-expression of God."[15] Or more directly,

> As *increatum*, the eternal Word lies at the very center of the mystery of the triune God. As *incarnatum*, the same Word lies at the center of creation, both in a metaphysical sense and in an historical sense. As *inspiratum*, the same Word resides at the center of the spiritual life by the power of the divine Spirit through whom the Word becomes the *verbum inspiratum* in the human heart.[16]

Additionally the incarnation of Christ through the hypostatic union reveals the mediating role of Christ. The remote context for the possibility of the incarnation is twofold: the reality of God as a "triune mystery of self-communicative love"[17] and the possibility of God's being a creator. Bonaventure argues that when humanity's capacity for a relationship with God is actualized by God, "the cre-

---

[13] Schaeffer, 1961: p. 306.
[14] Hayes, 1994: p. 58.
[15] Hayes, 1994: p. 83.
[16] Hayes, 1994: p. 84.
[17] Hayes, 1994: p. 87.

ated order finds its highest form of fulfillment: the hypostatic union. Christ is the purest actualization of a potential that lies at the heart of the created order."[18] Thus in the incarnation of the eternal Word as the incarnated Word, we have the union of the created and uncreated, the human and the divine, the finite and the infinite.

3. Bonaventure's Vision of Human Dignity

When we use the phrase "I'm in the middle of a project" or words to that effect, we generally connote that we are quite busy. Sometimes the phrase, given a particular hostile inflection, suggests that we are about to be overtaken by events and that we want to escape this middle as soon as possible. Between the rock and the hard place is not a position of comfort. We also use the term of the middle to describe someone who either has not or cannot make a decision. We all know people who perpetually seem to be in the middle—"on the fence," we say. And the middle frequently suggests a compromise position, again a stance that has negative undertones. In all these instances the phrase "the middle" has a negative connotation. It indicates a place from which we want to escape either because of the chaos there or because it suggests a compromised position.

Yet it is this middle position that Bonaventure has defined as the ground of human dignity. As Schaeffer says, "The central idea of the present study [which] finds its best and shortest expression in the formula *homo in medio constitutus*—man is placed at the center."[19] This formula both locates the position of humans within the world and also gives the metaphysical grounding to their status and role. We now turn to Bonaventure's positive account of what it means to be "in the middle."

A. Metaphysical dimensions

God as the creator and the fountain-fullness of all is revealed in the creation of the multiplicity of entities and in the order that exists in creation. For Bonaventure, such an order is structural:

---

[18] Hayes, 1994: p. 71.
[19] Schaeffer, 1960: p. 279.

The most perfect form of creation is not a world in which every being is equally perfect; it is the present order with its harmonious gradation, because it is in this condition the best manifestation of the divine power, wisdom, and goodness of the Creator.[20]

Such an order reflects the very image of the Trinity by manifesting God's power, wisdom, and goodness.

Creation manifests the *power* of God by revealing the greatness of extension, i.e., in the quantity and variety of creatures as well as in the creation of beings with opposite natures. A particular dimension of God's power is that it not only unites extremes—matter and spirit—but also creates a union between them.

Creation manifests the *wisdom* of God by manifesting a sufficient order. Bonaventure states this as follows:

But the wisdom of an artist is manifested in the perfection of *order*, and every order necessarily has a *lowest* level, a *highest* level, and an *intermediate* level. If therefore, the lowest level is the purely *corporeal* nature, the highest level the *spiritual* nature, and the intermediate level is *composed of both*, then the wisdom of God would not be shown *perfectly* unless [God] had made *all these levels*.[21]

God's goodness is manifest through diffusion and communication of itself to another. This is, on the one hand, another demonstration of the powerful first principle that Bonaventure evokes so frequently: *"bonum est diffusivum sui."* On the other hand, this diffusion of goodness is specified through an act of communication. While the act of creation communicates life and the capacity to know, Bonaventure states a more specific form of communication: "This more immediate and perfect manifestation consists in a reproduction and *dramatic presentation of the act of communication itself* somewhere in creation."[22]

The human is the locus of the critical act of communication and reveals the human as both the completion and consummation of God's work of creation: situated as the critical link that unites the two extremes of creation. And Bonaventure sees in the human both the completion and consummation of God's work of creation.

Because the first principle was most powerful, wise, and good in production, and because [God] has made this manifest in all his

[20] Schaeffer, 1960: p. 293.
[21] *II Sent.* I, 2, i, 2; fund. 2; quoted in Schaeffer, 1960: p. 298.
[22] Schaeffer, 1960: p. 309.

effects in a certain way, he ought to manifest this most impressive-
ly in his last and most noble effect. Such is man, whom he produced
last among all creatures so that in man he should appear most
potently, and the accomplishment of the divine works should be
reflected in him.[23]

B. *The Status of the Human*

All of creation, which manifests the divine goodness by virtue of
its existence and destiny, is ordained to God as its final end, and is to
participate in God's glory at the end of time. All of created reality is
equal with respect to this. But Bonaventure makes a distinction with
respect to how creatures participate in this divine goodness: there is
immediate participation with the spiritual beings and mediate participation with the material world.[24] This mode of participation is
either because by their nature they are made to *participate* as are the
angels or because by their nature they *serve* those who participate as
do the animals and the rest of inanimate creation.

These distinctions lead Bonaventure to the conclusion that the
human, because of the status of being constituted in the middle,
functions as "the mediator between the corporeal creatures and God
who alone is the ultimate end of all things."[25] This leads to a twofold
vocation: the human is the highest creature to whom all of creation
is directed and is the one through whom creation receives its full participation in the kingdom of God.

1. *Humanity's role within created reality*

Bonaventure's position is that all of created reality is directed to
humankind. On this basis he describes humans as monarchs of the
visible universe because the creature which reconciles the greatest
extremes in itself most perfectly manifests the power, wisdom, and
goodness of God and because of his doctrine of the plurality of corporeal forms in material creatures, which says that each form is
"essentially *ordained* towards the next higher one."[26]

---

[23] *Breviloquium* II, 10.
[24] Schaeffer, 1960: p. 312.
[25] Schaeffer, 1960: p. 313.
[26] Schaeffer, 1961: p. 319.

Thus Bonaventure can say:

> All desire of sensitive and corporeal nature is designed and intend-
> ed so that the soul, a form existing, living, sentient, and intelligent,
> as if in the mode of an intelligent orbit, leads back to its beginning
> in which it is perfected and beatified.
>
> And because through its origin the soul tends toward freedom of
> choice, it excels in this regard all corporeal power by its very free-
> dom of choice. Through this all things are born to serve it, and
> nothing can rule it except God alone, not fate nor the power of the
> star's position.
>
> Wherefore it is unquestionably true that we are "the end of all
> things which exist," and all corporeal matter was made for human
> service so that by all these things humankind may ascend to loving
> and praising the Creator of the universe, whose providence dis-
> poses of all.[27]

Thus the material universe reaches its fulfillment in humanity and humanity reaches its fulfillment in God. Through this mediating act of humans, therefore, the material world reaches and will ulti-mately be transformed by the glory of God. In reaching its final end of union with God, humankind, through its bodily dimension, brings created reality to participation in the glory of God.

2. Humankind's return of creation to God

Although the image of God in humans ordains them to God, gives them the capacity of entering a relation with God, and enables them to achieve beatification in God, the realization of the possibili-ty is impossible without God's direct intervention. Although the image of God imprinted in humankind gives us the natural disposi-tion for such a reality, the actualization awaits the initiative of God. The actualization constitutes the closing of the circle opened at cre-ation and now closed through redemption.

The first phase of this, according to Schaefer, is the formation of the supernatural image in humans. This is accomplished through the infusion of sanctifying grace, which elevates the soul and develops a supernatural structure of virtues within the individual person. The second phase is the transformation of the three distinct structural elements of the image of God in humans by sanctifying grace: intel-

---

[27] *Breviloquium*, 2, 3-5.

lect, memory, and will. Thus is the person in his or her entirety total-ly transformed through grace so that the image of God within each shines forth again.

This transformation continues at the end of life, where one finds one's ultimate fulfillment in what Bonaventure calls *deiformitas*: an infusion of sanctifying grace that disposes one to find total fulfill-ment in the continuous act of loving God.

> Hence in man's reward that godliness of glory (*deiformitas*) is given him by which he is conformed to God, sees God clearly with his reason, loves God fully with his will, and retains him forever in his memory. Thus the whole soul lives, the whole soul is richly endowed in its three powers, the whole soul is joined to God, is united to him and rests in him, finding in him all good, peace, light, and eternal sufficiency. Hence, situated "in the state of all good in a perfect gathering" and achieving eternal life, man is said to be happy and glorious.[28]

Finally, the full reality of redemption and the restoration of humankind to its original place in God's plan requires the resurrec-tion of the body and its reunion with the soul. One reason for this is that it is not souls that are redeemed but the person who is composed of both. For the soul "has a tendency naturally implanted to rejoin the body"[29] and in the union of body and soul, "the desire of matter for higher forms comes to rest."[30] Thus final perfection is achieved in the reunion of the soul and body.

The other consequence of this is that through the resurrection of the body and its participation in the restoration of all in God, the whole of creation too can participate in this final glorification. Just as through the sin of the first humans the world was subjected to dis-order, so now in the restoration of original justice in humans the world too is set right once again. Because the human body is com-posed of the elements of the world, the cosmos finds its representa-tion before the throne of God. And though the world of plants and animals will pass away because its function is fulfilled—because humans can now see God directly instead of indirectly through the exemplars and vestiges of the created world—plants and animals also participate in the final glory through humankind, which bears a

---

[28] *Breviloquium*, 7, 3.
[29] *Breviloquium*, 7, 4.
[30] Schaeffer, 1961: p. 375.

likeness to every creature. Since humans are "the focal point in the order of creation ...[their]... redemption and beatification restore and perfect this order and bring it to a final completion."[31]

> Finally, because the world ought to be consumed when man faces consummation, and man is to be consumed when the number of the elect in glory shall be complete and all tend to this state as their ultimate and complete end, it follows that upon the completion of that process there must be an end to the motion of celestial nature and quiet in it, and likewise elemental transmutations must cease and consequently generation both animal and vegetative must cease. Since all these matters are subordinated to the most noble form, which is the rational soul, hence, by virtue of its place among spirits, its status and complement must be established in other precedents. Hence the celestial bodies in a quiet and a fullness of light are said to be rewarded. The elements which no longer have the power of multiplying by a mutual transmutation are said to perish not alone as regards their substance but as regards their mutual activity and passivity, and most especially as regards their active qualities. Things vegetative and things sensitive, since they do not possess the power of perpetual life and eternal duration, for such is the degree of their nobility, must be consumed in their own natures and yet in such a way that they are saved in their principles and somehow in likeness, namely, in man who has a likeness to every kind of creature. Hence in man's renovation and glorification we can speak of the renovation of all and in some fashion of the reward of all.[32]

4. Conclusions: Bonaventure's Vision and Our World

The vision of Bonaventure is striking, but the question of its contemporary relevance is a valid one. It is, from a contemporary perspective, not only anthropocentric but also manifest speciesism with the claim that humans are monarchs of the universe and that animals are to serve us. Additionally, the presence of hierarchy, both metaphysical and social in his system, is both foreign to us and problematic in the context of contemporary understanding. We need to leave this part of his system behind, but if we can get beyond his language and expressions, Bonaventure displays a compelling profundity of thought.

---

[31] Schaeffer, 1961: p. 380.
[32] *Breviloquium*, 7, 4, 7.

A. Human Dignity

Bonaventure grounds human dignity in terms of the location of humans within the created order and our function within that order. For Bonaventure, this meant that humans, who were created last, according to the biblical narrative, are highest in the order of creation and that the function of humans is to be mediators by representing the world before God and ensuring the participation of all of reality in redemption. Finally, our dignity consists in the capacity for *deiformitas*, the infusion of grace that totally transforms and restores the tarnished image of God in humans and leads to the total fulfillment of the human in a continuous act of loving God.

This vision of human dignity allows Bonaventure: to affirm humans, but not at the expense of nature; to articulate a vocation for humans, but one inclusive of creation; to provide a positive relation between humans and nature, which can ground an ecological ethic. For Bonaventure, such a position is not a claim to power. Rather it is a position of service: to God, to one's neighbor, and to nature. Position, for Bonaventure, does not confer power—it calls to service.

1. Humans and nature

One of the significant dimensions of Bonaventure's thought is the place of nature in his overall scheme. Nature is a locus of revelation, a book given us by the graciousness of the Creator that we might learn of the Creator. The ground of this is the doctrine of exemplarism through which Bonaventure argues that what is created bears the likeness of its Maker and provides a way of understanding qualities of this Maker. Because the Creator has left personal traces in what has been made, we can work our way back to an understanding of who this Creator is.

Second, nature is the means through which the incarnation becomes possible. There are two reasons for this. First, matter is prerequisite of human existence. Second, the reconciliation of opposites shows the greatest wisdom and in the incarnation we have the reconciliation of infinite and finite, spirit and matter, divinity and humanity. Matter has a value beyond the instrumental for it is taken up into a most intimate relation with the Divinity itself.

Third, humans are embedded in nature as deeply as any other created entity. Indeed, we are animated flesh. Through our bodiliness we participate in the mineral world and the animal world.

Although Bonaventure predates the theory of evolution, this theory captures a real sense of the continuity of humans with nature.

For Bonaventure, such continuity is not a random or chance event. Our materiality looks beyond itself. It is transformed through the form so that the form of an entity both gives it its perfection and prepares it for the next higher form. The matter of our reality is not left behind or rejected as we develop. We do not have a Cartesian dichotomization of mind and machine, but rather the bringing of matter into the heart of reality.

2. The human vocation

Bonaventure's vision of the human vocation can be found in his understanding of Francis, who so submitted to the presence of grace in his life that it completely filled and shaped him. Thus in the life of Francis we can see a restoration of the original relation between God and humans, and between humans and nature.

Bonaventure alludes to two events that demonstrate this. First is the taming of the wolf and the calming of storms at Gubbio. Francis said that if people repented and remained faithful to God, these plagues of nature would cease. And so they did. Second is the cauterizing of Francis to relieve the pain in his eyes. Francis made the sign of the cross over the hot iron and prayed, and then it was applied. Afterward Francis reported that he felt neither heat nor pain. Bonaventure provides the theological interpretation:

> The man of God had attained to such a degree of purity that his flesh was subject to his spirit, and his spirit to God in a wonderful harmony and agreement, and all creatures were thus in marvelous subjection to his will and command, who was himself the faithful servant of the Creator.[33]

Thus as we actualize our redemption initiated at baptism, we enter more and more into the order intended by God. As we do this, we begin to actualize this reality in our own lives. This will evoke a response of respect and reverence to nature, not one of dominance and dominion. Stewardship is actualized not by lording it over creation but by appreciating the goodness of nature and by being its voice before God.

---

[33] Schaeffer, 1961: p. 327.

3. An ecological ethic

The critical difference between Bonaventure and the ecological ethic so prevalent in the West today is that Bonaventure presents an ethic of restoration and responsibility as opposed to the traditional ethic of dominance and exploitation. In the Bonaventurian vision, the shift to dominance was one of the fruits of sin that brought about a distorted relation with animals. First, the clouding of vision by sin prevented us from seeing clearly how animals reflected the beauty of God in their existence and diversity. Second, animals were no longer to serve human needs or, if wild, to be a punishment for sin and an opportunity to learn patience. Sin disrupted not only the relation between God and humankind, but also the order within nature itself.

Although redemption has repaired the broken relation between God and humanity, the effects of sin remain and affect our daily lives. However, as Schaeffer summarizes Bonaventure, "The more the re-formation of man progresses and approaches the state of original innocence, so much the more is also restored the original relationship of the animals and other creatures to man."[34]

We do not repeat the error of King Solomon, who basically loved knowledge for its own sake and the marvels of creation in themselves. Such knowledge is vanity: making created reality an end and not a means; forgetting that creation does not subsist in itself but only through the creative power of God; making creation independent and forgetting its primal dependence. We do not repeat the error of Lucifer.

For if Lucifer, in contemplating this Truth, had led back from the knowledge of creatures to the unity of the Father, he would have turned dusk into dawn and would have enjoyed daylight. But because he fell for the love and desire of his own excellence, he lost the day. And Adam did the same.[35]

B. Concluding Pastoral Implications

The view of human nature that Bonaventure offers is a profound challenge to our contemporary American way of life.

---

[34] Schaeffer, 1961: p. 326.
[35] *Collationes in Hexameron*, 1, 17; quoted in deVinck, 1970: pp. 9-10.

First, it is a challenge to the way we act with respect to nature. This caution is not based on an order of nature deemed to be inviolate or normative for human action. Rather it is a caution that recognizes that what we see is not the totality of reality. Bonaventure's vision is that the whole is greater than the sum of the parts. This is an argument against reductionism, but it is also an affirmation of the profound potentialities of matter. Recall Bonaventure's position on seminal reasons: "There are in matter the germs of forms upon which the action which is to develop them will operate.... Matter was created pregnant with a something from which the agent draws out the form."[36]

Louis Mackey captures a different dimension of this in discussing the limits of the epistemological theories of realism and nominalism:

> The realist, who demeans singulars in what he takes to be the interest of universals, and the nominalist, who consigns universals to oblivion to save the honor of the singular both commit fallacies of the misplaced concreteness.... St. Bonaventure would have said that both realist and nominalist err by mistaking the present scene—creatures in isolation from God—for the whole show. They regard creatures as things-in-themselves (which they are not) instead of seeing them as signs and expressions of the eternal art (which they are).[37]

To see the present scene as the whole show or to mistake what is for what might be is to miss, as Hopkins phrases it, "the dearest freshness deep down things." Such a perspective does not prohibit interventions in nature. Rather it cautions us that such interventions go beyond what is seen or what can be modeled even through the most sophisticated imaging technologies. Such interventions touch but a part of what reality is and to miss that is to miss the potential of reality. Such a recognition of the potentials of nature and our embeddedness within it can lead to a continuous conversion of heart so that we can once again "read the Book of Creation, [to] receive the full service of things below him, and to be in this way their decisive mediator on the way to God."[38]

---

[36] Gilson, 1938: p. 269.
[37] Mackey, 1979: p. 140.
[38] Schaeffer, 1961: p. 332.

Second, Bonaventure's vision is a challenge to how we view ourselves and others. Our dignity comes from being an image of God. For Bonaventure this consists in our having been created in the image of the Trinity with mind, knowledge, and love. As created this means that

> man is right when his intelligence coincides with the supreme truth in knowing, [when] his will conforms to the supreme loving, and [when] his power is united to the supreme power in acting. Now this is when man is turned to God in his total self.[39]

However, we know that we are not fully turned to God. Although we have turned from God, we retain the image and still desire this totality of Goodness. This image is restored through the redemptive work of Christ: "As Incarnate Word, Christ reestablishes man as Trinitarian image and with the Spirit brings him back to the unity of the Father."[40] Thus at the most profound level of our being we are shaped by the hand of the Creator and reflect the innermost dynamism of the Trinity.

This perspective can serve as the basis for a transformation in how we view ourselves and others. Although we were created in the image of God, we fell from grace and are in the process of conversion so that this image can once again appear within us and transform our lives. This is true of each of us and is the basis for, first, understanding why we act as we do, and second, what we can expect of each other. We act as we do because the process of transformation is not complete within us. Thus we forget our true vocation of service to others and creation. Yet we may expect the best because of our vocation to *deiformitas*.

Third, our dignity is not a prize or something to be clung to. It is a vocation. And the vocation consists in our being the voice of creation. Because of our being created "in the middle," we stand in a unique place and participate in both the spiritual and material dimensions of creation. The monarchical status that Bonaventure bestows on us and his statement that we are the apex of the material world is not a claim of human pride gone wild. It is not the basis for power or dominion over creation. It is, rather, an accurate meta-

---

[39] *II Sentences*, proem.; quoted in Cousins, 1977: p. 128.
[40] Cousins, 1977: p. 130.

physical description of where Bonaventure sees us located within the world of creation.

The vocation of monarchy is exercised through our freedom in which we recognize our ordination to God. Thus the order intended by God is realized: the world, which was made for us, serves us and we in turn serve the One who made the heavens and the earth—and humanity as well.[41] Such a vocation is captured well in the words of Teilhard de Chardin:

> May the might of those invincible hands direct and transfigure for the great world you have in mind that earthly travail which I have gathered into my heart and now offer you in its entirety. Remold it, rectify it, recast it down to the depths from whence it springs. You know how your creatures can come into being only, like shoot from stem, as part of an endlessly renewed process of evolution.
>
> Do you now therefore, speaking through my lips, pronounce over this earthly travail your twofold efficacious word: the word without which all that our wisdom and our experience have built up must totter and crumble—the word through which all our most far-reaching speculations and our encounter with the universe are come together into a unity. Over every living thing which is to spring up, to grow, to flower, to ripen during this day, say again the words: This is my Body. And over every death-force which waits in readiness to corrode, to wither, to cut down, speak again your commanding words which express the supreme mystery of faith: This is my Blood.[42]

Or, as DeBenedictis expresses it: "Thus, having been placed in a world pregnant with the divine imprint, man has been assigned the role of leading the world back to its Author by seeing him, praising him, and loving him in all things."[43]

---

[41] Schaeffer, 1961: p. 323.
[42] Teilhard de Chardin, 1961: pp. 22-23.
[43] DeBenedictis, 1946: p. 44.

REFERENCES

Bellah, Robert, and Richard Madsen, William Sullivan, Ann Swidler, and Steven Tipton, *Habits of the Heart: Individualism and Commitment in American Life*. Berkeley, California: University of California Press, 1985.

Cousins, Ewert, *Bonaventure and the Coincidence of Opposites*. Chicago: Franciscan Herald Press, 1977.

DeBenedictis, Matthew, O.F.M., *The Social Thought of St. Bonaventure*. Washington: The Catholic University of America Press, 1946.

de Vinck, Jos , *Collations on the Six Days*. Translation. Paterson, New Jersey: St. Anthony Guild Press, 1970.

Gilson, Étienne, *The Philosophy of St. Bonaventure*. Translated by Illtyd Trethowan. Paterson, New Jersey: St. Anthony Guild Press, 1965.

Hayes, Zachary, O.F.M., "St. Bonaventure: Mystery of the Triune God," pp. 39-126 in *The History of Franciscan Theology*. Edited by Kenan B. Osborne, O.F.M. St. Bonaventure, New York: The Franciscan Institute, 1994.

Mackey, Louis, "Singular and Universal: A Franciscan Perspective," pp. 130-150 in Franciscan Studies 39 (1979).

Schaeffer, Alexander, O.F.M., "The Position and Function of Man in the Created World According to St. Bonaventure," Chapters I and II, pp. 261-316 in Franciscan Studies 20 (1960).

————, "The Position and Function of Man in the Created World According to St. Bonaventure," Chapters II and IV, pp. 230-382 in Franciscan Studies 21 (1961).

Teilhard de Chardin, Pierre, S.J., "Mass Over the World," in *Hymn of the Universe*. New York: Harper and Row, 1961.

5

Ministry, Sacramentality and Symbolism

John Burkhard, O.F.M. Conv.

Pastoral ministry in the church today is multifaceted. Former contrasts between clergy and laity, men and women in ministry, lifelong and temporary service, though still very much a part of the landscape and still producing tensions, are no longer dominant. The ecclesiological scene is far more diverse and pluriform than these oversimplified dualities permit us to express. Men and women move in and out of various ministries, leaving one behind and taking up another. This liberty has been dictated by the vision of the Second Vatican Council as well as by a society in North America that has changed dramatically in recent decades. There is no end to the situations that call for ministerial response from Christians, and "official ministry" can no longer respond to all these pressing human needs. Today's Catholic can no longer be defined on the basis of adherence to creed alone, as important as orthodoxy of belief may be; equally important are the concrete actions that flow from committed discipleship. Ministry calls for action directed beyond the church and toward society. What, then, is ministry and the conditions for its exercise? What, too, is the role of the pastoral leader in a situation where ministry is so various and, of necessity, often unstructured?

The Second Vatican Council and postconciliar theological reflection offer us a number of helpful hints in dealing with this complex issue. Then, too, the charism of Francis tells us much about ministry and pastoral leadership. In the pages that follow, I draw on these currents of conciliar and Franciscan thought, focusing in particular on the sacramental character of the church and its ministry and using the notion of symbol as a hermeneutical key.

1. Symbol Theory

Without question, a major philosophical development of the twentieth century has been the rediscovery of the role of symbols in human life and the various symbolisms or symbol systems that have arisen. Major thinkers have turned to symbolic modes of expression as either primary or as a necessary complement to reason.[1] Catholic theology has felt the effects of this widespread and powerful movement as well, and particularly since the Second World War has begun to incorporate it in all areas of Catholic life and thought.[2] Biblical and liturgical studies could serve here as clear exemplifications of a much wider acceptance and incorporation of symbolic thinking into contemporary Catholicism.[3] This movement will continue to be strong in religious life and thought for the foreseeable future. How, we naturally ask, does symbolic expression influence the present understanding of Christian identity and Christian ministry? Before I provide a tentative answer to these questions, let us look more closely at just what is meant by a symbol.

All authors distinguish the symbol from a sign, with which it shares certain characteristics but then differs from it on essential points. Both symbols and signs are indicators of reality, but they deal with reality differently. The following chart will attempt to show several of their differences.

The Contrast of Sign and Symbol

SIGN	SYMBOL
1. Aims at clarity and denotation.	1. Aims at richness of meaning and connotation.
2. Organizes the reality of our world.	2. Reflects the depth of our world.
3. Deals with conscious reality.	3. Deals with conscious and unconscious reality.
4. Appropriate to understanding and communicating knowledge.	4. Appropriate to expressing human experience and emotions.
5. Single-layered and univocal.	5. Multilayered and polyvalent.
6. Delights in directness of meaning and uses a palette of black and white.	6. Delights in nuances, shades of meaning, ambiguity, resonances, shapes and forms, and employs a full palette of colors.
7. Operates directly and by isolating human operations.	7. Operates dialectically and dialogically.

---

[1] Eliade, 1963, 1991; Ricoeur, 1967; Dillistone, 1986.
[2] Rahner, 1966; Dulles, 1980; Happel, 1990; Cooke, 1990.
[3] Cooke, 1983; Power, 1984; Fink, 1990; Duffy, 1991.

8. Thrives in the physical sciences, law, logic, mathematics, medicine, lexicography, etc.	8. Thrives in the human sciences, art, poetry, music, anthropology, rhetoric, literature, politics, psychology, sociology, etc.
9. Strives for one-to-one correspondence.	9. Delights in complexity of meanings.
10. A conscious activity and given to constant revision.	10. Draws on the unconscious and tradition.
11. Aims at focused, discursive reasoning, separating out differences in reality.	11. Aims at uniting complex reality in an encompassing whole or totality.

From this selective listing of characteristics, it should be evident that we humans depend heavily upon both the significative and the symbolic. Society is ordered by both activities, and no judgment is rendered as to the superiority of one over the other. Yet one will be more appropriate in a certain situation than the other. It is from this perspective of relative utility that (generally) the more symbolical will show its usefulness in the areas of worship, preaching, pastoral situations, and theology.

Symbolic thinking need not be antirational, but can be seen as complementary to, and in many respects as more foundational to, the human search for meaning and truth. It is important to see that symbolic and discursive reasoning are reciprocally coordinated to one another. I take this as the point Paul Ricoeur has tried to make with his oft-quoted remark that "the symbol gives rise to thought."[4]

Symbols act as mediators of a reality that is complex, rich, profound, and elusive, and which, therefore, is not capable of being seized entirely by a definition or a concept. Some realities, or certain aspects of reality, defy simple objectification or categorization and can come to us only in the mode of symbol. God is mystery and not another object at the summit of things we can know.[5] Rather, God is the encompassing presence, ground or horizon of all our objective knowledge.[6] But even here, we can point to innumerable other aspects of human experience as defying our codification and cataloguing. Symbols and symbolic complexes in the form of myths, epics, sagas, and religious rites are far more effective in bringing us human beings into a life-giving contact with that deeper reality.

---

[4] Ricoeur, 1967: pp. 347-57.
[5] Rahner, 1978: pp. 57-66.
[6] O'Meara, 1975: pp. 405-10, 416-20.

Light in all its forms (sun, moon, stars, candle or fire, electric sources, and sight) is perhaps a particularly accessible example of what is meant here. Light points to a further reality or a reality beyond its manifestation as its source. It elicits reactions of seeing (both physically and metaphorically), of finding one's way, of invention, of discovering meaning or a purpose, of the question of truth. Light, therefore, is more than its physical manifestation and its explanation as a phenomenon of nature.

Symbols can act as mediators of the richness and depth of reality because in the mind of some theologians they participate in the reality immediately expressed (e.g., physical light) and the other realities mediated (e.g., knowledge).[7] Not all theologians share, or at least invoke, the argument of participation as an explanation of the fullness of a symbol, but all point in the direction of undisclosed depth of reality. All indicate that our rationalistic model of understanding is beginning to show serious signs of inadequacy as we look to other modes of expression.

Other theologians, again, would point in the direction of a dialectical process at work in symbolic communication. A symbol operates on the basis of an inherent tension between the primary signifier (e.g., physical light) and what is signified (e.g., knowledge).[8] In some way, the concept of the "other" must be introduced to explain the tension that symbols produce. Some reality, in fact it would appear a great deal of reality, is tension-laden and tension-producing. This helps to explain the dynamic character of symbols. The states of being which symbols produce are active, generative, creative, renewing, and transforming.

2. The Human Person as Symbol

Consider now how this theory of symbol is realized in several areas of thought. As we shall see, some reality evidences an extraordinary richness when looked at from the perspective of its symbolic character. I propose to look at our bodies as symbols, before moving on to sacramental reality, the church, and Christ. There is a continuity among these diverse realities, both secular and religious.

---

[7] Tillich, 1951: pp. 122f., 238-47.
[8] Haight, 1990: pp. 132-35.

As human beings, we have an immediate experience of symbol in ourselves, particularly in the experience of our bodies.[9] Scripture scholars have long pointed out to us that the biblical understanding of the human person is one of dynamic unity and not of dualistic dichotomy.[10] In biblical terms, the "body" refers to the whole person and not simply to one aspect of being human. The body is not a part of who I am (and the "lower" part at that) but represents me in my totality. I truly am my body to the extent that my human nature demands external symbolization. The sense of dynamic realization in any symbol comes to expression in my bodiliness. My spiritual nature does not exist apart from my physicalness or bodiliness.[11] The one dimension symbolizes the other, not merely to the extent that it intimates the other, but rather inasmuch as it truly realizes or effects the other. The tension or dialectical character of a symbol can be seen clearly in our unity of matter and spirit. The body, then, is a primary symbol for us.

To be human, therefore, is to be body. Our physicalness and our corporeality can never be understood by us as pure inconveniences, stages to be sloughed off or escaped, "lower" aspects of our being to be transcended or sublimated. Our transcendence is experienced in our corporeality, and this means that the whole of human experience is open to transcendence and to mediating transcendence to us. Concretely, therefore, our bodies as symbols are our self-expressions in the experience of pleasure and pain. Both come our way, and both are genuine experiences of our corporeality, and as such both are symbolic expressions of our full personhood. Because of a certain onesidedness often encountered in Christianity that expresses itself as suspicion of the pleasurable, the full scope of our bodiliness has not been the norm. Unfortunately, this has generally meant wild swings between positive and negative expressions of enthusiasm (e.g., Montanism, Manicheism, Pelagianism, Jansenism, etc.), and has made it particularly difficult for our contemporaries to understand the true value and place of ascetical practices in Christianity. It has even skewed the whole understanding of penance for us. Likewise, this misunderstanding has made it extremely difficult to accept pleasure and playfulness. Nowhere, perhaps, does this come to more acute expression than in the experience of our sexuality, both in sexual expression and in the life of our imagination.

---

[9] Ross, 1989: pp. 14-18, 21-24.
[10] Gundry, 1987: p. 3-8.
[11] Braine, 1992: 326-39, 532-45.

A second aspect of our bodiliness as symbol of our full humanity is the important area of the ordinariness of our lives. Because we find it so difficult to discover meaning in our very ordinariness, we are constantly scrambling for newer, higher experiences, and we tend to ignore and bypass the wealth of meaning to be found in our everyday corporeal acts and functions. Karl Rahner, in particular, has formulated a whole spirituality for our contemporary society that acknowledges the power and integrative potential of the ordinariness of our lives. He refers to such common actions as seeing, laughing, eating, sleeping, working, moving about, etc.[12] David N. Power, too, has pointed to the day-to-day, non-dramatic character of the elements of liturgical actions, taken from ordinary elements such as oil, water, bread, table wine, singing, dance, etc.[13] Because of the highly ritualized context in which we encounter these elements, we tend to forget their simplicity and what that simplicity might mean for us in pointing to the sacredness of the ordinary. More recently, drawing on the growing number of thinkers who are examining the depths of meaning in our everyday experience, Elizabeth A. Dreyer has applied the theory to a broad range of human actions.[14] Heroic life and heroic virtue is found not only on the summits of our experience but in the valleys and on the ascents and slopes.

A third, and for our purposes, our final consideration of the symbolic character of our bodiliness, is our sexual or gender differences. This is an area that has been neglected by theologians for too long and which is clearly pertinent on this very issue. It is also an area not without its ambiguity.[15] The Enlightenment had so stressed the dignity of the human person as a universal expression that the particularity of the human person as male or female tended to be passed over, until recent years. Our human bodiliness is not a generic, sexless physical expression. The dynamism and tension inherent in any symbol comes to particular expression in the human species. Humanity is realized perfectly neither in its male nor in its female expression taken in isolation, but only in the dynamic interaction of men and women. Of course, this comes to immediate expression in

---

[12] Rahner, 1967: pp. 13-43; and Rahner 1976(2): pp. 169-76.
[13] Power, 1984: pp. 96, 127f.
[14] Dreyer, 1994.
[15] Ross, 1989: pp. 13-14.

sexual intercourse and in societies' (and couples') concern for the survival of humanity (and the family). But it is much more complex than the issue of the procreation of the race. It involves an openness, an interactivity, and a mutuality of men and women at all levels. To be human involves not only the co-existence of persons but a true co-existence of the sexes. Neither sex alone expresses humanity fully or is its higher expression, but each does so only in terms of the complementarity of the other. The symbolism of our bodiliness is sexually determined through and through. Awareness of this fact can lead to true mutuality, respect, avoidance of exploitation and domination, love of each child born, and acceptance of the vulnerability of each sex. The ancient use of the term *symbolon* comes to powerful expression in the reciprocity and relationality of the sexes. Originally, the term was used to denote an object that was broken into two pieces by two contractors, only to have the two pieces fitted together again upon the fulfillment of the contract.[16]

Francis showed a keen awareness of the depth of meaning in the human body. Francis's stripping of himself to stand disrobed before the bishop of Assisi and lying naked on the earth as he died reveal a natural acceptance of his human state and his need to be cared for by others. The modification of penitential practices by Francis for his followers also reveals a realistic sense of their human needs and the limits of bodily mortification. Stories told about Francis, moreover, show us a man whose sexual imagination was quite active, not harshly repressed. Finally, Francis's friendship with Clare and his need for feminine companionship, led to his cofounding with Clare of the Second Order. In Francis's mind, neither sex held a monopoly on the life of Christian discipleship. Following Jesus and the apostolic community was an activity open equally to women and men.

3. Sacraments as Elements of a Symbol System

At the base of our anthropological structure, therefore, is the symbol. We engage in symbolic understanding and expression (e.g., in language) because we ourselves are symbols. We should, therefore, look at specifically religious activity from the point of view of its underlying symbolization. Just because sacraments are explicitly

---

[16] Dillistone, 1986: p. 14.

religious activities does not exempt them from symbolization. Religious acts are not on an entirely other plane of human activity, but express another dimension of human activity. Religious acts, then, will also participate in symbolic expression and symbolic causality.[17]

If we look at the sacraments as religious symbols, we see them along the line of a continuum that considers the sacraments in their plurality and in their rootedness in our human nature. Sacramentality is the conscious, reflexive expression of our innate religious symbolization. It is present before we advert to it and when we cannot exhaust its meaning. In our life of faith, we yearn for sacramental, symbolic expression. Pronouncements, creeds, propositions, theologoumena, theological systems, gnosticisms, and enlightenments are not enough in themselves. Only when they in turn are taken up into doxological and praxiological expressions are they consummated. Our sacramental life, therefore, must not be segregated from our lives in their wholeness, as though it existed in a separate, higher, privileged sphere.

Because we human beings are not reducible to our individuality, subjectivity, interiority, or consciousness, but are also by nature members of a society, symbols play an essential role in constituting this society.[18] We employ the term "culture" to state all those features that express the total reality of any given society: common values and meanings, customs, language, public celebrations, shared mythology, religion, systems of morality and mores, political institutions, educational system, legislative codes, etc.[19] In societies whose cultures are marked by pluralism, we even speak of "subcultures" coexisting within the broader cultural system. The human being, who is a symbol and hence is symbol-making and symbol-expressive, turns to a whole system of symbols to express the complexity, diversity and richness of the human experience in its cultural context. Thus, symbols are found in networks of interconnecting and mutually elucidating activities. Today, when we speak of symbols we generally mean a symbol that functions not in isolation but in its cultural complex.

---

[17] Lane, 1981: pp. 12-21.
[18] Cohen, 1985: pp. 97-118.
[19] Amalorpavadass, 1987: pp. 201-203.

Now, if we restrict ourselves to a consideration of our religious activity, we see that what we Catholics call seven sacraments is really a symbol system. The religious experiences we have, both individual and corporate, fit into a broader picture of reality. The experiences of birth, life, illness and frailty, healing, death, self-commitment, erring and failure, reaching majority, and service to the corporate body or church are some important aspects of our religious experience. They, together with the all-important symbol of the "word of God," are the basic framework of our Christian symbol system.[20] Furthermore, because our Catholic sacramental system is an "open system," other meaningful religious experiences can find their rightful place in our religious culture (e.g., religious life in its limitless diversity of charisms, lifestyles, and apostolates; celibacy for the reign of God; rites of passage at critical junctures in life; etc.).

What is important to realize about the sacraments as elements in a symbol system is that the general sacramentality of our lives vastly exceeds the scope of these individual sacraments themselves.[21] More of our lives is symbolically expressive of our religious experience and yearnings than the sacraments alone can represent.[22] To put it in other theological terms, grace is present and operative in the full array of our spiritual lives, e.g., in moments of prayer and in actions performed in behalf of justice. But what the sacraments (and the word of God) do for us is mediate to our consciousness the underlying sacramentality of all reality: God's abiding presence in the world, other persons, and human events, and the omnipresence and largesse of grace.[23] In any symbol system, religious or otherwise, some symbols will perform an integrating, focusing, and consciously reflexive function for the system as a whole. Some symbols exemplify a "surplus quality" in their inherently greater openness to reality. Of necessity, they point beyond themselves. Thus, the sacraments focus spiritual reality for us and bring us to a keener insight and commitment to the sacredness of the ordinary and the routine. Sacraments are life-giving, life-confirming, transforming, and hermeneutical events of grace.

---

[20] Rahner 1976(1): pp. 137-44.
[21] Rahner 1976(2): pp. 169-78.
[22] Tracy, 1981.
[23] Rahner, 1976(2): pp. 166-69.

4. The Church as Symbol

In their individuality and inexhaustible richness, sacraments point beyond themselves to the underlying unity of human solidarity. And this brings us to our next point regarding religious symbols, namely, that they are related to a yet more fundamental symbolic reality, which is the church. There is a unity, albeit a dynamic and tensive one, among our religious symbols.

Since the Second Vatican Council, we have become more comfortable with referring to the mystery character of the church. Every definition fails to express the full reality of our experience of the church. In this regard, we have come to see the role of symbols in expressing (though not exhausting) the nature of the church. The church itself is an inexhaustible, dynamic, and tension-laden symbol.[24] All its concrete symbols coalesce and conspire to constitute an underlying symbolic reality.

The church is a community of disciples of the Risen Lord.[25] Absolute priority must be given to Jesus, the Christ and Lord. The actuality of his presence forms the solidarity of women and men in community. Jesus's presence to his disciples is what is fundamental, and this actual presence comes to symbolic expression both in the community of disciples itself and in their concrete acts of discipleship. This intimate and mutual relationship between the Lord and believers is what the various biblical images of the church attempt to express: body of Christ, temple of the Spirit, people of God, vine and the branches, the flock and its shepherd, etc. From the point of view of symbol theory, too, this approach to the church makes sense. Each and every symbol, and the whole of a culture's symbol system, is the attempt to mediate ultimate reality to a society. The symbols are not ends in themselves. So, behind our Christian symbols and their sacramental expressions stands the person of Christ.

But the church is a symbol in another sense, one also intimately connected with Christ. The church is a symbol of God's ultimate purpose for all humankind. In a word, according to the teaching of the Dogmatic Constitution on the Church of the Second Vatican Council (Article 5), the church is a symbol for the reign of God. As such, the

---

[24] Rahner, 1976(2): pp. 179-81; Kasper, 1989: pp. 122-25.
[25] Dulles, 1982: pp. 7-14.

church has a role and a function to fulfill; it does not exist for itself. In this sense, the church is not the absolute reality, but a servant of the absoluteness of God's purpose and plan. Once again, like any symbol, the church must enter into a dynamic, self-dispossessing relationship with other realities that are not themselves church. The anti-triumphalism of Vatican II attempts to bring the church back to essentials. The church, then, is the sacrament of humankind and its ultimate destiny.[26]

These ideas remind us of the deep compatibility of Vatican II's ecclesiology and Francis's understanding of his Christian faith. As unique as Francis's personality was, he was never an individualist when it came to salvation. Francis knew that redemption was a corporate reality, not something to be pursued by individuals in isolation. This is the meaning of Julian of Speyer's reference to Francis as *vir catholicus et totus apostolicus*. It is not a phrase that would understand Francis as the ultimate organization man. Francis's faith went deeper than the externals of allegiance, loyalty, and unquestioning submission. Francis's love for the church, despite its flaws, which were evident to him as well, was legendary because its source was a deep confidence in the fact that the Lord continued to live in the midst of the church through his Spirit.

5. Christ the Symbol

One more stage on the continuum remains to be considered. Can we bring this pattern of symbolic action back even to the person of Christ? Is Christ, too, a symbol, albeit the most profound one from our faith perspective? And can the other symbolisms we have discussed find their foundation in this historical person? Such questions bring us to the very heart of the matter of what sacramentality is.

The classic definition of Chalcedon (451) that Christ is a unity of person in two complete natures has generally been understood and explained from the substantialist philosophical mindset that (with few exceptions) was regnant from antiquity to the nineteenth century. In that century, an opening to history and the category of the historical introduced new possibilities of thought. New, non-substantialist and non-rationalistic, philosophies appeared. One such

---

[26] *Dogmatic Constitution on the Church*, Articles 1, 9 and 48.

current of thought in Roman Catholic circles was the turning to transcendental method or transcendental Thomism. Twentieth-century transcendentalism has drawn heavily on the notion of symbol and symbolic understanding, exploiting in particular its dynamic and dialectical traits.[27] In turn, transcendentalism has opened up an understanding of Chalcedon's Christological definition as hypostatic union in symbolic terms.

Without becoming overly esoteric, let me state that the relationship of divinity to humanity in the subject Jesus of Nazareth is analogous to that of body and soul according to the monistic and symbolic understanding of the human person: each in its measure, but only together, symbolizes and thus in some way truly constitutes the other. The human is open to the divine, and yet only as symbolized by the divine in the historical (i.e., incarnate) Jesus. The divine determines and defines the human as its partner. The hypostatic union, then, in Christ is not an entirely unique phenomenon. Though it defines Jesus Christ, it does so in terms of establishing a universal order or ontology of the human as graced. According to this understanding, in the power of Jesus's life, death and resurrection, each person (but understood here as male and female open to one another) is hypostatically constituted.[28] When created reality is seen from the perspective of its being graced, some such reorienting of reality is demanded. Instead of exclusivities, one turns to inclusive categories, mutually conditioning and constituting categories, symbolic categories. Christologically speaking, all symbolic reality is Christic because the hypostatic union is the ultimate paradigm of what a symbol is.

It is not possible within the scope of this paper to develop further why and how this is the case. However, it does mean that in a Christian perspective, there is a spiral of ascending symbols that sees reality as dynamic, inclusive, complementary, and unified. The church as the fundamental sacrament of humankind called to the kingdom of justice, peace, and salvation is ultimately founded in Christ as the primordial sacrament of the human and the divine.[29] The sacramentality of the church, therefore, and not simply as exer-

---

[27] Dulles, 1980; Haight, 1990: pp. 129-66.
[28] Rahner, 1978: pp. 212-28, 285-93.
[29] Kasper, 1989: pp. 119-22.

cised in the celebration of one or another of the seven sacraments, is founded in the a priori nature of the church as symbolic reality. The church's concrete actions are symbolic because it is symbol in action.

Again, Francis's profound insights into the incarnate order and into the absolute preeminence of Christ are enduring in their perceptiveness. Francis saw the incarnate Christ at the heart of the universe, reconciling human divisions expressed by wars, hostilities, violence, socioeconomic stratification, national and religious differences, etc. His vision of fraternity/sorority is not just an idea of a group's shared interests or preferences, but is a symbolic expression of human solidarity. Francis's understanding of fraternity/sorority has a universal, transcultural quality to it.

6. Some Conclusions

What is ministry and pastoral leadership, considered from the vantage point of the underlying sacramentality of the church? And what could we possibly mean nowadays by sacramentality in a world increasingly experienced by us as thoroughly secular, technological, and fragmented? Perhaps, at the conclusion of our general observations, we are now in a position to offer several more specific points for reflection.

First, from broadening our understanding of sacramentality, we have come to see the preeminence of the role of the general sacramentality of life. This understanding leads us to gain a deeper sense of the wholeness and unity of our lives. The ordinary is, in fact, very sacred, just as specific sacred actions celebrate the sacredness of the whole of life. We need not experience ourselves as radically dichotomized between religious and secular activities. Both are occasions of meeting the transcendent, and the one leads to the other's mode of mediating transcendence. There is something deeply satisfying for us today in avoiding the sense of fragmentation and competition involved in separating reality into what is profane and secular and what is sacred and transcendent. In our complex and fast-paced lives, we yearn for this sense of continuity and reciprocity.

Concretely, the sense of general sacramentality might come to expression for us Franciscans in the following two ways in particular. First, we are challenged both by Francis's vision of the goodness of our bodies and our sexuality and by the complementarity-in-equality of both sexes. We are called to express reverence for each person without regard for gender, social status, religion, ethnicity, economic power, or authority. But we will also work for a society that is open and inclusive of all, giving each person the chance to contribute to society at large by accepting and realizing his or her potentialities and by working for the removal of barriers that lock people into socially marginal roles. Second, from the perspective of the value of the ordinary in our lives, fraternity/sorority will not appear to be a mere accessory to what is really important. We will see the quality and vitality of our community life as essential because it truly is a sacramental expression of human solidarity and the social character of salvation. We encounter these lofty theological truths in our common lives with our sisters and brothers. The implications of this idea cannot be spelled out in this essay, and are perhaps best left to the friars/sisters themselves to flesh out in study, discussion, and concrete experiments, but the vision of Francis, Clare, and their first followers stands as a powerful challenge to our religious presuppositions and acts as a stimulus to our imaginations.

Second, all the ideas developed above on basic symbolism, general sacramentality, and the sacramentality of the church have a great deal to say to us Franciscans about ministry today. The change in perspective from the priority of specialized sacramentality to general sacramentality must call forth a change in accent among Franciscans from a more or less exclusive concern with specialized (read here "ordained") ministry to global ministry or ministry shared in by all called thereto in the church. I cannot here spell out in detail my understanding of the extent of such global ministry, but suffice it to say that in our circumstances today, it will be far more inclusive than a handful of the ordained and another handful of their collaborators. Some will be ordained, some will be trained for specific ministries, but many others will have neither ordination nor specialized training. What I think is more to the point at hand is that ministry will necessarily be a collaborative effort from its very inception. No one today will really argue against this point in theory. The real issue is finding the ways to translate this insight into actions. However we do this concretely, it will not be done without sustained commitment to this guiding principle and without the friars/sisters being held accountable to the principle by the community's leadership. Admission of new members to the order and the placing of friars/sisters in specific pastoral assignments will have to be done in

the light of this principle. What forms might such collaborative sharing take? Again, let me indicate two possibilities.

The first must include involving both men and women in ministry. This should be clear from our anthropological principles on
human symbolism and its male-female relationality. Here there can
be no question of inferiority or exclusion of one or the other. The
complementarity of our human symbolism calls for both. We have
gained a more adequate anthropological understanding and a
greater awareness of the historical moment of ministry today. What
we lack is sufficient retrieval of the tradition of ministry. Thus, we
shall have to examine the tradition of ministry much more fully than
we have done to date. And secondly, in matters of ministry, too, we
Franciscans are thrown back to the issue of fraternity/sorority. Here
as well, we are challenged to see ministry as activity to which all the
brothers and sisters are called. Ordained ministry will have to cede
ground to ministry understood more globally. That means greater
sharing in ministry with all the friars and sisters on the part of the
ordained. Community resources for education and training, for
instance, will have to be allocated more broadly and equitably.
Insights into ministry by all must be encouraged and welcomed.
Obstacles in law to a fuller sharing in the ministries within the order
will need to be removed. The ministry to each other as brothers and
sisters will have to be recognized as central to Franciscan identity
and our charismatic gift to the whole church. Fraternity/sorority,
then, is at the very heart of ministry as constitutive of it for
Franciscans.

One final observation. Francis's love for the church exemplified
a prophetic and a poetic witness as a consequence of his total commitment to the gospel. Prophets and poets are seers: they "see" coming reality before others, and so must live in the eschatological
tension of the "already and not yet." On the one hand, such an attitude calls us to loving, prophetic critique of all that has not yet surrendered to the demands of conversion, while on the other hand, it
celebrates the beginnings, however humble and rudimentary, of genuine conversion. I think Francis's spirit of love of the church and his
conviction that he was also called to help reform it, is an apt example of what I have tried to develop in the dialectical, tension-laden
character of a symbol. Francis was such a symbol in his day. Are we
such symbols for our church and society in our day?

REFERENCES

Amalorpavadrass, D.S. "Church and Culture," pp. 201-206 in *The New Dictionary of Theology*. Edited by J.A. Komonchak, M. Collins, and D.A. Lane. Wilmington, Delaware: Michael Glazier, 1987.

Braine, David, *The Human Person: Animal and Spirit*. Notre Dame, Indiana: University of Notre Dame Press, 1992.

Cohen, Anthony P., *The Symbolic Construction of Community*. London and New York: Routledge, 1985.

Cooke, Bernard, *Sacraments and Sacramentality*. Mystic, Connecticut: Twenty-Third Publications, 1983.

————, *The Distancing of God: The Ambiguity of Symbol in History and Theology*. Minneapolis: Fortress, 1990.

Dillistone, F.W., *The Power of Symbols in Religion and Culture*. New York: Crossroad, 1986.

Dreyer, Elizabeth A., *Earth Crammed with Heaven: A Spirituality of Everyday Life*. New York: Paulist, 1994.

Duffy, Regis A., "Sacraments in General," Volume 2, pp. 183-210 in *Systematic Theology: Roman Catholic Perspectives*, two volumes, edited by. F. S. Fiorenza and J. P. Galvin. Minneapolis: Fortress, 1991.

Dulles, Avery, "The Symbolic Structure of Revelation," pp. 51-73 in Theological Studies 41 (1980).

————, "Imaging the Church for the 1980s," pp. 1-18 in *A Church To Believe In: Discipleship and the Dynamics of Freedom*. New York: Crossroad, 1982.

Eliade, Mircea, *Patterns of Comparative Religion*. Translated by Rosemary Sheed. Cleveland and New York: World Publishing Company, 1963. (Original English copyright by Sheed and Ward, 1958.)

————, *Images and Symbols: Studies in Symbolism*. Translated by Philip Mairet. Princeton: Princeton University Press, 1991. (Original English copyright by Harvill, 1961.)

Fink, Peter E., "Sacramental Theology after Vatican II," pp. 1107-14 in *The New Dictionary of Sacramental Worship*. Edited by Peter E. Fink. Collegeville: Liturgical Press, 1990.

Gundry, Robert H., *"Soma" in Biblical Theology With Emphasis on*

Pauline Anthropology. Grand Rapids: Akademie/Zondervan, 1987. (Original copyright by Cambridge University Press, 1976.)

Haight, Roger, *Dynamics of Theology*. New York: Paulist, 1990.

Happel, Stephen, "Symbol," pp. 1237-45 in *The New Dictionary of Sacramental Worship*. Edited by Peter E. Fink. Collegeville: Liturgical Press, 1990.

Kasper, Walter, "The Church as a Universal Sacrament of Salvation," pp. 111-28 in *Theology and Church*. Translated by Margaret Kohl. New York: Crossroad, 1989.

Lane, Dermot A., *The Experience of God: An Invitation to Do Theology*. New York: Paulist, 1981.

O'Meara, Thomas F., "Toward a Subjective Theology of Revelation," pp. 401-27 in *Theological Studies* 36 (1975).

Power, David N., *Unsearchable Riches: The Symbolic Nature of Liturgy*. New York: Pueblo, 1984.

Rahner, Karl., "The Theology of the Symbol, " vol. 4, pp. 221-52 in *Theological Investigations*. Baltimore: Helicon, 1966.

————, *Belief Today*. New York: Sheed and Ward, 1967.

————, "What Is a Sacrament?" vol. 14, pp. 135-48 in *Theological Investigations*. New York: Seabury, 1976 (1).

————, "Considerations on the Active Role of the Person in the Sacramental Event," vol. 14, pp. 161-84 in *Theological Investigations*. New York: Seabury, 1976 (2).

————, *Foundations of Christian Faith: An Introduction to the Idea of Christianity*, translated by William V. Dych. New York: Seabury, 1978.

Ricoeur, Paul, *The Symbolism of Evil*, translated by Emerson Buchanan. Boston: Beacon Press, 1967.

Ross, Susan A., "'Then Honor God in Your Body' (1 Cor.6:20): Feminist and Sacramental Theology on the Body," pp. 7-27 in *Horizons* 19 (1989).

Tillich, Paul, *Systematic Theology*. Volume l. Chicago: University of Chicago Press, 1951.

Tracy, David, *The Analogical Imagination: Christian Theology and the Cultureof Pluralism*. New York: Crossroad, 1981.

6

Fraternity and Sorority in Franciscan Leadership

Helen Rolfson, O.S.F.

T he followers of Francis of Assisi have long been associated with the ever-necessary renovation of the church. When Francis first heard the call to "repair my house, which, as you see, is falling into ruins," these words heard in prayer before the crucifix of San Damiano became the *Leitmotiv* and summary of his life-work as it was remembered by his followers. Pictorially, it was translated into Giotto's memorable fresco of Pope Innocent III's dream of the poor friar Francis propping up the crumbling church of the Lateran.[1]

In this essay, I propose to reflect upon some aspects of the Franciscan approach to renovation of ecclesial life from the perspective of the ideals of fraternity/sorority, with a view to its role in our respective missions and styles of leadership, for the renewal to which Francis was called was not of his order, but of the church itself. This reflection is intrinsically related to the question of "who" for Francis and Clare constituted the church. While they had an almost unparalleled respect for clergy and had ceaseless contacts with the hierarchical leaders, they were convinced that they were "in the church, of the church"; saw themselves *as* church; and lived as "brothers" and "sisters" through the grace of Christ. Though it may not always have felt like a grace to him, Francis said, "The Lord gave me brothers."[2] And Clare's own *Testament* reflects a similar sentiment when she speaks of "the few sisters whom the Lord had given me soon after my conversion."[3] Clare saw her enclosed community as intrinsically related to the church at large: "For the Lord himself has set us as an example and mirror for others, but also for our [own] sisters whom the Lord has called to our way of life, so that they in turn will be a mirror and example to those living in the world."[4]

---

[1] *LM* 9.
[2] *Test.*
[3] *TestCL*, 7.
[4] *TestCL*, 6.

The ideal of "brotherhood" among friars was quite strikingly promoted from the very beginning as was that of "sisterhood" among the followers of Clare. The stories we pass on about our roots not only deliver a tradition; they describe to ourselves and others who we are and who we want to be. The striving for unity among brethren by bonds of mutual love is demonstrated in story after story of the early tradition. The relationship of brother to brother in love took into account service, obedience, forgiveness:

> Francis's brotherhood was not determined by place, ministry, nationality. It was a reality determined by the deeper, more penetrating principle of the Holy Spirit.... In both Rules, Francis expresses a sensitivity to the "itinerant" aspect of a brother's life. The brothers were indeed, in the world, on the road, and traveling about in order to proclaim the gospel. Therefore, brotherhood had to be expressed in whatever place they found themselves and intensified through a loving obedience in which the minister and subject were eager to pray with, visit, and serve one another. It is difficult to lose sight of this dynamism of the gospel brotherhood in the writings of St. Francis. Yet it is consoling to notice tensions and struggles in expressing the ideal in everyday life. Sin was a reality that Francis saw as an enervating factor in the relationships of the brothers.... Francis encourages the ministers to love the sinful brother unconditionally so that he may be drawn to God."[5]

The ideal of fraternal relationships of brother to brother was clear as was that of sister to sister in mutual love. Even as abbess, "mother" Clare insisted on being "sister," not "lady abbess," to her community. Our language has preserved the terminology of "fraternity" as the inheritance of both the men and the women of the Franciscan family. (The lot of the term "sorority" has been less specific and today has unfortunately something of the ring of a college dorm to it. As a result, women of the Franciscan family have commonly used the term "fraternity," not "sorority," to describe mutual relationships within their religious communities. However, I use it here in the significance which it is given as the feminine expression of "fraternity," including the nuances inherent to these terms by their use in male or female communities.) "Fraternity" and "sorority" serve as sacramental relationships (in the broad sense: the Franciscan sister or brother is meant to be an embodiment of that love of one's neighbor in the church, which marks every Christian. However, it is not sepa-

---

[5] Armstrong/Brady, "Introduction," *FAC*, 18.

rate from the way that Francis and Clare saw themselves as related to Christ. Because we are the children of the one Father, and in a special way incorporated through baptism into the Son of that Father, through Christ our Brother, the primordial implication is that of being "brother" or "sister" of the Lord himself. It is through the lens of the primacy of Christ that Francis uses the term not only personally, but for all of nature. One whom he calls "brother" is first and foremost related to the Lord, and then by grace to the rest of creation. These terms, far from being accidental, or simple commonplaces, are bearers of ecclesiological significance.

This much seems rather evident. But in an age looking to collaborative styles of leadership in ministry, we must also ask whether our tradition provides any model for viewing relationship of brother to sister and vice versa.

Traditions about the Beginnings: First and Second Orders

From the beginning, the friars were continually associated with sisters, for good or for ill. A widely held and often-propagated mythology of the intimate friendship (not to say romance: witness the film *Brother Sun, Sister Moon*) between Francis and Clare is hard to substantiate from the early sources. The thirteenth and fourteenth century accounts demonstrate a certain ambiguity about the relationship between "brothers" and "sisters." If a solid tradition of fraternity did indeed emerge among the friars, it was not always seen as a relationship extending to their religious sisters. One of the disciples of Francis, Stephen of Narni, tells us of a disconcerting incident:

> Francis did not want to be the friend of any woman. Blessed Clare alone seems to have been the object of a certain predilection on his part. When he spoke with her, or when he spoke of her, he did not call her by her name, but he called her Christiana. He took care of her and of her monastery. He never concerned himself to found other monasteries himself, even though, in his own time, some monasteries were built, through the intervention of others. One day he remarked that they called the women who lived in community in those monasteries "sisters"; he was profoundly troubled by this and said: "The Lord has willed us not to have spouses; and so the devil has procured sisters for us!"[6]

---

[6] Thomas of Pavia (+1280-84), quoted in Vorreux, SFA, *Documents*, 1335; my translation.

The parallel with Francis's *Testament* (v.14), in which Francis readily acknowledges that it was the Lord who gave him brothers, appears almost intentional. Yet the *Vita Secunda* (8:13) of Celano recounts that the newly-converted Francis, busy with the repair of San Damiano, ecstatically sings out, in French, a prophecy of the future monastery of consecrated virgins that was to take root there. Clare, who happily called herself Francis's "little plant," or better, "footprint" (*plantula*),[7] remarks that it was "by the will of God and our most blessed Father Francis" that the Poor Ladies settled at San Damiano. Clare makes a great deal of this providential destiny:

> For almost immediately after his conversion, while he had neither brothers nor companions, when he was building the Church of San Damiano, in which he was totally filled with divine consolation, he was led to abandon the world completely. This holy man, in the great joy and enlightenment of the Holy Spirit, made a prophecy about us that the Lord fulfilled later. Climbing the wall of the church, he shouted in French to some poor people who were standing nearby: "Come and help me build the monastery of San Damiano, because ladies will dwell here who will glorify our heavenly Father throughout his holy church by their celebrated and holy manner of life."

Francis, their father and brother, also wrote a "Form of Life" for them.[8] Thomas of Celano[9], however, is a witness to a certain antifeminist approach that reminds one of many an ancient monastic tale. It speaks of the danger of women, who can lead astray even the elect. The friar is counseled to avoid association with women, on the example of Francis himself, to whom women were definitely "unwelcome." (With the exception of Clare and Lady [Brother!] Jacoba, what other women had Francis's unhesitating trust?) "Indeed, a woman was so unwelcome to him that you would think that his caution was not a warning or an example but rather a dread or a horror," Thomas observes. Women are characterized here as "importunate," "loquacious," a "contagion," an "impediment" to those seeking perfection, a danger to both weak and strong among the brethren, and providing "no profit but only great loss, at least of time."[10]

---

[7] Blessing attributed to St. Clare. *FAC*, 233.
[8] Cf. *TestCL* 4,5,9,10; cf. also *L3S* 24.
[9] *2Cel*.
[10] *2Cel* 78.

This is certainly not the only time such attitudes crept into the tradition, but they need to be recalled, and rethought. In any case, Francis wanted his brethren to avoid scandal, to live uprightly before God, with pure hearts and minds. Fraternity was hard enough in the male or female community without putting oneself in the way of stumbling blocks. Just as in our own day, because of the danger of certain scandals, new rules of conduct almost equivalent to ancient abstemiousness are entering ministerial practice and express the current tension between the desire to express genuine affection and the risk of lawsuits. The innocent simplicity of the chaste dove must be balanced with the prudent shrewdness of the serpent. It was probably not for nothing that Francis felt he had to severely reprimand some of the brethren who showed themselves too willing to visit the women's monasteries:

> One brother went in the winter to a certain monastery on an errand of sympathy, not knowing the saint's strong will about not going on such visits. After the fact had become known to the saint, he made the brother walk several miles naked in the cold and deep snow.[11]

One might well question Francis's use of authority in his leadership here. Does this perhaps give us an idea of how Francis himself first learned exercise of authority from his own severe father? Whereas Clare's use of authority seems to emanate gentleness and a foot-washing spirit, Francis's use of disciplinary action with dull or refractory brethren seems to differ considerably from Clare's style, as being sometimes quite harsh. While he did indeed exhibit some "motherly" moments in the care of his brethren, his severity in the exercise of authority is something of which Francis had more than one occasion to repent. However, Francis expressed his genuine love for the Poor Ladies, in spite of his general avoidance of them:

> Not to have called them would not have been a wrong; not to care for them once they have been called would be the greatest unkindness.... I do not want anyone to offer himself of his own accord to visit them, but I command that unwilling and most reluctant brothers be appointed to take care of them, provided they be spiritual men, proved by a worthy and long religious life.[12]

---

[11] *2Cel* 156.
[12] *2Cel* 155.

It may have been important for Francis to call for "unwilling and most reluctant brothers" as the most appropriate friars to minister to the sisters, but from the angle of the objects of such ministry, such a prescription could conceivably appear quite unedifyingly unchristian. But Francis protests his love of the sisters, humbly aware of his own fragility. The poignant stories of his building a "snow family" and the episode of "rolling in the roses," both undertaken to quench the fire of an already ardent nature (familiar *topoi* in ancient hagiography), are witnesses to his classic struggle. There is no evidence of Clare's battles with herself in the search for the just relationship between the sexes, and it is probably foolhardy to speculate on the reason for the lack. In any case, the tradition has been remarkably close-mouthed about women's view of the "danger" of men in this area, while extant spiritual literature, written by men for men, is full of warnings not even to look at a woman. (An exception is an *apophthegma* from the desert tradition that tells of an abba and his disciple who, on seeing an amma and her disciple coming in the distance, give them a wide berth, whereupon the amma responded: "If you kept your eyes where they belonged, you would not even have noticed we were women!")

Early Second and Third Order Members

In the time of Francis, as we know, many groups of people, such as the Humiliati, seeking a more gospel-oriented, gospel-inspired life in Christ were mushrooming, and in some way threatening the established order of things. Many, wanting to see more of Jesus than Judas in the face of the church, were hypercritical of the hierarchy, and assumed what we would call today "a prophetic stance." The desire to engage in public preaching was very much part of this sort of mission. In some of these groups, the role of the women involved direct collaboration with their masculine counterparts, on the road with the wandering preachers.

The risk of scandal in male-female relations was—and is— always present. In asserting his right to have the help of some devout women, St. Paul had argued that he was "not at all inferior to these super-apostles" (2 Corinthians 12:11). But sometimes cultural assumptions question the very possibility of chaste relationships between women and men, not to mention those in single-sex environments. A priest giving retreats for sisters in Zaïre, whose house was quite separate from that of the male missionaries, once told me that the groundskeeper for the sisters had come up to him privately to ask: "How do they do it?" "What?" "Manage to get together. I've worked here for twenty-five years and have kept them under close surveillance, but have not been able to figure out how it can happen, but it surely must." Legends of tunnels are not dead!

Women, ever determined not to shrink in the face of the difficulties of the apostolate, have confronted many a cultural challenge throughout history. Often authorities sensed that their enthusiasm could go easily out of control and work to the detriment of the mission of Christ. The "safer" route was to have strict separation of the sexes, giving men the predominantly "active" role and leaving the more "passive" role to the women. Their life "behind the scenes" was one of support, of backup in a spiritual sense, to the role of the men "in the field." This is one of the tensions presently experienced by many of the Clares. The question is frequently raised as to whether the original intention of the living out of their charism was strictly linked with enclosure, or was that same enclosure for those women merely a cultural necessity? The promise Francis makes to the Clares seems to be more one of protection than of collaboration, when he says "I promise you personally and in the name of my friars that I will always have the same loving care and special solicitude for you as for them."[13]

Consequently, the Franciscan women in the time of Francis himself were largely people such as Clare and her mother and sisters—where her own mother has become "sister"—living in the cloistered seclusion of San Damiano, spending themselves as tabernacle lamps in a life of contemplation and mutual love. It was to Clare-the-contemplative that Francis sent an inquiry to resolve his own spiritual doubts regarding his deep inclinations toward a life of contemplation.[14] Bonaventure's LM 12 has him first consulting his own friars, then sending two friars to Clare; she, inspired by the Spirit, agreed with Brother Sylvester in confirming Francis's preaching vocation. When the Clares are sometimes seen as the "contemplatives" whose vocation is to support the friars' "active" apostolate by their prayers, we have but to think how close it came for Francis, too, to have "gone contemplative."

---

[13] *FormViv.*
[14] *Fior* 18.

Third Order men and women were known for their charitable activity for the poor and downtrodden in society. This is a role that nobility often played, to the great edification of others (cf. Elizabeth of Hungary, for example, or Agnes of Prague). They knew that "What you do to the least of my brethren, you do unto me" (Matthew 25), something that Francis himself had experienced in his encounter with the leper, and the subsequent work of his brothers in "going among lepers." Early Third Order women contemplated the Passion of Christ, and wept over it in living color. Yet they seldom or never had the opportunity of preaching or of "going on mission" in the direct sense. Their experience of what it is to be "church" is a quite different thing from that which was experienced by men. But, like the later Thérèse of Lisieux, they, too, discovered their true vocation: love.

Some of the initial stresses in the First Order seemed to have arisen over care of, and relationship to, the feminine branch, the Clares of the Second Order. These are the same tensions that the Cistercians had had for a century or more before Francis. They saw that chaplaincy duties, and protection of the women's branch, risked detouring them from the exigencies of their own vocation, especially when monasteries multiplied rapidly. The dependency of the women was not only a *desirable thing* in thirteenth-century society, but also a *burden* to those who had care of them.

Influence of Post-Vatican II Ecclesiology

Vatican II enunciated principles of an ecclesiology of *communio*, the first time that such a view was officially propagated. To live out this ecclesiology in praxis is a challenge for all of us in the church, and, by that fact also a challenge for Franciscan men and women to enflesh. The pattern of striving to live as "brother" and "sister" to each other and to the world we serve in our various ways is admirably suited to that model of the church.

What is involved in this *communio*? It is an ecclesiology of mutuality, collaboration, of dialogue, in obedience to the gospel.

The Essentialist Model

The essentialist model reflects an ecclesiology of the pyramid— the familiar model of the pope at the top, followed by the descending order of hierarchy of clerics, and at the bottom, the "faithful," the laity. The essentialist model of the church has two poles: those in authority and those who obey; those who define the faith and those who profess it; sacred and profane are separate; *fuga mundi* is therefore the spiritual attitude which seems most preferred; in popular parlance, the authority figures are often identified as "the church." Doctrinal definitions are spoken of as "immutable." The task of the theologian here is one of finding the right words to explain to the "faithful" the immutable truth that has been chiseled out by a series of dogmatic proclamations. Correction is given from above to those below. Holiness is a question of keeping oneself "unspotted from this world," literally. "Catholic Action" is a participation in the mission of the hierarchy. The "signs of the times" as seen here are almost all negative warnings to take cover while there is still time. At present, it is fair to say that we are experiencing a time of crisis in the church, a crisis principally over the tension between this model and that of *communio*.

The Communio *Model*

Beginning with the Constitution on the Sacred Liturgy, and continuing with the documents of the Second Vatican Council, especially those on the church, and the church in the modern world, a new view of interrelationships within the church comes to light. Authority as service is stressed, with a more horizontal, non-dualistic view of the world. In this model, the pyramid is upended, or even better described by the model of the circle with Christ in the center; openness to the world, not flight, is acknowledged. Here, the "world" that calls the Christian to engagement *qua* Christian is not the Johannine ensemble of all that is opposed to the reign of God, but rather refers to the building ground for constructing that reign of God. Spirituality here is not so much characterized by "inwardness" and "individuality" as by "discernment" and recognition of being a member of "the people of God" in which all the members of the Body, no matter what their role of service, are the "faithful." The incarnational model plays a large part in this *communio* ecclesiology with its resultant spirituality. Catholics here are invited to be alert to "the signs of the times," and, living in the Spirit given to the whole church, make the necessary and courageous adaptations. Openness to "the other" in ecumenism is also characteristic of the new stance. Indeed, a sea change had come about in the way that it became possible for the church to see herself.

Effects on Franciscan Life

Religious, and, I dare say, religious women in a very emphatic way, have often been in the vanguard of the upheavals caused by the adaptations brought about in the wake of the council. Among these, of course, are to be found "sorores" and "fratres" of the Franciscan family. These religious men and women were anything but indifferent to the council's invitation to profound spiritual renewal. Who can tell the hours of discussion and prayer, the cautious and incautious launchings into experiments of all kinds in order to live the gospel more faithfully in resonance with the Spirit which was felt to be blowing so forcefully through the church? And who can measure the anguish of many who, in the throes of the discernments required in casting out into the deep, felt that "they have taken away the Body of my Lord and I know not where to find him"? Or who, discovering a new world view, found that they had sought religious life under what seemed to be "false pretenses"? It was also a period in which religious women in particular began to reach their majority (psychologically speaking), and refused henceforth to be treated like minors. The new winds of change blew many right out the door. Discussions of the whole religious community went on and on, on a revamping of the religious life *in toto,* with principles of *communio,* service, subsidiarity, and more ringing in their ears. The decisions themselves were often taken in a way quite different from those of chapter gatherings which had taken place preceding the council, in which a few made policy for the many. *Communio* required participation, not mere receptivity. In women's communities, the very title "superior" became abhorrent, as it rang of the old hierarchical, static model; it was soon exchanged for titles more apt to express one's ministry to the community. Those communities who opted to call the superior "president" are now finding it less satisfactory, not etymologically (for it simply means one who "sits in front" or who "chairs"), but for its political connotations.

In hagiography, the roles of saintliness have seemed quite clear for the women: they could be religious, martyrs, virgins, widows. In the pre-Vatican II church, as well as in the contemporary "restoration" mentality, some of the saintly models held out to religious display a world view quite different from Vatican II ecclesiology of *communio,* with virtues of obedience and humble submission seemingly being preferred to values such as creativity, loving critique of the church, or engagement in political action. We have but to look at the *vitae* of those canonized or beatified by the present pope to won-der if a Vatican II-shaped religious will ever make it to the altars. This is just to underline the fact that those committed to *communio* ecclesiology in "fraternity/sorority" may not even have the consola-tion of the support of the spiritual models they may have been used to before. In fact they may not even have the consolation of the old sources of spiritual support at all, except that which is found in their faithful rootedness in Christ and in the "fraternity/sorority" of their communities.

For the Franciscan brethren, their "place" (one of Francis's favorite words) in the church is not subject to too many questions. But, because of the feminist movement, it is becoming increasingly difficult for women to delineate for themselves their proper relation-ship to the church. Language which presumes that women can in no way mirror Christ is also self-defeating.

Even the pope's encyclical *Mulieris dignitatem*, or "The Place of Women in the Church," for all its laudable intentions, seems to imply that "the place" is quite limited. They know where they *don't* belong, in other words. What men are concerned about their "place" in the church? It may seem self-evident to them. But it remains for us as men and women to delineate and to forge a "place" in creative rela-tionship to each other for the sake of the gospel.

These characteristics are only a few indications of the vast impli-cations for religious life of living according to a new way of "being church." I submit that the Franciscan models of "sorority" and "fra-ternity" are ideally suited for the sisters and brothers of the three orders who obediently "return to the sources," to find congenial models in their own spiritual tradition. Our "story" tells us who we are. Let us take, by way of illustration, what happened in many a Franciscan religious community of women, since I know that best. There, this "return to the sources," through critical study of the "real" Francis and Clare, spurred a great élan of discovery: the sister previously titled deferentially as "general superior" came to be addressed as "sister" and not as "mother"; the sisters discovered a new Francis (not the romantic Francis, and not Sabatier's Protestant Francis, but the Francis of the critical texts) and they finally discov-ered Clare as more than an appendage to Francis, for new studies bring to light that Clare should be considered a major religious fig-ure in her own right. The prototypes of today's Franciscan women tell them better who they are, not only as "sisters" to each other in the community but also as members of and sisters to the ecclesial community with its task before and in the world as contemporary disciples and lovers of the Lord Jesus.

How Can We Help Each Other in the Crisis of "Restoration"?

The model of *communio* corresponded to a much changed world view. Catholics had begun to see the value of coming out of a ghetto mentality that previously had been the result of political and social circumstances. Once out, however, some wanted to retreat to the security they had known before within the *societas perfecta*, as the church had been described. The crisis now consists precisely in the many current efforts to achieve a "restoration" of pre-Vatican II ordering, with its attendant hierarchical view of the church. In the thirty years that have elapsed since the council, we have had the chance to observe several indications of this effort to "take back the church" from the people of God.

It is perhaps safe to say that some religious communities, in somehow weathering that storm, have proceeded to a stage of "second naïveté," a new reassessment of their situation, and can be of help (in spite of—or even because of?—the figures of the advancing average age of their respective communities) to brothers and sisters who, for one reason or another, have not—yet!—experienced such radical change. They can encourage them not to retreat into havens of security, not to cut off dialogue, not to be enticed by the frequent public praise, attention, and yes, even money, given to the reactionaries.

After Vatican II, religious men and women have also found themselves collaborating in unprecedented ways with other religious communities, with other churches, and with believers and unbelievers, men and women, those who are engaged with the church, the indifferent, and those who are disaffected from it, in direct and indirect ways. They have been called to discernment in their own vocational commitments on a regular basis. At the present time, with the rise of feminism, for which many religious women have found themselves in the vanguard, religious men and women alike are being called to reexamine their commitment to and understanding of "church."

This is true for religious of all stripes, but it is particularly important for Franciscans, whose founder found it so important to be true sons and daughters of the church. Can we do this with the same creativity, joy, and commitment that our spiritual ancestors displayed?

The Twentieth, Going on Twenty-first Century

It is probably not helpful for Franciscans to be overly concerned about survival as Franciscans. We do have a duty, stemming from our vocation, however, to see that we do all in our power to live in vibrant and evangelical fidelity in our respective communities. There is no guarantee that even very *good* communities will go on and on. The point is, while survival is important if we are to carry on our mode of evangelical witness, survival itself is not the primordial goal of religious life.

Leadership should also take into account that it is only too tempting to consider success in attracting vocations as a sign that the community is doing something right (God's will). This may not necessarily be the case. Some of our communities, even very good ones, will go through the death and dying process earlier than others. Rather, it is the vitality of the gospel message that is in question today. We agree that the twentieth century requires other methods to share the Good News that is Christ himself. Christ is not necessarily best preached today by thirteenth-century methods. The gospel-inspired dedication of the Franciscan message is as urgent as ever, if not more so.

In the light of the urgent task that we have before us to be faithful to the mission of Jesus in Franciscan "fraternity/ sorority" and genuine *communio,* I conclude by proposing some questions we might ask ourselves as we engage in leadership and ministry today as members of the Franciscan family:

1. In what ways can and do we collaborate as Franciscan leaders for the good of the whole church? for the upbuilding of the reign of God? In an age in which religious change is occurring at lightning speed, and is only paralleled by the increasing lack of theological and philosophical training on the part of candidates for religious orders, how can leaders assure that religious of every age keep intellectually and theologically alive and up to date?

2. How can we use the gifts of Franciscan leadership and commitment in such a way that our very collaboration as a "priestly people" is a witness to the reign of God we preach? What limitations do we see in working apart instead of together? What conditions do we

need to envisage in furthering our mutual collaboration? Are there cultural barriers today which hinder the desired collaboration?

3. How can we reawaken a lively and deep love for the church on the part of women who have begun to feel more and more alienated from that church? and in particular, our "sisters" engaged in a Franciscan apostolate? The urgency of this task will certainly not escape those in leadership positions. How does a Franciscan best relate to the local church and its leaders? How does a Franciscan best critique the church he or she loves?

4. Do we need a new hagiography? What models of collaboration and religious leadership, whether ancient or modern, can we find and underline? Are there some models that, holy as they were in a given time and place, are to be eschewed today? How do we tell the "story" of our own community roots? Has that story undergone reinterpretation after the benefit of post-Vatican II renewals?

5. Do we need a new view of ecumenism, bringing not only churches, but men and women, especially our own "fratres" and "sorores" into much-needed dialogue, as well as to reconciliation, for the service of the whole Body of Christ? How can Franciscan fraternity/sorority promote the ecclesiology of *communio*, which seems the model most akin to these Franciscan values?

6. How can we pray together in sorority/ fraternity? Can we help each other find the words needed? What patterns of piety or spirituality can we promote for those in our communities in order to help them live better an ecclesiology of *communio?* Are there some models which we would not hold out, or even discourage?

7. Can we find language in which to speak to one another in mutual support in our ministries? How does a soror /frater respond to those within a community who have harmed it in some way?

8. How can Franciscan leadership as soror or frater help us to vocational discernment for candidates? or to the hard choices that need to be made in love? Do our constitutions allow our leaders room for creativity as well as collaboration? As leaders, how do we keep from hiding behind "fraternity" when real decisions have to be made, and made now? How do we best handle scandals which arise in our communities in a way that is itself a witness to love, truth, and discretion?

9. How do we find meaningful ways to relate to those who wish to associate in some way with our communities without taking any permanent commitment to them? This may also relate to our relationship with ex-members, some of whom may be wishing for some sign of healing of past hurts, reconciliation. Do they perhaps see sisterhood/ brotherhood in a new or changed way? How can we dialogue most fruitfully with these who have in the past shared our sister/brotherhoods, and in such a way that members of the communities themselves do not feel neglected?

10. How does Franciscan fraternity/sorority in leadership face the question, only too urgent for some of our communities now, of the death of an institution? How can we best "assist the sick and the dying" collaboratively? lovingly? How can we work together, not as forced through circumstances of diminishment of personnel and resources, but motivated by the gospel imperative?

In the course of this essay, various terms have come up again and again: *communio*, sorority/fraternity, dialogue, ecclesiology, tradition, reconciliation. The Franciscan tradition, both as to Francis and to Clare, is very rich in models for all of these. When we read positively the signs of the times today in the spirit we have inherited from Francis and Clare, new and revitalized patterns of leadership will emerge. And in so doing, we may indeed contribute, in hope and fidelity, to that rebuilding of the church, true to our roots, open to the future, and to what the Lord asks of us and of no one else in history.

7

Contemporary Ecclesiology and the Franciscan Tradition

William McConville, O.F.M.

David Tracy, the distinguished Catholic theologian at the University of Chicago, recounts a wonderful interchange which took place between the late archbishop of Chicago, John Cardinal Cody, and himself. The occasion was the imminent arrival of Hans Küng to lecture at the university. Cody summoned Tracy into his presence to express his displeasure. When asked what the subject of the lecture was to be, Tracy responded: "Belief in God." Cody breathed a sigh of relief and said: "Oh, is that all? I thought he was going to speak about the church." In a way that he never intended, the cardinal was signaling just how central, indeed contentious, the subject of the church had become in theological discussion in the latter half of the twentieth century.

A humorous bit of dialogue from Woody Allen's film *Hannah and Her Sisters* sharpens the tension between God and the church. A character, played by Allen, has mistakenly conceived the notion that he has been miraculously healed of a fatal illness. He decides to "get religion" and fixes on the Catholic Church. We soon find him in discussion with a cleric. The priest says to him: "Now, let me understand this. You don't believe in God, but you want to join the Catholic Church. Is that correct?" The potential catechumen answers: "That's right, but you do have a wonderful structure." Is this, in part, the legacy of a baroque ecclesiology's vigorous defense of the visibility of the church?

I do not have to remind you how much attention is given to the tensions within that structure by the media. I was in Ireland during the 1993 visit to Denver by Pope John Paul II. Given what I read in the papers and what I saw on some of the news programs that made their way to Irish television, I must agree with E. J. Dionne, a columnist for the Washington Post. He noted that, on the basis of what one heard on television or read in the newspapers, the only issues of import in the Catholic Church were those connected with gender or dissent in matters of sexual ethics. As significant as these are, they do not begin to exhaust the mystery at the heart of the church and the profound transformation in the self-understanding of the church that had begun before the Second Vatican Council, received direction and official stamp at the council, and has continued in the thirty years since the council concluded its official sessions.

The topic I have been assigned is a vast one. Thus I have structured and focused its development as follows. First, I will look briefly at the shape of the ecclesiological renewal that was occasioned by the Second Vatican council, sketching the themes that emerged out of the council and some of the tensions that are characteristic of the post-conciliar period. Second, I will attempt to highlight, without being in any way exhaustive, some of the ways in which the Franciscan tradition has contributed to, and been shaped by, the renewal. Finally, I will offer some reflections as to how some themes within the Franciscan tradition can contribute to what I have called an "ecclesiadicy," a consideration of the tragic dimension of ecclesial belonging.

Ecclesiology of Vatican II and Its Reception

It is safe to say that certain periods in the history of the church have their overarching theological preoccupations. Without radically oversimplifying one can legitimately say that the patristic era and its councils was dominated by Trinitarian and Christological concerns. The period of the Reformation was one of intense preoccupation with questions about grace, freedom, and redemption, while the post-Enlightenment period saw the church grappling with the challenge to faith posed by rationalism and revolutionary politics. In our time, particularly as a result of Vatican II, it is safe to describe the central theological theme of our time as the mystery of the church. As Peter Hebblethwaite's biography of Paul VI demonstrated, it was Cardinal Montini, assisted by Cardinals Suenens, Alfrink, and Döpfner, who saved a floundering council by focusing the disparate themes of the council on that of the church. The centrality of *Lumen Gentium* and *Gaudium et Spes* points to the success of those efforts, along with documents on bishops, presbyters, laity, religious, ecumenism, and the liturgy.

Permit me to recall briefly the central motifs of this ecclesiological renewal. First is the affirmation of the centrality of the reign of God and the more nuanced reflection on the relationship of the church to it. To use a phrase which the council did not use, but which reflects accurately its understanding, the church is the *sacramental servant* of the reign of God.[1] This decidedly non-triumphalistic way of understanding the church recognizes that the church, although poor and sinful, is integral to the reality of the reign of God, but does not monopolize its presence or activity in the world. Second, the seemingly arcane debate over whether the church of Christ is the Catholic Church or subsists in the Catholic Church opened up amazingly fruitful ecumenical possibilities as it recognized the realities of the church of Christ present outside of the Catholic Church. Third, the recovery of the importance of the ministry of the bishop and thus of the significance of the local or particular church served to redress, as Joseph (now Cardinal) Ratzinger noted at the time of the council, a one-sided emphasis on papal primacy and universality. Thus the notion of collegial governance was revitalized, as a thoughtful retrieval of patristic sources challenged the assumptions of a baroque ecclesiology. Fourth, the relationship between the church and the world was reconfigured. There is a fascinating metamorphosis of the church from "embattled fortress" under Pio Nono (who for all practical purposes excommunicated the world of the nineteenth century) to the church of John XXIII and Paul VI as the "sacrament of dialogue" with the modern world. Thus the church declared its solidarity with the hopes and dreams, the pain and suffering of modern men and women; spoke compellingly to the dignity and freedom of the human person; affirmed the values of democracy and human interdependence; and was clear that its rootedness in the gospel impelled it to be of service to the social and political order. Notably absent from the conciliar documents was the triumphal language of Christendom.

After the council officially completed its work, the exhilarating and painful process of "reception" began, and it has continued for the last thirty years. During this period certain ecclesial themes emerged with great vigor as the people of God sought to apply the teaching of the council to life in local churches. One area in which a dramatic transformation took place was in the theology of mission. Drawing deeply on the conciliar vision of salvation, the local church, and the commitment of the church to human development, the the-

---

[1] O'Meara, 1983: p. 33.

ology of mission found itself attending to three central issues: *Inculturation*—How does the gospel become incarnate in a particular culture?; *Dialogue*—How does the church couple its commitment to proclaim the gospel with a recognition of the presence of God in the lives of Hindu, Buddhist, or Muslim men and women; and *Liberation*—What is the relationship between salvation and the process of human liberation? This last question emerged with great insistence in the Latin American church as it sought to appropriate the dynamism of the council for its own pastoral situation. Thus the watershed bishops' conference held in Medellin, Colombia, in 1968 placed the poor at the center of the church; the church in Latin America was to be for, with, and of the poor. It was here that liberation theology found its official warrant. Thus the realities of cultural pluralism, poverty and oppression, and the presence of vital non-Christian religious traditions posed dramatic challenges to the church's understanding of its pastoral ministry in the world.

And, of course, there have been ongoing contentious debates within the church that have been the occasions of much pain and bitterness. Let me remind you of the most prominent of these. How is the church to be understood as the people of God and as a hierarchical communion? How can its structure embody or "sacramentalize" adequately both of these dimensions? Given that the universal church is not simply a loose confederation of local churches and that the local church is not simply a section or a fragment of an international organization, how is the church to function as a communion? How can the rights and responsibilities of local churches be protected and enhanced? (This, of course, has enormous implications for the ecumenical movement, as the current debates about *communio* have shown.) How can the ecclesial magisterium teach authoritatively as it seeks to engage the intelligence and freedom of the people of God? What are the possibilities and limits of dissent? How is the ministry of the church to be structured so that the church's mission in service of the reign of God can be most effectively accomplished. Who should be allowed to share in this ministry? Only celibate men? Only men? Clearly not so, say many women within the church. The debate about the role of women within the church, while occasioned perhaps by questions about women and ministry, has become a much larger and more radical discussion about patriarchy, oppression, and the lack of attentiveness to the experience and voices of women. Finally, there is the recurring debate about the relationship between the church and the political order. The issue is not so much that the church should not be involved, but rather who should be involved ("the cleric or religious woman in politics question") and how should the church's position on various issues respect the pluralism within a given nation or community.

The Franciscan Response

The council challenged religious orders to engage in a process of renewal that was similar to that of the council itself: to return to their sources, particularly the charism of their founders, and to read the signs of the times, to determine how they could most effectively be of service to the church and the reign of God. Like so many conciliar mandates this challenge took religious communities in ways that neither the council fathers nor religious superiors could have anticipated. It was also to have profound implications for the mission and ministry of the church.

Franciscans of every stripe engaged with great seriousness in the retrieval and, while discovering the world of tangled roots and muddied sources (Eric Doyle's artful phrase) that characterize the early Franciscan movement, found their encounter with Francis of Assisi to be enormously liberating. In more recent years, of course, owing to the pioneering research of scholars like Regis Armstrong, O.F.M. Cap., and Margaret Carney, O.S.F., and the added impetus provided by the eight hundredth anniversary of her birth, the importance of Clare of Assisi in the origination and shaping of the charism has been appropriately recognized.

I will leave the substantive accounts of those retrievals of the Franciscan charism to others, but I would like to make the following points in regard to current ecclesiological discussions. Francis's fidelity to the movement of the Spirit in his life, his refusal to be fitted into preexisting structures, his aggressive defense of his way of life before the highest ecclesiastical authorities, his identification of the Holy Spirit as the minister general of the order, yet his profound respect for the magisterial and sacramental mediation of the church, and his refusal to countenance anything which would alienate him or his followers from the Catholic faith, threw into sharp relief for his followers the troublesome question of the relationship between institution and charism. For Francis and his followers there could be no churchless gospel or a churchless brotherhood and sisterhood, and yet at the same time this church was to be no closed system or absolute institution which could not be moved by the sovereign Spirit of freedom and grace. Sophisticated commentators like Yves Congar, the great Dominican ecclesiologist, have noted that pneumatology, while clearly influencing the conciliar texts, was not as powerful an influence as Christology on the conciliar agenda, and yet the ongoing renewal of the church requires that it be given significantly more attention. It is precisely a phenomenon such as the Franciscan movement, if it is faithful to its origins, that will not let the institutional church forget the necessity of the charismatic and prophetic dimensions of religious life for its continuing vitality. But have Franciscans themselves forgotten this? A cursory review of the General Constitutions of the Franciscans, the Capuchins, the Conventuals, and the Poor Clares, as well as the Rule of the Third Order Regular reveals almost no references to the charismatic or prophetic dimension of Franciscan life and ministry for the life of the church, no sense that those who are the bearers of the Franciscan tradition commit themselves to exercising their unique mission within the church, and not simply on behalf of it.

Reading General Constitutions is one thing, being attentive to the lives of Franciscan women and men is quite something else. It is in the lives of countless committed followers of Francis that the ecclesial renewal called for by the council has been carried out and, in these very lives, that the ecclesiology of tomorrow is being brought to birth. In the liturgical celebrations of African Poor Clares, as they move majestically and rhythmically around their chapels, the invitation to the inculturation of the gospel is wonderfully choreographed. When Franciscan brothers and sisters live in practical solidarity with the poor, they witness to the fact that, as *Gaudium et Spes* attested, the grief and anguish of the poor are the grief and anguish of the followers of Christ. They testify dramatically, as Leonardo Boff suggests, to the twofold loyalty of the Franciscan tradition: to the poor and to the church. When friars work collaboratively in ministries with the laity, a whole new praxis of ministry is being established which will, in fact, result in a quite different ecclesiology. Finally, within this context, I would like to remind you of the comprehensive and insightful *Correspondence Course on the Franciscan Missionary Charism*, known in this country as *Build with Living Stones*. This project, which appeared in English in 1987 and was revised in 1989, involved men and women from every part of the Franciscan family and from every part of the globe. It sought to address many of the themes that are at the center of contemporary ecclesiological discussion—Christ and the unity of the human family, contemplation and action, issues of peace and poverty, the dialogues with technology, secularism, Marxism, and Islam—from the point of view of the Franciscan sources and the experience of contemporary Franciscan men and women. It is, I believe, an underutilized resource. The text will undergo major revision during the next several years, when the men and women who have been using and reflecting on the texts offer their perspectives and corrections. This is a process analogous to consulting the *sensus fidelium* on matters about which they have wisdom. Somewhere there is a lesson for the wider church here.

Buehlmann and Boff

There are, however, certain individuals who, because of their vision and their capacity to articulate that vision, have been especially prominent in bringing the dimensions of the Franciscan tradition to bear on issues of moment within ecclesiology. Through their books and their lectures they had great influence not only within the Franciscan Order but in the wider church as well. Without a prejudice to any number of other Franciscan thinkers I must mention Walbert Buehlmann, O.F.M. Cap., and Leonardo Boff.

Buehlmann, a Swiss Capuchin who had served as a missionary in Africa, as a professor of missiology in both Fribourg and Rome, and as the secretary general for missions for the Capuchin Franciscans, began to receive international recognition in 1976 with the publication of his provocative book, *The Coming of the Third Church*. The argument of the book was two-fold. On the one hand, Buehlmann sought to provide the empirical data to justify Karl Rahner's thesis that the Catholic Church had truly become a world church, a communion of local churches marked by an increasing cultural pluriformity, and not simply a worldwide extension of Latin Catholicism. Certainly the numbers would indicate a great shift in regard to where Catholics are to be found. By the year 2000 almost two-thirds of Catholics will be found south of the equator. On the other hand, Buehlmann sought to exemplify his view that in this emerging "third church" will be important resources for the renewal of the entire church, as these churches themselves struggle with the great mission themes: inculturation, dialogue, and liberation. He is convinced, as I am, that the renewal of the church, its structures and its ministries, will come most radically from the renewal of its sense of mission. His subsequent works have continued to advance this agenda, particularly his attention to the dialogue with world religions, as well as his more autobiographical pieces that describe in great detail his struggle with disapproving and suspicious ecclesiastical officials.

Buehlmann, along with other Franciscans such as Arnulf Camps, has enriched this important discussion within the church from a particularly Franciscan point of view. I refer, of course, to the way in which the early Franciscan experience and vision of mission, as described in Chapter 16 of the Rule of 1221 (*Regula nonbullata*) provided a dramatic alternative to traditional missionary activity in the thirteenth century and continues to be a challenge to the manner in which Franciscans and indeed all Christians are to go *among* (and not simply *to*) nonbelievers. The importance of preaching the gospel and offering the sacraments is coupled with an emphasis on fraternal and sororal presence, and respectful participation in the life of the people. The call to service, to vulnerability, and to presence provides a credible context for the proclamation of the word. If this text is brought together, as Buehlmann and others do, with the marvelous story about St. Francis and the sultan, there emerges an especially powerful resource for renewing the Christian understanding of mission. (Francis himself remains, of course, the unsurpassable resource. I am fascinated by the testimony of an Asian theologian like Aloys Pieris, who contends that Francis is one of the few religious figures who can bridge the gap between Christianity and Buddhism: his way of holiness transcends confessional boundaries.)

It is impossible to speak about contemporary ecclesiology and the Franciscan tradition without speaking about Leonardo Boff. His writing in the area of liberation theology, his struggles with the Vatican, and his subsequent decision to leave the friars gave him an international reputation not shared by many of his sisters and brothers. It is hard for me not to believe that his passionate commitment to bring to his people the hope and the reality of an integral liberation, a liberation which transformed structures as well as the human heart, was not nourished by his commitment to the Franciscan life. Although I assume he is not a candidate for canonization, he does embody the kind of intellectual which is recognizably Franciscan—an organic intellectual, to borrow the phrase from Gramsci. His academic, intellectual, or theological concerns are never far removed from the hopes and aspirations, anguish and grief of the people. I think it is important to note also that the vindication of the importance of the theology of liberation, for which Boff and many others had worked so hard, was effected by the support and advocacy of two extraordinary Brazilian Franciscans, Aloisio Cardinal Lorscheider and Paulo Evaristo Cardinal Arns, two modern-day Ugolinos.

In his specifically ecclesiological works Boff often draws on the Franciscan tradition. As he seeks to legitimate the necessity of criticism in the face of institutional pathologies or perhaps dysfunctionalities, he reminds his readers of the pointed and harsh rhetoric that Anthony of Padua and Bernardine of Siena leveled against prominent prelates. His major thrust, however, is to explore the ways in which the base Christian communities, key places of ecclesiogenesis, reflect Francis's vision for the communal life of his followers within the church—fully Catholic, yet living with the tension of obedience and nonconformism, embodying a geniunely collegial and fraternal life, alive to the movement of the Spirit, fed by the word of God, in solidarity with the poor, and committed to mission in the service of the reign of God. This all sounds terribly utopian, but Boff reminds us that there has always been a utopian strain within our shared tradition as Franciscans. While that can prove dangerous or even destructive, such hopes are therapeutic as many of us settle into cynical complacency or stoical inactivity.

Ecclesial Suffering

There are many in the church today who can hardly be called complacent, but they cannot justly be characterized as hopeful either. This brings me to my final theme. There are countless men and women who are suffering because of the church, not on behalf of it, to use Flannery O'Connor's nicely turned phrase. There are sources of this suffering that should not surprise us. After all, the church has always been filled with sinners and the church itself can be described as a reality which is at once sinful and holy. Sinners, of what ever level of responsibility and of however exalted a ministerial state, can inflict pain on fellow members of the Body of Christ. Many have walked away because they have felt violated or have been overwhelmed by the gap between rhetoric and reality. It has always been thus. Francis's call for reformation, for metanoia, is a constant reminder as to the fragility of our own discipleship as well as to our responsiblity to edify, to build up, and not to tear down.

I find that the simple words "Come home" which describe a Franciscan ministry of welcome and reconciliation for wounded and alienated Catholics to be a marvelous expression of Franciscan ecclesiology in action. This is Franciscan pastoral life at its best. The friars are seen to be attentive, listening, compassionate, and companionable, and countless men and women have responded. This approach was aptly described by a Franciscan pastor who was asked why his parish was flourishing, why it was perceived to be the premier parish in the diocese. The friar replied: "We treat people with dignity and we don't put obstacles in their way." I found it striking that in Patricia Hampl's wonderful memoir, *Virgin Time*, it is a Poor Clare sister whose wise and humane counsel draws the author back into communion with the church.

There is, however, another aspect to the reality of suffering within the church today. It goes beyond the simple fact of sinfulness. It occurred to me, as I struggled to understand this aspect of ecclesial pain, that it had something of the tragic about it, that there is a tragic dimension to ecclesial belonging. What do I mean by this? In large measure it is connected with the fact that the church, although it is the people of God, the Body of Christ, and the Temple of the Spirit, is all of these things as a human reality. Thus, the church is finite, historical, and in possession of a limited but real freedom as it shapes its concrete manifestations in history. Thus it is conceivable that those who participate in the life of the church can suffer because of the presence or the absence of change, or because of the asceticism demanded by time. There is also the possibility that suffering can flow from the conflict of two goods, both of which are necessary to the life and vitality of the church, but which in a given epoch or context are impossible to reconcile. Raymond Williams has pointed out that the tragic interpretation of life often occurs in times of transition where, on the one hand, inherited beliefs are both prized and questioned, and yet, on the other hand, it is difficult to square these beliefs with newly and vividly experienced contradictions and possibilities. This seems to me to characterize so much of contemporary Catholicism, e.g., the struggle over the place of women, the conflict over unity and diversity, the debates about sexuality.

This kind of pain and suffering requires that we develop an "ecclesiadicy." By this I mean discourse about the church which attends in a special way to the sinful or tragic dimensions of the church, which seeks to reflect on the reality of the church in the face of this suffering, and thus to offer hope. It seems to me that the Franciscan tradition can contribute to the formulation of this ecclesiadicy in three ways. The first is that, given the intimate connection between Francis and the cross and the sensitivity to victims which flows from this closeness, Franciscans must keep alive the stories of suffering. Thus the enduring humanity and finiteness of the church must not be lost sight of. Any temptations to hard-edged moralism or triumphalism must be resisted. Second, those who suffer need the comfort and support of communities where they can be accompanied in their pain and in their struggle. Franciscans have had a gift for welcoming such people. I am not suggesting the development of sectarian or gnostic groups but the creation of shared spaces, communities of reflection and prayer, where men and women can survive, wait, and speak the stories of grace and hope.

And, finally—and this may sound precious—Franciscans can bring their sense of the importance of beauty to our current situation. This struck me when I read *The Dork of Cork* by Chet Raymo. It is a story told by a bastard dwarf whose life is concerned with the struggle between beauty and brokenness. He finds beauty, of course, in the world of the night sky and much of the book traces his discovery of that beauty. The other strain in the book is his grappling with brokenness, his own physical deformation as well as the moral and psychological flawedness of the people who share his life. The dwarf's name is Francis. If, in some way, we can reappropriate contemplation's "look of love," we can come to recognize the beauty of God's gracious presence in the lives of countless men and women who struggle to believe, hope, and love. Such was Francis's angle of vision. It is one of his most precious gifts to those of us, dwarfs all, who follow after him.

124   *William McConville, O.F.M.*

REFERENCES

Boff, Leonardo, and Walbert Buehlmann, *Build Up My Church.* Chicago: Interprovincial Secretariat for the Missions, 1984.

Boff, Leonardo, *Church: Charism and Power.* New York: Crossroad, 1985.

————, *Ecclesiogenesis.* Maryknoll, New York: Orbis Books, 1986.

Buehlmann, Walbert, *The Coming of the Third Church.* Maryknoll, New York: Orbis Books, 1976.

Flannery, Austin, *The Documents of Vatican II.* New York: Pillar Books, 1975.

Hampl, Patricia, *Virgin Time.* New York: Farrar, Straus and Giroux, 1992.

Hebblethwaite, Peter, *Paul VI.* New York: Paulist Press, 1993.

McConville, William, *"The Sinful, the Tragic, and Ecclesiadicy."* Unpublished paper, 1989.

Mueller, Andreas, *Build With Living Stones.* et al. 1987-1989.

O'Meara, Thomas, *Theology of Ministry.* New York: Paulist Press, 1983.

Pieris, Aloysius, *Love Meets Wisdom.* Maryknoll, New York: Orbis Books, 1988.

Raymo, Chet, *The Dork of Cork.* New York: Warner Books, 1993.

Williams, Raymond, *Modern Tragedy.* Stanford: Stanford University Press, 1966.

8

Hermitage or Marketplace?
The Search for an Authentic Franciscan
Locus in the World

Michael F. Cusato, O.F.M.

It is almost axiomatic to note that the monumental social changes
of the 1960s have had an enormous impact upon the church: its
life, its teaching, its institutions, its understanding of its role and
mission in the world. The symbol of this new wind of change blowing in the church is, of course, the Second Vatican Council.
Moreover, the subsequent changes wrought within the church contributed to even further changes in society itself, fostering a symbiotic, but tense, relationship of change between the Catholic Church
and the world into which it has historically been inserted.

One of the institutions of the church in the United States that has
been most strongly affected by these decades of change has been the
religious life. The Order of Friars Minor is no exception.[1] The
changes have prompted the American Franciscan provinces to
undertake both a close examination of the situation in which they
currently find themselves and the drafting of realistic plans for their
future life.

A Current Problem: The Impact of Decreasing Numbers on Ministry

One of the most visible effects of the changes following the
Second Vatican Council has been the slow exodus from the church of
thousands of previously church-going Catholics, an exodus that has
been only slightly reversed in recent years. The exodus, moreover,
has had its parallel in religious communities, as hundreds of men
and women have left the vowed life to live out their Christian com-

---

[1] In this presentation, I am concerned solely with the First Order of the
Franciscan family.

mitment—or sometimes explicitly to abandon it—in a world free of the structures and demands of the religious life. The withdrawals have had a profound impact upon the ministries performed by religious communities, creating an atmosphere of crisis within them as they face the future. This crisis[2] in ministry serves as the point of departure for my reflections.

Franciscan provinces have had to face the hard fact that many of the ministries in which the friars have faithfully served the people of God for decades are no longer tenable *as they presently exist*. We simply do not have the manpower to continue in them as we have in the past. Over the last two decades, a variety of provisions have been adopted to meet the situation: consolidation of parochial resources where possible, relinquishment of untenable ministries to dioceses; adaptation to new roles and methods of ministering where required; continuing education for friars where appropriate; and inclusion of and collaboration with the laity where acceptable.

No one can accuse provincial administrations of a lack of good will, honest intent, or heroic effort in their attempts to grapple with the problem. Their efforts have borne much fruit, but the same problem persists today as the number of friars available for ministry continues to decline. Despite enormous expenditures of energy and money, provinces are still faced with a variety of serious and pressing questions: Which ministries can we still keep? How are we to staff them? What does the future hold for these (or other) ministries? In other words: What can we realistically do?

The gravity and apparent intractability of these problems has created doubt and questioning among the friars themselves not only about the future life of the community but also, by implication, about the value of their previous and present work. Faced with often bleak but honest assessments of the future, friars can become dispirited and bitter about life in the fraternity and the present state of the church. How can that which had seemed so solid and certain when they had entered religious life possibly be falling apart around them? Some friars wonder: Do we have a future?

---

[2] The term "crisis" is certainly overused and abused in contemporary American discourse. I use the term here in its root meaning in Greek: *krinein* = to separate, to decide. Hence, the "crisis in ministry" is a situation in which some serious decision-making about the future is being demanded.

Some Current Thinking on Possible Solutions to this Problem

How then should we respond to this crisis in ministry so as to prepare and provide for the future? A number of friars advocate revitalizing our ministry by recovering the truly distinctive elements of the Franciscan approach to the spiritual concerns of ordinary people. The task, in other words, is to retrieve our "ministerial charism," the special gift that we—and no one else—offer to the church. Our object is to recover that which we have historically done best in ministry and to apply it creatively to a contemporary church and world radically different from that of the thirteenth or even the sixteenth century. But such thinking rests, I believe, upon two false suppositions that either weaken or ultimately undermine the desired outcome.

The first false supposition is that there is indeed a distinctive or unique notion of Franciscan pastoral leadership and, further, that this uniqueness consists in the belief that the authentic place for the Friars Minor to be in the world is "in the marketplace."[3] This assertion is true only in a qualified sense. It is true that in the thirteenth century, the Friars Minor stood apart from the older religious orders by the friars' presence and preaching in the marketplaces of towns and villages. (In contrast, the monastic communities largely remained, by charism, behind cloister walls.) But this presence in the marketplace was a general characteristic of the mendicant movement as a whole, not the private or exclusive preserve of the Friars Minor. Hence, the claim that the uniqueness of the Franciscan ministerial charism resides in our being "in the marketplace" is somewhat misleading.

---

[3] For an example of this perspective, see Dominic Monti, "'What Is Ours To Do?' The Roots of Franciscan Ministry," Friar Lines, 2.3 (Spring 1990): pp. 1-20, *passim*. Support for such a position, based on a case study of the friars' preaching in late thirteenth-century Florence, is found in the recent work of Daniel Lesnick, *Preaching in Medieval Florence* (Athens, Georgia: University of Georgia Press, 1989). However, in support of his thesis that the distinguishing characteristic of the mendicants was their preaching in the marketplace, Lesnick presents only a partial picture of the Friars Minor at Santa Croce. Florence was also one of the seedbeds for the Franciscan Spirituals, who opposed the increasing assimilation of the friars' lifestyle to that of the marketplace. For a corrective, see the review of Lesnick's book by Paul Lachance, Church History, 60 (1991), pp. 532-534.

In addition and more important, what exactly do we mean when we claim that the friars' place is *"in the marketplace"*? The question is important because the controversies that threatened to destroy the Franciscan movement in the first century of its existence revolved not simply around the question of poverty but, more fundamentally, around differing interpretations of how a Friar Minor was to be "in the world" and "for the world" without being "of the world." The relationship of the friars to the marketplace thus needs to be clarified. As we shall see, not all friars were persuaded that the marketplace was the authentic locus of the true Friar Minor.

The second false supposition is that the solution to the contemporary crisis facing the various provinces is indeed to be found in a renewal of ministry: that is, in the manner in which we conceive of, structure, and ultimately exercise our ministry. Here, the relative failure of previous efforts and strategies formulated along the lines of ministerial renewal should be instructive.

We have already noted that the current crisis in ministry is closely related to the declining number of friars available for these ministries. We must ask ourselves: If, in spite of all our best efforts over the last twenty years to consolidate or relinquish ministries and to adapt and reeducate ourselves, the number of our vocations has still continued to decline, does that not indicate that we, Friars Minor, are simply failing to attract new members to our way of life and work? And does it not also indicate that the reason for this failure to attract others to ourselves—beyond the impact which societal turmoil has had upon the church at large—is that young men apparently see little that is evangelically *distinctive* and *compelling* about our way of life in our friaries, a life style that might bespeak the challenge of the gospel and inspire them to "leave all things" to follow Christ in the way of Francis?[4]

I believe that there is a direct correlation. The root crisis in Franciscan communities today is only secondarily one of *ministry*; the primary crisis is one of *identity*.[5] Faced with the daily realities of

---

[4] I find it instructive that as the order moved into the cities and into larger convents in the 1240s and 1250s, forsaking its precarious position as social *minores*, men who previously would have been attracted to the Friars Minor were attracted to newer religious movements—the Friars of the Sack in southern France, the Servites and Apostolic Friars in central Italy—who were living more closely to the conditions of the poor.

life and ministry, provincial administrations naturally ask themselves the question: How are we to do what we need to do? That is,
how can we be faithful to the ministries that we have been given or
chosen as our task in the church? And yet, perhaps the deeper question we must ask is: How can we be what we are called to be? That
is, not only what are we to do, but who are we supposed to be? To
put it literally: What *in the world* are we supposed to be?

Rather than trying to retrieve a ministerial charism supposedly
unique to the order, it seems to me wiser, though far more difficult,
to seek to renew that which is truly unique to us and our gift to the
church: our particular identity as Friars Minor, formed by the call of
the charism. This is what friars bring to ministry that is unique to
them alone. Refine and refocus our ministerial skills and we can
become better ministers, but not necessarily better friars; renew our
minorite charism and we can become better friars as well as better
ministers. In addition, our witness may become more evangelically
compelling, attracting to our life the quality of men we desire to have
with us on the journey. One can thus legitimately ask: Is it not more
appropriate to be refounding (our ministry) through our identity,
rather than to be refounding (our identity) through our ministry?

The Question from the Perspective of History:
The First Decades of Franciscan Existence (1210-1274)

In the sixteenth chapter of the *Regula non bullata*[6], Francis
instructs those who have been given permission to go on mission
among the Muslims that there are two ways in which they can conduct themselves "spiritually": the first is "for the Lord's sake [to]
accept the authority of every human institution" (1 Peter 2:13), that
is, to be Friars Minor, to be who they are; the second is to proclaim
the word of God as God inspires them. Francis assumes that both
kinds of friars have something to "say": a "word" to announce that
can be either vocal (preaching) or nonvocal (the example of one's
life).

---

[5] It is important to point out that I am not referring to the tension between
ministry and fraternity (the community life of the friars). By "identity," I
mean that which a Friar Minor is to be before the world: hence, the
question of charism.

[6] *RegNB*: 16: 268-269; Flood and Matura, 1975: pp. 86-87.

Ministry presupposes that one has something to witness to, something to "say": some "word" to announce or some action to render to the one to whom one wishes to minister. That "word", moreover, is grounded in, indeed flows out of, one's experience of God. Otherwise, the minister would simply be, to borrow an image from Paul, "a noisy gong or a clanging cymbal" (1 Corinthians 13:1). Ministry, to be both effective and authentic, requires as its prerequisite: spirituality, spiritual identity, vocation.

We can begin our presentation on Franciscan identity and ministry by asking two questions that attempt to go to the heart of these two issues: What did Francis and his friars have to "say" to the world around them? and, How was this "word" grounded in their experience of God?

A Response to the Discovery of an Evangelical Truth: "To Do Penance"

Understanding the spiritual experience of another is always a difficult task. Fortunately we have at our disposal some later reflections by Francis, dictated shortly before his death, on the experience that reoriented his life in a wholly new direction: his encounter with the lepers. We can do no better than to cite his own words:

> This is how God inspired me, brother Francis, to embark upon a life of penance. When I was in sin, the sight of lepers nauseated me ... but then God himself led me into their company.... After that I did not wait long before leaving the world[7].

What did the encounter with the lepers mean to Francis and what within it became valid for those who followed him?

We are accustomed to reading this experience as one in which Francis encountered the person of Christ. Yet this was not the whole truth of the experience.[8] If we could draw back the veil of piety through which we tend to see this seminal experience of the founder, we might be able to appreciate it for the profoundly human encounter that it was. Francis, repelled by the sight of lepers, found himself one day in their midst. This time, however, through the

---

[7] *Test*: 1-2, 4; Habig, 1973: p. 67.

[8] The conventional readings are largely based on the hagiographical accounts of Celano and Bonaventure, accounts whose intent is to highlight Francis's relationship with Christ and thereby demonstrate Francis's sanctity.

power of grace, he was able to see the leper no longer as a repulsive object but rather as a human person, indeed a suffering human being. Suddenly his eyes were opened to truly see persons whom he had been socialized by Assisi to avoid and ignore, to account as nothing, as human beings like himself, people of dignity and value. Moreover now, through these very people whom he had been taught to account as having no significance whatsoever, Francis began to see the face of Christ, the suffering Christ. Therefore, contrary to what he had been taught by Assisi, Francis came to recognize that all men and women, even the seemingly most insignificant and repulsive among them, were bearers of the presence of Christ: all are brothers and sisters one to another, *fratres et sorores* of the same creator God.

In the encounter with the lepers, Francis discovered an evangelical truth that would form the very foundation of his spirituality and of the movement that would form around him: the insight of the universal fraternity of all creation under the same God. Once Francis had been given this crucial insight, he further came to recognize that everything that breaks the bonds of this fraternity (through blindness, willful ignorance, or acts of injustice) is precisely what constitutes sin. Indeed, it is in this experience of encountering Christ through the poor and forgotten of Assisi that Francis realized, as he tells us in his *Testament*, that he himself had been "in sin."

To understand the nature of his sin is also to understand the nature of his penance, that is, the specific content of the "life of penance" that he would embrace after this encounter. Put succinctly, to "do penance" is to change the way one sees the world and the truth that the world would have us believe. To "do penance" is nothing more—but nothing less—than to live in the Truth, not as the world teaches it but as it is revealed by Christ in the Gospel. For the truth the world teaches is a "narrative of the lie."[9] Assisi had taught him to spurn and despise those marginal people who were of no account to the growing wealth and power of the new commune. But Jesus in the gospels announces a different Truth about such human beings, as Francis instructs his followers in the opening of Chapter 9 of the *Regula non bullata*:

---

[9] The apt phrase originates with Robert Schreiter, *Reconciliation: Mission and Ministry in a Changing Social Order*. Maryknoll, New York: Orbis Books, 1992, pp. 29-39.

> Let all the brothers strive to follow the humility and poverty of our Lord Jesus Christ.... And they should rejoice when they find themselves among social outcasts and the despised, the poor and helpless, the sick and the lepers and those who beg by the wayside.[10]

The world of Assisi considered such people to be of no account, of no use to it in its rise to power and glory. But through his experience among the lepers, Francis had seen that the truths and values trumpeted by Assisi were not necessarily those heralded by the Gospel. Brought face to face with such a contradiction, as he tells us, "It was not long before I left the world."

This statement from the *Testament* is an extremely significant indicator of the specific orientation which Francis's life would take after his encounter with the lepers. What does it mean "to leave the world"? Our post-Vatican II reaction to the monastic suspicion of the world leads us to dismiss out of hand any talk of "leaving the world"; indeed the challenge of the post-Vatican II church is precisely the opposite: to engage the world, not run away from it! Yet, if we are to take seriously our historical retrieval of the *intentio* of Francis and his followers, we must likewise take seriously those aspects that perhaps strike us as the most strange and jarring.

Francis "left the world" in two ways. First, and more generally, he abandoned values that were in conflict with the truths of the gospel. Second, and more pointedly, he and his early followers left the city of Assisi, never to return again as residents, to live apart from its system, in an environment where they could construct for themselves an evangelical, truth-filled world of their own: a religious community. This physical relocation outside the city, tucked away in hidden or remote areas[11], will be an extremely important datum to take account of as our survey of the early history of the community unfolds.

Finally, this relocation of the friars outside Assisi had not only a geographical and spiritual component but also a social component. Belief in the universal fraternity of all creatures also led Francis and his followers to consciously separate themselves consciously from everything that divided human beings, every form of power that

---

[10] *RegNB*: 9; Flood and Matura, 1975: pp. 76-77.

[11] *Eremi*, the word used in the *Regula non bullata* for such places, initially referred not to hermitages in our sense of the term (i.e., places for contemplation), but simply to remote, desolate, and abandoned places.

tended to rupture the human community by placing one over or against the other. And in medieval society, one of the things that gave a person power over others—besides the brute force of sword—was the ownership of property and possessions. As they surrendered their possessions, the friars surrendered their social rank and value in medieval society. As a result, the friars deliberately placed themselves among those who had no status, voice, or power in society: they decided to live as the poor among the poor. Henceforth, they would be not only a community of *fratres* but also a fraternity of *minores*. They would be, therefore, *fratres minores*.

A Corollary to this Discovery: Where To Live and Work

Having discovered, through the work of grace, the evangelical truth of the universal fraternity of creation and its implication for living as poor men (and women) among the poor, Francis and his followers set out to live and structure their lives in accord with this insight. And there is a remarkable consistency between their values and their actions. The friars now had something to "say": a "word" to share with their fellow citizens in the world of Assisi. How did they share it and what exactly did they share?

Francis and his companions had left the world of Assisi, locating themselves, after a short time, next to the abandoned Church of Our Lady of the Angels. Yet they did not cut themselves off entirely from the "world" they had just left They went into the city or to nearby locales each day to work and earn their keep, returning by night to their dwelling well outside the city on the plain.[12] This interplay between *eremus* and *civitas*, between the Porziuncola and Assisi, is precisely what impressed Jacques de Vitry, who was passing through the area en route to the Holy Land:

> As for the brothers themselves, ... during the day they go into the cities and villages, giving themselves over to the active life of the apostolate; at night, they return to their *eremus* or withdraw into solitude to live the contemplative life.[13]

The friars shuttled back and forth between their distanced dwelling and the city, but always returning at night to the commu-

---

[12] In his work on the dynamics of the early life of the friars, David Flood insists on the friars' need to earn a daily subsistence, using as his proof the concrete admonitions given in *RegNB* 7 and 8 (Flood, 1975: pp. 23-24).

[13] Huygens, 1991: p. 75; Habig, 1973: p. 1608.

134 Michael F. Cusato, O.F.M.

nity for fraternal support and to share together in prayer the joys and pains of their experiences. Note the crucial nuance: the friars frequented the marketplace of Assisi but did not live there.

Why not? The friars could have chosen to live closer to the town itself (as did the women associated with their movement)[14], but they did not. Hence, unless we wish to posit that the Porziuncola was the only possible available residence for the friars, I believe it is important to highlight that the friars had made a conscious decision and a deliberate choice to remain at a distance from the city. Indeed, by imposing a physical distance between themselves and the city, the brothers were deliberately removing themselves from an environment which they considered to be not only in certain ways antithetical to the gospel but harmful to the clarity of that new evangelical vision which they had recently been given. Distance provided the friars with perspective on the false values of Assisi and protection of the integrity of their movement.

Yet it would be misleading to paint a purely economic picture of the relationship of the early community to Assisi. The brothers went into the cities of the region not only to gain subsistence for the day but also to share this "word" that they had been given by God. These were men with a mission. And their mission was to share the same call they received when their eyes were opened to a world of injustice and inequity. Their "word" was to call others, by word or by the example of their lives of humility, to do penance, that is, to change the way one *sees the world* by learning to see it through the eyes of those who suffer and are neglected by the larger society; and to change the way one *lives in the world*, to use the goods of creation at one's disposal in such a way that all may have the necessities of life. This is at base what Francis meant by doing penance. This was the substance of his penitential movement and the substance of the penitential preaching of the early friars for which Innocent III granted permission in 1210.

From Penitential Preaching to Ecclesiastical Ministry

It is possible to ferret out the general contours of the content of the penitential preaching of this first generation of friars through a

---

[14] The reasons for this are connected to the medieval attitude towards women and sexuality.

close examination of the early sources.[15] But instead of giving a detailed exposition of that content here, suffice it to say only that there is an astonishing consistency between the socioeconomic roots of penance noted above and the "word" the friars had for their contemporaries.[16]

Penitential preaching represented the primary vocal form of proclamation employed by the early friars during the first decade of the order's existence. This is particularly understandable given the predominant social composition of the fraternity prior to 1220. Drawing its recruits primarily from the middle and poorer classes, whose members may (or may not) have had the basic tools of literacy, the early fraternity was a predominantly lay phenomenon for which the act of penitential (as opposed to doctrinal) preaching would have been an appropriate expression for its evangelical fervor. However, as the community began to extend itself beyond the confines of the Spoleto Valley into Italy and then beyond the Alps, two important changes occurred within the fraternity itself: changes engendered by the very fact of growth and expansion.

First, the order began attracting men from different backgrounds and cultures who were less familiar with the socioeconomic roots of the original vision of the Rule and who brought to the community another set of presuppositions about the spiritual and religious life. Among the newcomers was a growing number of clerics who had been trained in the ecclesiastical environment of the cathedral schools. Such men read the minorite experience through the lens of their classical education and tended to conceive of themselves less as penitential preachers than as ecclesiastical ministers with a public role to play in the ministry of the church. Both of these differences gradually pointed the Franciscan movement in a new direction.

Second, the very growth of the number of friars created serious problems of space and subsistence for the community. How could the hermitages of old accommodate so many new recruits? How were they to find the food necessary to sustain such large numbers when their habitations were generally quite removed from the centers of population and commerce?

---

[15] Notably the two *Lives of Celano*, the *Anonymous of Perugia*, and the *Legend of Perugia*.

[16] Cf. *EpFid*, *EpRect*, *RegNB* 11, *1 Cel* 35-36, *2 Cel* 37, *LP* 110. Much of the friars' preaching manifests the contention that civil conflicts are often the result of social injustice and economic inequity.

Beginning in the late 1220s and into the 1230s, the two new developments led many in the community to leave the isolated hermitages in order to relocate on lands at the edges of the cities, usually along the old city walls, settling in convents constructed for their use by spiritually minded patrons. The move to the marketplace had solid advantages: the friars were now closer to those who would be both the source of their alms and the focus of their ministry.

The classic summation of the justifications advanced by the community's leaders for this historic break with the early friars' practice is the *quaestio* found in the Bonaventurian (or pseudo-Bonaventurian) "Determinations of Questions on the Rule of the Friars Minor."[17] The *quaestio* has as its explanatory title "Why the friars live more frequently in the cities and towns" and is an attempt to respond to the following question about the lifestyle of the Minors:

> Since religious ought to endeavor more intently to separate themselves from the tumult of the world and to live in solitary habitations, why is it that you have accustomed yourselves more intently to living in the cities and towns? To the point, while providing more efficiently for yourselves here, you are actually living more restlessly and disobediently here."[18]

The author then gives three explanations or justifications for the residence of the friars within or next to the towns: the efficacy of their pastoral ministry; the material necessity of alms; and the need of security for precious items like books and liturgical articles. The explanations seem reasonable and convincing.[19]

Nevertheless, the move to the cities was accompanied by a shift in the life style of the friars. The adoption of "conventualism," as historians call it, involved residence in large convents on significant

---

[17] There is some dispute as to how much of the *Determinationes* was actually penned by Bonaventure himself. Whatever its authorship, it is certainly a thirteenth-century work. See Luigi Pellegrini, "L'ordine francescano e la società cittadina in epoca bonaventura. Un'analisi del *Determinationes questionum super Regulam fratrum minorum*," Laurentianum 15 (1974), pp. 154-200. (Revised and reedited under the title "Nel contesto cittadino: realtà e giustificazione teorica" in his *Insediamenti francescani nell'Italia del Duecento* (Rome: 1984), pp.123-53.)

[18] Bonaventure: pp. 340-341.

[19] See the ground-breaking article of Jacques Le Goff on the settlement of the mendicant orders within the walls of the Italian communes burgeoning in the thirteenth century: "Ordres mendiants et urbanisation dans la France médiévale. État de l'enquête," Annales économies, sociétés, civilisations 25 (1970): pp. 924-946, here at p. 929.

plots of land, the pursuit of studies, and an active engagement in the clerical apostolate. Settled now in the marketplace with episcopal or papal permission to build (first oratories, then later conventual churches designed for preaching), the friars became involved in the more institutionalized, ecclesiastical ministries of doctrinal preaching, hearing confessions, and burying the dead.

Now there is no question that through these new ministries (and through the papacy's use of the order for a host of other activities), the Friars Minor, among others, made enormous contributions to the life of the church of the thirteenth century. Unfolding a significant ministry of the word, they transformed the church of their day. They became an integral part of the marketplace, a leaven in the new world of the communes. And yet, not all friars were in agreement with these new directions, for not all had left the hermitages.[20]

The Debate over the Marketplace: The Opposition of the Friar-Hermits

A significant segment of the order contested the gradual foundation of minorite communities in the marketplace.[21] This relocation, moreover, was viewed as part of a larger picture, as yet another deviation of the order from the original vision and practices of the founder, a further drifting away from the "humility and poverty of our Lord Jesus Christ," prescribed in the *Regula non bullata*[22]: that is, a renunciation of their status as social and economic *minores* through their slow but gradual reinsertion into positions of importance and power in the church and society. For the friar-critics, the papal use of

---

[20] The opposition to the new directions taken by the order was centered primarily in the hermitages of the Spoleto Valley, where a growing number of friars who considered themselves "companions of Francis" had taken up residence, especially after 1221. Following Francis's death and especially during the 1230s, they came to be considered the focal point of the opposition.

[21] It is almost impossible to determine a precise measure of this opposition camp, but one can hazard the guess that it comprised a group of friars who were increasingly in the minority. Conversely, those who spearheaded the changes were increasingly the new clerics who had entered the order in steadily growing numbers, articulate men who were swiftly rising to positions of leadership in the community. Suffice it to say that, whatever the numerical strength of the opposition, it had a certain amount of moral prestige behind it due to its association with the "companions of Francis" and its ability to root its views in both the intentions of Francis and the practice of the early friars.

[22] *RegNB* 9.

the order to revitalize the church and the relocation of the friars within the cities are, to a large extent, two sides of the same coin of betrayal.

The most important and cohesive expression of this opposition—and indeed the most eloquent—is the compelling document known as the *Sacrum commercium beati Francisci cum domina Paupertate.*[23] The *Sacrum commercium* is a highly polemical document, written as a direct challenge to the new directions which the order had been taking since the late 1220s in violation, according to the author's view, of both the *Rule*[24] and *Testament* of Francis. For him, the symbol of the new orientation of the order was the recent construction of the great basilica of Saint Francis just outside the city of Assisi with its adjacent papal palace and Franciscan convent completing the complex.[25] He viewed this project as a blatant betrayal of the "humility and poverty of Christ" desired by the founder and unmistakably enunciated in the documents of the community—*Quo elongati* notwithstanding![26]

It is important, however, not to read this text as being primarily about *material* poverty alone. Rather, the *Sacrum commercium* concerns itself more broadly with the movement of the friars away from the posture of *minoritas*, understand first and foremost in its socio-economic sense: to be and to remain among the poor and despised of society, calling others by word and example to use the goods of creation on the basis of necessity so that all the people of God can

---

[23] A new critical edition of the text has recently been published: *Sacrum commercium sancti Francisci cum domina Paupertate*, edited by Stefano Brufani (Assisi: 1990). My own work on this critical document remains as yet unpublished (Cusato, I, 1991: pp. 316-386). Contrary to most scholarship on the *SC*, I date the document in the mid-1230s (probably 1235-1238) and consider the author to have been Caesar of Spire (d. winter 1238-1239). Furthermore, whereas most view the work as an exaltation of the purity of Franciscan poverty as opposed to the failed poverty of the monastic orders, I read it, after chapter 38, as a stinging critique of Franciscan poverty gone awry.

[24] Reference is made both directly and indirectly to the *RegNB*.

[25] It is important to keep in mind that the mastermind of this complex was Brother Elias (responsible for having brought Caesar of Spire into the order in Syria!). Hence, the issue which inspired the opposition was much larger than the question of the clericalization of the order: it concerned the very nature and role of the order in society.

[26] The papal bull *Quo elongati* (September 28, 1230) had decreed that the exhortations in the *Testament* (mostly concerning poverty) were not legally binding on the friars. The *Sacrum commercium* identifies it as one of the key villains.

have access to necessities of life. It is only secondarily that the expenses incurred in the building of the basilica or in the escalating levels of the life style of the friars becomes an issue: such breaches of poverty are only outward manifestations of an inner refusal to remain *minor*.[27]

The author gives voice to the arguments proffered by the leaders of the community in defense of the new directions in which they were orienting the order. They, through Avarice's handmaid Discretion, try to reason with the voices of opposition:

> Do not show yourselves so unbending before society and do not despise in this way the honor they show you; rather show your-selves affable to them and do not outwardly spurn the glory they offer you, but do so at most inwardly. It is good to have the friend-ship of kings, acquaintance with civil leaders and familiarity with the great for when they honor and revere you, when they rise and come to meet you, many who see this will be more easily turned to God by their example.[28]

But such flattering associations eventually have a more concrete effect upon the values and life style of those rubbing elbows with the rich and famous:

> And they began at last to fawn upon the powers of civil society, coming to be wedded to them, as it were, that they might empty their purses, extend their own buildings, and multiply the very things they had completely renounced. They sold their words of advice to the rich, ... they frequented the courts of kings and princes with great eagerness so that they might "join house to house and lay field to field." And now they have grown rich and strong upon the earth....[29]

Hence, friar-hermits such as Caesar of Spire[30] believed that their confreres had surrendered that distance which had been so critical for seeing the world and the truth clearly. Having first erased the *physical* distance which they had imposed between themselves and the marketplace, the friars were quickly losing all sense of *spiritual*

---

[27] The key paragraphs are in the Great Discourse of Lady Poverty, particularly chapters. 38 to 52.

[28] Brufani, 1990, c. 20: p. 157; Habig, c. 43: p. 1578.

[29] Brufani, c. 23: p. 162-163; Habig, 1973, c. 49: p. 1582.

[30] I should note that the identity of the "companions of Francis" and the issue of the relationship of Caesar to the companions are complex and important questions. Any attempt to oversimplify matters and to rigidly identify two opposing camps tends to further complicate the issue.

distance from the world and its values. They were no longer able to discriminate between the truth of the gospel and the truth of the world. Located in the marketplace and involved with the great of the world, such friars were no longer seeing the world through the eyes of the despised and neglected (that is, through the eyes of the poor Christ). Indeed, the experience of Francis among the lepers had revealed to him (and to those who would enter into the experience) both the violence which was being doing to the poor of the world (by neglect and injustice) and the clever "narrative of the lie" which the world had constructed around itself in order to justify its actions. The friar-hermits now saw their own community leaders weaving a *"narrative of the lie"* of their own, laid out in the various justifications of their new policies and belied by their large convents, tracts of lands, contacts with the mighty and pursuit of university degrees in Paris.[31] We find ourselves before a critical struggle of identity within the order over what it means to be a Friar Minor in the world and for the world.

In Defense of the Marketplace: The Response of the Clerics

In spite of the vigor of this opposition and its arguments against the involvement of the friars in increasingly visible ecclesiastical and political roles, by the 1250s the voices of opposition had been largely quieted. Caesar had died in early 1239 while under house arrest; his followers, lacking the eloquence of their master, were easily scattered and silenced, drifting into relative obscurity. The companions themselves (Leo, Rufino and Angelo) never actually constituted a cohesive movement of opposition.

Perhaps the most outspoken critic of the changing lifestyle of the community was the Provençal cleric Hugh of Digne.[32] Consistent with the perspective which we have outlined here, Hugh's critique centered around the friars' betrayal of their profession of humility:

---

[31] We should recall that recipients of a university degree were considered *maiores* by medieval society, an interesting dilemma for the *fratres minores*.

[32] Hugh has erroneously been called "the father of the Spirituals." For an overview of this neglected figure, see David Flood, *Hugh of Digne's Rule Commentary* (Grottaferrata: 1979); Jacques Paul, "Hugues de Digne," in *Les Franciscains d'Oc, Cahiers de Fanjeaux, 10* (Toulouse: 1975) pp. 69-97; and Alessandra Sisto, *Figure del primo francescanesimo in Provenza. Ugo e Douceline di Digne* (Florence: Leo S. Olschki, 1971).

their status as social *minores*. This blurring of their identity was occurring because the friars had become accustomed to associating and working with the most powerful figures of church and civil society.[33] Nevertheless, as a cleric, Hugh sees a more active, participatory role for the friars in the daily lives of the people than Caesar had envisioned. Where he parts company with the new directions in ministry being set in place by the leadership of the order, however, is not so much over the friars' involvement in ministry *per se* but over their assumption, indeed usurpation, of tasks and roles which properly belong to parish priests (like baptizing and burying the dead). On the contrary, he sees the role of the order in ministry primarily in terms of preaching. And the content of that preaching was to be none other than the evangelical truth revealed to their founder—and accepted by the friars at profession—of "the humility and poverty of our Lord Jesus Christ". Moreover, if their message of humility was to be effective, their own lives must not give the lie to their words: they must be *minores* in word as well as in deed.

By the 1250s, it is increasingly the voice of the clerics in the community which comes to the fore in defense of the friars' ministry in the church, and no one was more eloquent in its defense than Bonaventure. Interestingly, the arguments of Bonaventure that emerged during the controversy with the secular masters at the University of Paris in defense of the public ministry of the friars would be the very same arguments used, a few years later, *within* the order to counter the continued opposition to the friars' involvement in the affairs of the church and world with its resulting dangers to *minoritas*. These arguments centered on one particular and preeminent theme, the usefulness of the friars to the church.

Perhaps Bonaventure's most graphic presentation of the ecclesial role of the Friars Minor is to be found in the treatise "Why do the Friars Minor Preach and Hear Confessions?" Here he states the issue quite clearly:

> In these last days ... the Holy See has instituted a means of assistance for obviating the dangers to perishing souls when, by divine arrangement, it established certain religious orders to undertake the office of preaching and hearing confessions—committed to

---

[33] In this regard, Hugh's famous sermon before the cardinals at the First Council of Lyons is revelatory (see *The Chronicle of Salimbene de Adam* [Binghamton, New York: Center for Medieval and Early Renaissance Studies, 1986] pp. 217-224, *passim*).

them because of the need of the people and because of the insufficiency of the priests....[34]

Then, after detailing these priestly insufficiencies, he continued:

> We are those poor men ... [who] must bring from the threshing floor of the church to the granary of the celestial homeland, those left behind, whom the parish priests ... have abandoned....[35]

But what kinds of ministries are the friars being called to perform within the church? In the aforementioned "Determinations" on the Rule, Bonaventure affirms that they have been charged "to build up the faith and virtues of the people by preaching doctrinal sermons and by the example of their virtuous living." A decade later, in the *Apologia pauperum*, the seraphic doctor will be even more specific, equating the ministry of the friars with the classic priestly functions:

> ... instructing [the faithful] in matters of faith, developing virtues, giving examples, interceding through prayers, healing injuries inflicted by enemies, warning against imminent dangers and repelling actual assaults.[36]

Hence, according to Bonaventure, the Friars Minor are to serve as assistants to the bishops and clergy to whom the pastoral ministry has been first and foremost entrusted. This pastoral orientation—which goes well beyond the ministerial activities sanctioned for the friars by Hugh of Digne—is precisely what makes the Minors "useful" to the church, useful, that is, in leading the people of God to salvation. That this, moreover, had become the predominant thinking among the leaders of the Franciscan Order and, indeed, had become the key criterion for admittance into the community is shown by the insertion of the following lines into the *Constitutions of Narbonne of 1260*:

> Since God has called us not only for our own salvation but also for the spiritual edification of others by way of example, counsel and salutary exhortation, we ordain that no one be received into our order unless he is such a cleric who has received competent instruction in grammar or logic, or unless he is a cleric or a layman whose entrance would cause note and bring good fame among the faithful and clergy.... If it is necessary to receive a candidate outside this norm, ... let not such a one be received without urgent necessity.[37]

---

[34] Bonaventure, 1898: p. 377.
[35] Bonaventure, 1898: p. 380.
[36] Bonaventure, 1898: p. 317.
[37] Bihl, 1941: p. 39.

By 1260, the friar-hermits, especially those who were not clerics and yet who remained committed to proclaiming the evangelical truth by the example of their lives and by the word of their penitential preaching, found themselves on the fringes of the order, marginalized by virtue of their "uselessness" to the salvific work of the church.

Finally, it is intriguing to note how Bonaventure squared his ideas with the early tradition of the fraternity. In his little treatise, the *Epistola de tribus quaestionibus*, written in the 1250s, Bonaventure was forced to respond to a critic outside the order who had raised the issue of the humility and penitential preaching of the early friars as counter-evidence to their active engagement in the parochial ministry. Drawing a parallel, he notes that just as the early Christian community had been born of simple fisherman and only later, when in need of defense, did it witness, by God's grace, the apologetic efforts of the patristic fathers to defend and explain the faith and a more visible engagement in the life of the Empire, so too the Friars Minor, born of simple men like Francis and his companions, now, under attack, had likewise acquired a more learned character and given itself to a more active engagement in the life of the church. This change in the character of the order, explicitly acknowledged by Bonaventure as an evolved version of the original inspiration, was equally, he contended, the product of divine inspiration and guidance.

With the emergence of the Franciscan Spirituals after 1274, the struggle between identity and ministry would be engaged yet again, with each camp constructing its own version of the "true tradition," while typifying its opponents' reading as a betrayal, a "narrative of the lie." By this time, however, the terrain of the battle had shifted and other issues had come into play, altering the character of the struggle.[38] But this is another chapter in the history of an order that in every age has wrestled unceasingly with the question of how to minister within the church while remaining faithful to its charism.

Contemporary Implications

The preceding has presented one way of accounting for the historical tension that existed in the Order of Friars Minor during its first decades of existence. There are other possible accounts, but one cannot deny that such tensions did, in fact, exist and that they repre-

---

[38] Cusato, III: p. 770; Moorman: pp. 177-187, 307-319.

sented a significant problem for the order. Hence, it is important to note that the resistance to the engagement of the friars in new ecclesial and political roles and its consequent impact upon the life of the community cannot simply be dismissed as the agitation of malcontents or fanatics. Indeed, some of the greatest figures of early Franciscanism—Caesar of Spire, Leo, Giles, Hugh of Digne, John of Parma, Peter Olivi, Angelo Clareno, Ubertino da Casale, and others —aligned themselves to some degree with the resistance.

When one attempts to learn from this tradition of struggle ways forward through the present realities facing Franciscan communities, one is at something of a loss. Part of the problem is that in the thirteenth century, the order was torn between choices that were still rather clear: the memory of an original tradition that was still possible to recover versus a contested adaptation of the original ideals to accomplish other, broader laudable goals. In the twentieth century, the choices seem more constrained: Do we seek to do better and improve on that which we have inherited from our brothers in the light of new and urgent realities. Or do we dare to dream more boldly and actually consider an authentic reform of the way we live (identity) so as to rethink where and how we work (ministry)? It is the latter approach that is advocated here.

Summary of Lessons from the Historical Record: What Are We to Do?

In order to see the world as it really is, one needs distance from the "narrative of the lie" (woven by the world) and proximity to the "narrative of the truth" (discovered by communities intent upon the gospel). One needs thus to recover an adversarial relationship with the world, embracing creation while hating the world, that is, every form of evil that denies and destroys the dignity of the human person.

In the Franciscan tradition, such a pursuit, voluntarily undertaken, is the daily commitment to "do penance."

Distance from the narrative of the lie is provided by one's social location. Crucial is where one chooses to place oneself in society, in what environment and among whom. Historically, the social location consciously chosen by the friars, assuring them that they would see the world differently, was among the poor and suffering, those most adversely affected by the powers of the world. Our social location was the choice of *minoritas*.

This social relocation seems to be aided by physical relocation. Living among the poor, which fosters a separation from the market-place, offers space for contemplation and reflection, a home base that is physically one's spiritual center and a communal springboard for one's daily work in the marketplace.

Implications for Action: How Are We To Get There?

Given the present state of our provinces, and the ministries we have inherited from the past and are are now engaged in, the lessons drawn from the early historical record might seem irrelevant, or worse, an indictment of our present way of life and of doing min-istry. My intent is not to impugn the good work which our confreres are doing in parishes, chaplaincies, schools, and so on. Far from it. But the tradition does raise some questions. Perhaps we need to revisit the supposed truth of the old dictum that Franciscan work is whatever a Franciscan does. Certainly, the friars of the order's first century of existence were not so glib. My aim has been to follow out the implications of the historical record and to note some ramifica-tions. Indeed, it is a call for reform. Allow me thus to propose a three-pronged approach for consideration:

For the immediate future: Reform is life-threatening. Most cannot and will not change. What can be done is to continue, in all of our fri-aries, the revival of contemplation and reflection that has already begun. But our vision should be grand: learning from the laity of South and Central America, let's reconceive of our friaries as base communities of gospel reflection, not simply places where morning and evening prayers are held.

For the near future: Provinces ought to foster, for those interested, the creation of intentional regional communities, located among the *minores* of society and centered not on a ministry but on the way of life of the Friars Minor.[39] The focus of such houses would thus not be on fraternity (our horizontal relations) but on the charism (how to do penance). To coin a phrase, I am advocating the creation of "pen-intentional" communities.

For the distant future: Provinces ought to commit themselves to a slow process of downward social mobility and to consider ways of

---

[39] *RegB* 1.

locating our residences in places which provide a "critical distance" from the marketplaces of our ministries. Is this a call to abolish corporate ministries (which imply an on-site presence)? I am not sure. More to the point, it is a call to rethink what we mean by minorite pastoral leadership. Ministerial leadership often implies a certain control over a given ministry so as to have beneficial influence. But minorite leadership seems to call us to have influence in particular situations by force of the evangelical word which we bear and the impress of our lives. I am being deliberately provocative here so that, in rethinking this question, we are not simply tinkering with how to switch ministerial models and to improve our ministerial professionalism.

Caesar of Spire, Hugh of Digne and Bonaventure each presented somewhat different models for "being in the world" as a Friar Minor. If we were to dream boldly and think along the lines of reform, the insights and criticisms of Caesar of Spire must be taken seriously while the model of Hugh of Digne seems to be the most consistent with the early tradition and the most appropriate manner of exercising a role of pastoral leadership in our world.

REFERENCES

Bihl, Michael, editor, "Statuta generalia ordinis edita in capitulis generalibus celebratis Narbonnae, an. 1260..." Archivum Franciscanum Historicum (1941) 34: 13-94.

Bonaventure, *Opera Omnia*, VIII. Quarrachi: Collegium S. Bonaventurae, 1898.

Brufani, Stefano, editor, *Sacrum commercium sancti Francisci cum domina Paupertate.* Medioevo Francescano. Testi, 1. Assisi: Edizioni Porziuncola, 1990.

Cusato, Michael F., *La renonciation au pouvoir chez les Frères Mineurs au 13e siècle.* 4 volumes. Paris: Unpublished dissertation, 1991.

Esser, Kajetan, editor, *Opuscula sancti patris Francisci Assisiensis.* Bibliotheca Franciscana Ascetica Medii Aevi, 12. Collegium S. Bonaventurae, 1978.

Flood, David, *Hugh of Digne's Rule Commentary.* Spicilegium Bonaventurianum, 14. Grottaferrata: Collegium S. Bonaventurae, 1979.

Flood, David, and Thadée Matura, *The Birth of a Movement: A Study of the First Rule of St. Francis.* Translated by Paul Schwartz and Paul Lachance. Chicago: Franciscan Herald Press, 1975.

Grundmann, Herbert, "Die Bulle 'Quo elongati' Papst Gregors IX." Archivum Franciscan Historicum 54: 3-25.

Habig, Marion A., editor, *St. Francis of Assisi. Writings and Early Biographies: An English Omnibus of the Sources for the Life of St. Francis.* Chicago: Franciscan Herald Press, 1973.

Huygens, R.B.C., éditeur, *Lettres de Jacques de Vitry. Édition critique.* Leyden: E.J. Brill, 1991.

Lachance, Paul, "Review of Lesnick, *Preaching in Medieval Florence.*" Church History 60 (1991), pp. 532-534.

Le Goff, Jacques, "Ordres mendiants et urbanisation dans la France médiévale: État de l'enquête." Annales économies, sociétés, civilisations, 25 (1970), pp. 924-946.

Lesnick, Daniel R., *Preaching in Medieval Florence: The Social World of Franciscan and Dominican Spirituality.* Athens, Georgia: University of Georgia Press, 1989.

Monti, Dominic, "'What is Ours to Do?': The Roots of Franciscan Ministry." Friar Lines 2.3 (Spring, 1990), pp. 1-20.

Moorman, John R. H., *A History of the Franciscan Order from its Origins to the Year 1517*. Oxford: Clarendon Press, 1968.

Paul, Jacques, "Hugues de Digne," pp. 69-97 in *Les Franciscains d'Oc*. Cahiers de Fanjeaux, 10. Toulouse: É. Privat., 1975.

Pellegrini, Luigi, "L'ordine francescano e la società cittadina in epoca bonaventuriana. Un'analisi del *Determinationes questionum super Regulam Fratrum Minorum*." pp. 154-200 in Laurentianum 15 (1974).

Salimbene, *The Chronicle of Salimbene de Adam*. Translated and edited by Joseph L. Baird et alia. Medieval & Renaissance Texts & Studies 40 (1986). Binghamton, New York: Center for Medieval and Early Renaissance Studies.

Schreiter, Robert, *Reconciliation: Mission and Ministry in a Changing Social Order*. Maryknoll, New York: Orbis Books, 1992.

Sisto, Alessandra, *Figure del primo francescanesimo in Provenza. Ugo e Douceline di Digne*. Biblioteca della Rivista di Storia e Letteratura Religiosa. Studi e Testi, 3. Florence: Leo S. Olschki, 1971.

9

Contemplation and Compassion:
A Franciscan Ministerial Spirituality

Michael W. Blastic, O.F.M. Conv.

1. Setting the Context

The reality of human suffering, physical, spiritual, or mental, challenges believers at the core of their religious convictions. Ministry to those who suffer involves the art of attending to the other in his or her pain, the ability to stand in solidarity with the other without judgment or criticism as the first step toward healing. It calls not for problem solving, which is perhaps the first reaction to the pain of another as evidenced in attempts to take the pain away, or worse to ignore it with statements such as "That's all right, it will get better," or, "You need to look at it in this way."

What this experience of suffering does call for, as Robert Schreiter suggests in his book *Reconciliation,* is an "orthopathema, a right way to suffer, when our orthodoxies have been shattered and our orthopraxies have come to naught."[1] The suffering to which ministry today must respond is as much emotional and structural as it is the result of physical violence. The signs of the times today must be read in the broken lives and tortured existence of ordinary men and women who struggle to hold on to their humanity in a non-human world.

The Franciscan tradition of contemplation and compassion provides a valuable resource for ministry in this context. It finds its own realized orthopathema in the experience of Francis and Clare of Assisi, an experience which discovered in the embrace of suffering, of one's own human condition, the very mystery of God. The Franciscan poet Jacopone of Todi (died 1306), living in the turbulent and dangerous period at the end of the thirteenth century, gives

---

[1] Schreiter, 1992: p. 37.

vivid expression to the essential content of this tradition in his laud,
The Three Stages of Divine Love:

> When the soul is in harmony with conscience
> It takes joy in the love of its neighbor.
> Then without doubt it is true love,
> Then we can call it charity.
>
> Love then joins love
> To his suffering brethren;
> And in his compassion he suffers more
> Than the man whose suffering he shares.
>
> While the brother who was suffering
> Finds respite from his pain,
> The compassionate man suffers anguish,
> Day and night without repose.
>
> No man can comprehend how this can be
> If the understanding is not infused in him by charity,
> That charity which lies hidden in suffering,
> Waiting to give birth.[2]

As Jacopone suggests, it is compassion that gives access to the
other without being intrusive, establishing a real connection with the
other by participation in the other's suffering. This way of being
human implies vulnerability, availability, solidarity, and empathetic
attachment, while at the same time respecting the integrity of the
experience of the other. Without providing solutions or answers,
compassion brings healing and health in that it allows the other to
stand in her or his pain and suffering while resisting evil, confusion
and surrender, in order to share in the experience of charity, which is
God.

This compassion which the Franciscan Jacopone celebrates is
nurtured by contemplation, the ability to see and recognize the charity hidden in suffering. In other words, contemplation allows one to
discover God in the other with the other, and invites participation.

---

[2] Jacopone da Todi, 1982: p. 235.

Compassion is a defining characteristic of Franciscan ministry understood as the ability to be with others in their pain as well as in their pleasure. This way of being is sustained in contemplation, the ability to be drawn out of oneself in attention, awareness, receptivity, and surrender to the other. This is the shape which "following in the footsteps of Jesus Christ" takes in the world. The object of contemplation for the Franciscan, as the tradition reveals, is the other in his or her suffering, concrete humanity—that is where Christ is found and met and followed.

Contemplation and compassion effect reconciliation. The primary reconciliation is the acceptance of one's own human condition as one marked by pain and suffering, incompleteness, fragility, and limits. As an examination of the Franciscan tradition will show, contemplation and compassion translate into real presence, eucharistic grace in the world. Transformation takes place not in the private recesses of the heart, but in the body and the blood, in the world, with passion with the other, in unity. At the same time, this describes and defines a style of ministry that is eminently Franciscan.

2. Examining the Tradition

Francis of Assisi

Raoul Manselli has commented that the novelty and uniqueness of Francis and his movement is to be sought not primarily in terms of his personal spirituality, but rather in the social configuration of his life, which characterized and expressed his spirituality. The urban context of the social life of Assisi was characterized both by wealth and by poverty; it was made up of both the propertied nobility and merchant class as well as those without property or resources who were homeless and lived on the margins of communal life. Thus, apart from the nobles and merchants dwelling within the city walls, there were those who found themselves outside the city walls, the sick and those abandoned to themselves, totally dependent for survival on the generosity of those inside the walls.

While the monks remained enclosed in their monasteries and had no direct contact with the faithful outside the monasteries, and while the canons regular were engaged in the *cura animarum*, Francis went to those on the margins to bring help—a word of comfort, material sustenance when it was available, and in the most extreme cases, simply a sharing in their suffering and unhappiness. This was, according to Manselli, what made Francis so different from religious movements that came before him, as well as what distinguished Francis from all movements, both heterodox and orthodox, contemporary to him.[3] In other words, Francis did not wait for people to come to him for help. He took the initiative and moved toward them to offer them assistance in response to their situation, an attitude and behavior that went beyond the norm of thinking and doing of his times. It was this that made it difficult for people, both ecclesiastics and seculars, to understand what he was about. In fact, as Francis's early biographers note, the social structures of the city itself were seen to be threatened by Francis's actions on behalf of the poor and sick.[4]

This consciousness of the need to attend to the poor and suffering, finds its source in Francis's experience of conversion. As Francis recounted in his *Testament*, his conversion was a relational and social experience, not a purely private affair between himself and God:

> The Lord granted me, Brother Francis, to begin to do penance in this way: While I was in sin, it seemed very bitter to me to see lepers. And the Lord himself led me among them and I had mercy upon them. And when I left them that which seemed bitter to me was changed into sweetness of soul and body; and afterward I lingered a little and left the world.[5]

At the end of his life when he dictated this text, Francis was explicit about the experience that gave meaning and direction to his life. His own "merchant" sensibilities were not only disturbed but clearly offended by the plight of the lepers, who were treated even by the church as if they were already dead.[6] His experience with the leper was overwhelming, upsetting his sensibilities, changing his

---

[3] Manselli, 1983: p. 197.

[4] This conflict provides the background for Francis's conversion, according to Thomas of Celano in his *Vita prima*, especially paragraphs 8-15. His father's anger and frustration at Francis's unheard of behavior both symbolizes and expresses the commune of Assisi's response to Francis's social protest.

[5] Armstrong, 1982: p. 154.

[6] Auspicius van Corstanje describes the liturgical ritual used to consign lepers to their "hospitals" outside the city walls, listing the rights and obligations of the lepers. The cell in which the leper would live is declared by the leper to be his "place of eternal rest" (Corstanje, 1977: p. 38-41). The Third Lateran Council, 1179, in canon 23, allows lepers to have their own churches with their own priest, since "they cannot dwell with the healthy or come to church with others...."

socially conditioned disgust into "sweetness of soul and body." Most important and central to Francis's own religious experience as he tells us, was that in meeting the leper, Francis met God—the suffering of the leper that God led Francis to embrace became for Francis a sweet embrace of God, a mystical experience of human exchange.[7] This movement out of himself toward the other became then the norm of Francis's action and mission, which describes and names Francis's understanding and experience of God.[8] Based on his experience with the leper, Francis began to understand the real meaning of the Incarnation. Above all for Francis, Jesus Christ was one who moved toward humanity in humility. His characteristic approach to the Incarnation is outlined in these words from the Second Version of the Letter to the Faithful:

> Through his angel, Saint Gabriel, the most high Father in heaven announced this Word of the Father—so worthy, so holy and glorious—in the womb of the holy and glorious Virgin Mary, from which he received the flesh of humanity and our frailty. Though he was rich beyond all other things (2 Corinthians 8:9), in this world he, together with the most blessed Virgin, his mother, willed to choose poverty.[9]

Francis describes the descent of God in Jesus into the world in terms of movement, movement from a position of glory and riches to one of frailty and poverty. For Francis, it is this movement of God in humility toward humans and their world which is salvific. The companions of Francis recounted how he would often say that

---

[7] The western contemplative tradition associates sweetness (*dulcis*) with mystical experience of God. Augustine uses this language in describing his mystical experience at Ostia with his mother Monica in his *Confessions* IX, x, 23-26. Edith Scholl studies the usage of the terms *dulcis* and *suavis* in the Cistercian sources (Scholl, 1992), a language and theology that would become familiar to the Franciscans through the presence and preaching of Cistercians at the general chapters of the friars and poor ladies as a result of the Fourth Lateran Council decree.

[8] Consult Michael Cusato's paper in this volume, "Hermitage or Marketplace: The Struggle for an Authentic Franciscan Locus in the World," p. 125, for a similar approach to the conversion of Francis and the life of penance.

[9] Armstrong, 1982: p. 67.

"although the Lord may work our salvation in his other festivals, yet, because he was born for us ... it was his concern to save us."[10]

Francis's Christology focuses on Jesus the "Word made flesh" in frailty and poverty, who in his suffering flesh reveals the glory of God.[11] Francis's experience of and approach to the Incarnation in terms of suffering and limitation, reflects the Victorine emphasis on Incarnation as compassion, rather than the Cistercian emphasis on Christ's humanity as the first step of a ladder leading up and above the world to the contemplation of the divinity.[12] It is the pattern of Jesus's life on earth that Francis holds out as model for Franciscan behavior and action because it is the life of Jesus in its very fragile humanity that is salvific. The rule and life of the Franciscan thus becomes life "according to the form of the Holy Gospel,"[13] by *following* "the teaching and footprints of our Lord Jesus Christ."[14]

This has concrete implications for Francis. For example, we should love our enemies because "our Lord Jesus Christ, whose footprints we must follow (cf. 1 Peter 2:2), called his betrayer 'friend' (cf. Matthew 26:20) and gave himself willingly to those who crucified him."[15] Franciscan life is determined by this following of Jesus, not merely as a spiritual reality within one's heart, but even more importantly as a physical expression in the body, reincarnating the actions of Jesus in a new context, moving toward humanity, brothers and sisters, in humility.

Francis clarifies this approach in his exhortation to preachers in

---

[10] Brooke, 1970: p. 283.

[11] Norbert Nguyen Van Khanh has demonstrated that the strongest New Testament influence on Francis's writings are the Johannine writings. He states that "a careful study of his writings leads us to conclude that, from the viewpoint of theological depth and by natural disposition, Francis was closer to John than we might imagine" (Khanh, 1994: p. 219). He bases this conclusion on the frequency of citations, the fact that Francis had the friars read from the Gospel According to John prior to his death, the precedence given to Johannine texts in Chapter 23 of the Early Rule, and by the Christological expressions of Johannine origin used by Francis (Khanh, 1994: pp. 217-224).

[12] Of the many Victorine texts that express this approach to the Incarnation, that of Richard of Saint Victor (died 1173), "The Four Degrees of Passionate Charity," is central, and would certainly have influenced Bonaventure's theology.

[13] *Test* 14; Armstrong, 1982: pp. 154-155.

[14] *RegNB* X:1; Armstrong, 1982: p. 109.

[15] *RegNB* XXII:2; Armstrong, 1982: p. 127.

Chapter 17 of the *Regula non bullata* as he contrasts the spirit of the flesh with the Spirit of the Lord. The spirit of the flesh desires attention and hence is all talk and no action. Francis comments, "The spirit of the flesh desires and is most eager to have words, but [cares] little to carry them out."[16] In contrast, the Spirit of the Lord

> wishes the flesh to be mortified and despised, worthless and rejected. And it strives for humility and patience, and the pure and simple and true peace of the spiritual person. And above all things it always longs for the divine fear and the divine wisdom and the divine love of the Father, and of the Son, and of the Holy Spirit.[17]

The Spirit of the Lord transforms human flesh into the flesh of Jesus Christ, a human flesh that is "mortified, despised, worthless, and rejected." These divine adjectives derive from the songs of the Suffering Servant in Isaiah, used by the gospel writers in narrating the passion of Jesus, and here used by Francis to describe the experience of following in the footsteps of Jesus Christ. True understanding of the gospel comes from experiencing the gospel, made possible by the working of the Spirit of the Lord.[18] This would suggest that for Francis, following in the footsteps of Jesus means compassion, a participation in the suffering of the other, not in a narrow sense understood in terms of pain for the sake of pain, but rather, in the

---

[16] *RegNB* XVII:11; Armstrong, 1982: p. 123.

[17] *RegNB* XVII: 14-16; Armstrong, 1982: p. 123. In the *Regula bullata* Francis exhorts his brothers to "pursue what they must desire above all things: to have the Spirit of the Lord and his holy manner of working, to pray always to him with a pure heart and to have humility, patience in persecution and weakness, and to love those who persecute us, find fault with us, or rebuke us, because the Lord says: 'Love your enemies and pray for those who persecute and slander you' (Matthew 5:44)" (*RegB* X:8-10; Armstrong, 1982: p. 144). Note the repetition of the virtues of humility and patience in the context of persecution, and the connection of these virtues with the behavior of Jesus in his passion as noted by Francis in *RegNB* XXIII:2.

[18] Francis's *Admonition* VII (Armstrong, 1982: p. 30) speaks of the same dynamic in terms of the interpretation of Scripture: "And those are given life by the spirit of Sacred Scripture who do not refer to themselves any text which they know or seek to know, but, by word and example, return everything to the most high Lord God to whom every good belongs." Here again the characteristic emphasis of Francis on enfleshing the meaning of Scripture in action (example) is underlined.

broadest sense of suffering as the human condition.[19]   Again, the experience with the leper for Francis was one of self-discovery in which he came to understand himself and his life in terms of the mission received to live according to the form of the gospel. The gospel, following the footsteps of Jesus Christ, describes the human condition, the real humanity embraced by God in the Incarnation of the Son. Compassion becomes another name for Christian living in the vocabulary of Franciscan life.

The Legend of the Three Companions

The author of the *Legend of the Three Companions* portrays Francis as a person of compassion.[20]   After narrating Francis's embrace of the leper, the author describes the experience in the dilapidated church of San Damiano where Francis received from the cross a mission to repair Christ's house, which was falling into ruin. The impact on Francis of hearing the Crucified speak to him is described by the author in the following words:

> From that hour his heart was stricken and wounded with melting love and compassion for the passion of Christ; and for the rest of his life he carried in it the wounds of the Lord Jesus. This was clearly proved later when the stigmata of those same wounds were miraculously impressed upon his own holy body for all to see.[21]

As described here at the beginning of Francis's conversion, the text

---

[19] Jurgen Moltmann comments that "Anyone who 'has compassion' participates in the suffering of the other, takes another person's suffering on himself, suffers for others by entering into community with them and bearing their burdens" (Moltmann, 1990: p. 179). This is an appropriate description of Francis's service of the lepers which characterized his conversion as described in his *Testament* 1-3 (Armstrong, 1982: p. 153).

[20] The dating of this text has been a point of controversy. I accept the dating of Pierre Beguin (1979). Beguin demonstrates convincingly the dependence of the text of the L3S on the *Anonymous of Perugia* which he dates between March 4, 1240 (the death of Brother Sylvester), and August 22, 1241 (the death of Gregory IX). Further, the L3S was used by Celano in compiling the *Vita secunda* in 1247. Therefore, the L3S was written between August 22, 1241, and 1247 (Beguin, 1979: pp. 9-20, 137-144). The critical edition of the L3S was prepared and published by Théophile Desbonnets (1974).

[21] L3S 14; Habig, 1973: p. 904.

goes on to say that it was the compassion which characterized his entire life that transformed his flesh into the image of the crucified Christ on Mount La Verna two years before his death:

> Rapt in divine contemplation, blessed Francis was absorbed in seraphic love and desire; and through the tenderness of his compassion he was transformed into a living crucifix. Thus the inmost desire of his burning love was fulfilled.[22]

For the author of this *Legend*, compassion describes the ability Francis had to reach through separateness and distance, to pass beyond and through externals and touch the very hearts of men and women. In particular, the text comments on the effectiveness of Francis's words, which

> were not greeted with ridicule, neither were they spoken in vain; for they possessed the strength of the Holy Spirit and went straight to the hearts of the listeners, rousing them to vehement astonishment.[23]

Here, the text describes a style of ministry that was motivated by and accomplished in compassion.

The text goes on to describe how Francis sent the friars out on mission telling them to prepare their hearts "to suffer everything humbly and patiently."[24] In other words, the friars were not sent out so much to "do" something for others, but rather, they were sent to "receive" from others, to bear the pain of others, to listen to the story of others, and in this receiving from them to connect their lives to the story of the gospel, of which the life of the friars attempted to exemplify the "form."

The mission and ministry of the Franciscan movement as articulated by Francis in this text, represents the lived experience of Francis and his brothers in their attempt to follow in the footsteps of Jesus Christ. Addressing the chapter of the friars at St. Mary of the Angels, Francis admonishes them with the following words:

> Since you speak of peace, all the more so must you have it in your hearts. Let none be provoked to anger or scandal by you, but rather

---

[22] L3S 69; Habig, 1973: p. 953.
[23] L3S 25; Habig, 1973: pp. 915-916.
[24] L3S 36; Habig, 1973: p. 925.

may they be drawn to peace and good will, to benignity and con-
cord through your gentleness. We have been called to heal wounds,
to unite what has fallen apart, and to bring home those who have
lost their way. Many who seem to us to be children of the devil will
still becomes Christ's disciples.[25]

The emphasis is placed on the behavior of the friars, the manner of
their relationships in the world, their gentleness in a ministry of
healing and reconciliation, which challenges the friars to open themselves to the truth of the other by going beyond the surface and penetrating to the heart. In short, the ministry of Franciscans is here
described as a "heart-to-heart" encounter. By entering into the experience of the other in compassion, one is able to penetrate beyond the
appearance all the way down to the reality, to the truth of the other
in contemplation.

This Franciscan style of ministry, though approached from a different perspective, yields the same meaning in an episode described in
Thomas of Celano's *Vita secunda*. It describes Francis's encounter with
a Dominican theologian who asks Francis to explain the saying of
Ezekiel 3:16-20, where the prophet is reminded that if he does not point
out the wicked person's sin, the death of the sinner will be held to be
the responsibility of the prophet. The traditional interpretation and
ecclesial use of the passage underlined the responsibility of the hierarchy to renounce sin as well as the sinner. Gregory VII used the text in
his letters to justify his active role in seating and unseating princes and
kings. The Waldensians used the text to justify their preaching against
the abuses of the clergy. Francis's exegesis is simple yet novel:

> If the passage is to be understood in a general meaning, I would
> take it that the servant of God should be so aflame in his life and
> his holiness that he would reprove all wicked men by the light of
> his example and by the words of his conversation. So, I say, the
> splendor of his life and the renown of his fame will proclaim to all
> their wickedness.[26]

Francis suggests here that the example of a life lived in poverty and

---

[25] L3S 58; Habig, 1973: pp. 942-943.
[26] *2 Cel* 103; Habig, 1973: p. 447.

service is the most effective call to conversion—more effective than words of condemnation. Example and conversation should be an invitation to holiness and coherence of living: "Let them not judge or condemn," exhorts Francis in his Rule. "And as the Lord says, they should not take notice of the little defects of others (cf. Matthew 7:3; Luke 6:41)."[27] This praxis of ministry and invitation to compassion places great emphasis on the need to recognize the other as an icon of Jesus Christ: engagement with the other is at the same time encounter with God. This characterizes Franciscan spirituality as focused out of the self and toward the other and defines it as encounter, meeting, being-with in compassion.

Thomas of Celano's Vita prima.

Thomas of Celano develops this aspect of Franciscan life and ministry in the latter part of Book I of the *Vita prima*, which culminates in the celebration of Christmas at Grecchio. In rebuking a friar who doubted and questioned the poverty of a beggar, Celano tells us, Francis was accustomed to say: "Who curses a poor man does an injury to Christ, whose noble image he wears, the image of him who made himself poor for us in this world."[28] The poor person for Francis was an icon of the poor Christ, as the leper was an icon of the suffering Christ. Both the poor and the lepers placed before the eyes of Francis, in a concrete, tangible way, the image of Jesus Christ whose footsteps Francis promised to follow. Thus, Celano insists, Francis looked outside of himself to discover the Christ he was called to follow.

This vision of Francis was directed even beyond the human icons of the poor and suffering Christ to the entire creation, as Celano remarks. "All things, especially those in which some allegorical similarity to the Son of God could be found, he would embrace more fondly and look upon more willingly."[29] Sheep, lambs, flowers, and even worms, revealed to Francis the presence of Jesus Christ. By looking at both concrete, particular human persons and these simple

---

[27] *RegNB* XI:10-11; Armstrong, 1982: p. 119. See also *RegNB* XVI:6; *RegB* II:17; *EpMin* 9-11, for parallel texts. For a discussion of 2 *Cel* 103 consult Miccoli (1991: pp. 115-147).

[28] 1 *Cel* 76; Habig, 1973: p. 293.

[29] 1 *Cel* 76; Habig, 1973: p. 293.

and tangible elements of creation, Francis came to know Christ better and was able to follow in the footsteps of Jesus more closely.

The celebration of Christmas at Grecchio connects Francis's attentiveness to creation with the mystery of the Incarnation. Francis's intention in recreating the scene of Jesus's birth in Bethlehem is explained by Celano with these words of Francis:

> For I wish to do something that will recall to memory the little Child who was born in Bethlehem and set before our bodily eyes in some way the inconveniences of his infant needs, how he lay in a manger, how, with an ox and an ass standing by, he lay upon the hay where he had been placed.[30]

The text goes on to describe in detail how Francis celebrated the Incarnation at Grecchio not with plaster statues but with real creatures, human and animal, who had real, concrete histories, and who lived real, tangible lives, and who in their concrete particularity "brought to life again" Christ Jesus, who stood available before everyone's bodily eyes.[31]

Celano returns to this focus on Francis's seeing in his description of the stigmata. Two years before he died, while at prayer on Mount La Verna, Francis "saw in the vision of God a man standing above him, like a seraph with six wings, his hands extended and his feet joined together and fixed to a cross."[32] It is interesting to note that Celano does not say that the seraph embraced the crucified Christ, but simply and more generally, a crucified man. Celano suggests that for Francis the vision of the seraph is the vision of human potential and identity, fully revealed and made clear in the life of Jesus Christ. In other words, the vision of the "man in God" on La Verna becomes for Francis an icon of humanity.

---

[30] *1 Cel* 84; Habig, 1973: p. 300.

[31] *1 Cel* 86 becomes explicit about this: "The gifts of the Almighty were multiplied there, and a wonderful vision was seen by a certain virtuous man. For he saw a little child lying in the manger lifeless, and he saw the holy man of God go up to it and rouse the child as from a deep sleep. This vision was not unfitting, for the Child Jesus had been forgotten in the hearts of many; but, by the working of his grace, he was brought to life again through his servant St. Francis and stamped upon their fervent memory" (Habig, 1973: p. 301).

[32] *1 Cel* 94; Habig, 1973: pp. 308-309.

Unable however to understand fully what the vision meant, and feeling both wonder and fear at the sight, Celano continues his narrative of Francis's experience:

> His soul was in great anxiety to find its meaning. And while he was thus unable to come to any understanding of it and the strangeness of the vision perplexed his heart, the marks of the nails began to appear in his hands and feet, just as he had seen them a little before in the crucified man above him.[33]

This "great mystery" in the life of Francis was first suggested by Celano at the point where Francis renounced his natural father before the bishop of Assisi. Here Celano reveals that the mystery enfleshed in the body of Francis in the stigmata was already a reality, a mystery that the bishop recognized but which remained unrealized until this point in Francis's life.[34] What Francis was doing from the moment of his conversion in the encounter and embrace of the leper until this moment on Mount La Verna was literally looking at what was outside himself—looking to the poor and sick and abandoned, as well as looking at lambs and flowers and worms, that is, at all of created reality. What Francis saw before his eyes transformed him into the image of what he saw, as the description of the stigmata dramatically recounts.

The transformation of Francis was not therefore the effect of that one-time experience of the vision of the crucified man on La Verna. Rather, all along the way Francis was following the footsteps of Jesus Christ in what he saw before his eyes. This contemplative vision of

---

[33] *1 Cel* 94; Habig, 1973: p. 309.

[34] *1 Cel* 15: "The bishop, however, sensing his disposition and admiring greatly his fervor and constancy, arose and drew him within his arms and covered him with the mantle he was wearing. He understood clearly that the counsel was of God, and he understood that the actions of the man of God that he had personally witnessed contained a mystery" (Habig, 1973: p. 241). It is important to note that Celano underlines that it is what Francis is doing, his actions, that contain a mystery. Celano later declares that this mystery is revealed in the stigmata: "For in truth, that venerable father was marked in five parts of his body with the marks of the passion and of the cross as though he had hung upon the cross with the Son of God. *This is a great mystery*, and shows forth the majesty of the prerogative of love" (*1 Cel* 90; Habig, 1973: p. 305).

Francis found expression in his compassion, his entering into and sharing the experience of the other, and here on La Verna, quite literally, the crucified man.

For Francis, this is connected to his experience of the eucharist. Francis's contemplation allowed him to penetrate through the appearance all the way down to the reality, which he celebrated in the eucharist as humility:

> See, daily he humbles himself as when he came from the royal throne into the womb of the Virgin; daily he comes to us in humble form; daily he comes down from the bosom of the Father upon the altar in the hands of the priest. ... So, as we see bread and wine with our bodily eyes, we too are to see and firmly believe them to be his most holy body and blood living and true.[35]

Here, humility is revealed as the true identity of Jesus Christ and thus of the human person. And the humility which Francis sees in the eucharist, in God's humbling movement toward humanity as the ongoing, present, continuing dynamic of the Incarnation, reveals Francis to himself. This becomes a central theme in his *Letter to the Entire Order*, in which he reflects on the role of the eucharist in the life of the brotherhood. He is so astounded by the mystery of the eucharist that at a certain point he breaks into poetic praise:

> That the Lord of the universe, God and the Son of God, so humbles himself that for our salvation he hides himself under the little form of bread! Look, brothers, at the humility of God and pour out your hearts before him! Humble yourselves as well, that you may be exalted by him.[36]

What Francis sees in the eucharist becomes the motivation and meaning for a lifestyle of humility, of following in the footsteps of Jesus Christ.

But even more central to Francis is the role of the eucharist in the mission and ministry of the brotherhood. In this same text, Francis, probably more clearly than in any other of his texts, describes this mission: "... He has sent you into the entire world for this reason; that in word and deed you may give witness to his voice and bring every-

---

[35] *Admonition* I:16-18, 21; Armstrong, 1982: pp. 26-27.
[36] *EpOrd* 27b-28; Armstrong, 1982: p. 58.

one to know that there is no one who is all-powerful except him."[37]
Francis then goes on to describe how this mission is to be carried out:

> Therefore, kissing your feet with all that love of which I am capable, I implore all of you brothers to show all possible reverence and honor to the most holy body and blood of our Lord Jesus Christ in whom that which is in the heavens and on the earth is brought to peace and is reconciled to the all-powerful God.[38]

The eucharist celebrates reconciliation achieved in the Incarnation, God's movement in humility toward the created world. Jesus Christ the reconciler reveals human identity to be humility. Therefore, Francis's contemplation of the eucharist leads to his embrace of creation in compassion. As reconciliation is achieved in Christ's life on earth, so reconciliation is achieved through the words and deeds of Francis in his engagement with God's world.

In summary, the mystery of God unfolded before Francis's eyes in the lives of every man and woman, and most clearly in the lives of those who were poor and those who suffered. In his relationship to these persons and to creation itself, Francis was taught how to contemplate God's own mystery as it unfolded before his eyes so that he in turn might become in compassion what he was in what he saw. The mystery of the stigmata, a mystery of love as Celano describes it, reveals the motivation and meaning of contemplation and compassion in Franciscan living.

Clare of Assisi

While the ministerial experience of Clare and her sisters was encompassed by the enclosure and took a very different form from that of Francis and his brothers, the role of contemplation and compassion in their life mirrors that of Francis and his brothers. Contemplation allowed Francis to participate compassionately in Christ's life, to follow in his footsteps, and to be transformed from "the lover into the beloved" in the stigmata. Clare of Assisi also lived this dynamic in the enclosure at San Damiano.[39] This Franciscan

---

[37] *EpOrd* 9; Armstrong, 1982: p. 56.
[38] *EpOrd* 12-13; Armstrong, 1982: p. 56.
[39] On Clare's approach to contemplation as a visual experience consult Johnson (1993).

approach to contemplation provides the context for an accurate understanding of the implications of what Clare is suggesting in the following passage from her *Testament:*

> When blessed Francis saw, however, that, although we were physically weak and frail, we did not shirk deprivation, poverty, hard work, trial, or the shame or the contempt of the world—rather, we considered them as great delights, as he had frequently examined us according to the example of the saints and his brothers—he greatly rejoiced in the Lord. And moved by compassion for us, he bound himself, both through himself and through his order, to always have the same loving care and special solicitude for us as for his own brothers.[40]

This text presents an important description of the succession of events and actions that involved Francis with the Poor Ladies in an ever deepening relationship. First, Clare underlines Francis's *seeing* of the Poor Ladies in the difficulties of their existence. Second, Francis is moved to *compassion* for the Poor Ladies. And third, compassion leads Francis to bind himself to the Poor Ladies in a personal relationship of care and solicitude. Thus, suggests Clare, what Francis saw engendered compassion, which in turn expressed itself in a connection, a linkage with the Poor Ladies that Clare names *care.*

What Francis saw was the concrete expression in the flesh and blood of the Poor Ladies, of their following in the footsteps of Jesus Christ. In short, Francis saw their commitment in their physical frailty and weakness, deprivation, poverty, hard work, trials, the bearing of shame and contempt. Francis saw in the Poor Ladies the visage, the image, the picture, the icon of the suffering servant, the crucified savior, Jesus Christ in his most human condition. Real human suffering, or better, the human condition embraced by Jesus Christ in the Incarnation as the most appropriate and most adequate vehicle for revealing God, is what Francis saw in his sisters at San Damiano. In embracing Jesus Christ through their commitment to follow in his footsteps, the sisters were embracing their own human condition, which at the same time was their most appropriate and adequate vehicle for identification with Jesus Christ.[41]

---

[40] *TestCl* 28-29; Armstrong, 1993: p. 58.

[41] Caroline Walker Bynum suggests that it is precisely in and through their bodies that women expressed their religious experience (Bynum, 1991: pp. 151-179).

This dynamic of contemplation and compassion leading to trans-formation describes the religious experience of Clare. She writes to Agnes:

> Gaze upon that mirror each day, O queen and spouse of Jesus Christ, and continually study your face within it, that you may adorn yourself within and without with beautiful robes.... Indeed, blessed poverty, holy humility, and inexpressible charity are reflect-ed in that mirror....[42]

The mirror which Clare invites Agnes to gaze into is the cross of San Damiano, the cross that spoke to Francis and commissioned him to rebuild a dilapidated house. In looking into this image of Christ, Agnes is invited to see her own reflection, as if she were looking at her own mystery. And Clare goes on to suggest that what Agnes will see there is something very familiar:

> Look at the border of this mirror, that is the poverty of him who was placed in a manger and wrapped in swaddling clothes.... Then at the surface of the mirror, consider the holy humility, the blessed poverty, the untold labors and burdens that he endured for the redemption of the whole human race. Then, in the depth of this same mirror, contemplate the ineffable charity that led him to suf-fer on the wood of the cross and to die there the most shameful kind of death.[43]

What Clare describes here are very ordinary human experiences—birth and poverty; the burdens and labors of life and humility; suf-fering, shame, death, and charity. These ordinary human experiences are salvific because they were embraced by Jesus.

There is a clear parallel between what Clare invites Agnes to do in looking at the mirror of the cross and what Clare suggests Francis sees when he looks at the Poor Sisters in their life at San Damiano. Both Francis and Agnes are seeing human life. Francis contemplates the life of the Poor Ladies, Agnes is invited to contemplate the life of Jesus Christ in the mirror of the cross. The juxtaposition of these two texts reveals an important Franciscan insight: Contemplation is the means for the discovery of the truly human without disguise. The humanity revealed in the fragile, weak flesh of Jesus Christ is the

---

[42] *4EpAg* 15-16, 18; Armstrong, 1993: p. 50.
[43] *4EpAg* 19, 22-23; Armstrong, 1993: pp. 50-51.

truth of human life. The adjectives which describe the life of Christ reflected in the mirror of the cross,[44] are the same adjectives which describe the life of the Poor Ladies in the mirror of the enclosure of San Damiano.[45] Clare does not stop at this point, however, and continues with an exclamation and exhortation to Agnes:

> Therefore, that mirror, suspended on the wood of the cross, urged those who pass by to consider, saying: "All you who pass by the way, look and see (*attendite et videte*) if there is any suffering like my suffering" (Lamentations 1:12).[46]

As the sisters dwelling together within the enclosure are called to be mirrors for each other and for the world, the question posed in this text from the cross with the words from Lamentations begs for an affirmative response: Clare is asking Agnes to embrace her own humanness, her identity, her own experience, as that which makes her most like Christ. At the same time, this text serves as a description of both Clare's and Francis's consciousness of their mission—in embracing their own humanness, weakness, and frailty, they are following in the footsteps of Christ. Contemplation leads to compassion in that what makes one most like Christ and hence, most the image and likeness of God, is one's own frail and fragile humanity.

It is this experience of contemplation and compassion that provides an essential context for understanding the role of enclosure for Clare and the Poor Ladies. The enclosure does not cut the sisters off from the world or shut the world out. Nor does the enclosure focus the attention of the sisters on the spiritual realm of the divine as opposed to the earthly realm of the natural. Rather, the enclosure is meant to foster real authentic humanity—its purpose is to protect humanness, its dignity, value, and worth.

Clare's description of the mirror parallels her experience of the enclosure. Poverty is the border, the "wall," as it defines the space of human reality without disguise; poverty defines a space where real humanity is protected, cherished and nurtured. Poverty encloses the Poor Ladies in their love and care for one another. In this sense, the enclosure provides the space for human life *sine glossa*, without gloss or clarification. The center of this enclosure is charity whose surface

---

[44] *4EpAg* 19, 22-23.
[45] *TestCl* 28-29.
[46] *4EpAg* 24-25; Armstrong, 1993: p. 51.

is humility. Hence, enclosure bears Christological meaning for Clare. She writes to Agnes:

> May you cling to his most sweet Mother, who gave birth to a Son whom the heavens could not contain. And yet she carried him in the little enclosure of her holy womb and held him on her virginal lap.[47]

The enclosure is thus the space where Christ is conceived in human flesh and is nurtured and grows in poverty, which, as Clare exclaims, "the Son of God never wished to abandon while he lived in the world."[48] And, "Out of love of the God who was placed poor in the crib, lived poor in the world, and remained naked on the cross,"[49] Clare insists on preserving poverty till the end.

It is this poverty, the border of the mirror of the enclosure, that gives Clare access to God. Most high poverty gives birth to and engenders Jesus Christ in the flesh and blood of the human person who contemplates the mystery of God. One enters into the mystery through compassion expressed in active charity, love, and care for others. This is the dynamic that defines the enclosure, and it is this which Francis sees and imitates in his compassion and care for the Poor Ladies. Here again, Francis becomes what he sees in the enclosure of San Damiano, just as he becomes what he sees in the stigmata.

3. Retrieving the Tradition

Patricia Hampl has commented: "The Franciscans read Francis and Clare not for stories but for signals."[50] This final section of the paper will look at the signals that the Franciscan tradition, examined above, makes available for us today.[51]

---

[47] *3EpAg* 18-19; Armstrong, 1993: p. 46.
[48] *TestCL* 35; Armstrong, 1993: p. 58.
[49] *TestCL* 45; Armstrong, 1993: p. 59.
[50] Hampl, 1992: p. 120.
[51] Zachary Hayes distinguishes between the religious experience of Francis and the theological reflection on this religious experience, emphasizing the need for attention to both of these elements which describe the Franciscan charism. See his paper in this volume, "Franciscan Tradition as a Wisdom Tradition," p. 27. Similar to Hampl, Hayes states in his paper, "If Francis bequeathed anything to later generations, his bequest would be a vision of human life and an insight into the meaning of the gospel that demands and deserves serious reflective thought."

Contemplation

For both Francis and Clare, contemplation was primarily a visual experience, something like a "penetrating gaze" that gets to the heart of reality. Recently, Elizabeth Johnson has described contemplation "as a way of seeing that leads to union. It arises from an experience of connection with the sacred at the very core of life."[52] This contemplative seeing functions for both Francis and Clare as the experienced fruit of poverty: it uncovers the truth, lifts the veil. As Francis was fond of repeating, "For what a man is before God, that he is and nothing more."[53] The truth which contemplation uncovers is anthropological and theological. The mirror of the cross functions to reveal that one's identity is discovered in the real humanity of Jesus Christ.

In this context the ministry of the Poor Ladies at San Damiano can be understood precisely in their being and becoming mirror and example for the world. Like Christ, the Poor Ladies show humans who they really are, they reveal the human person to him/herself. In their life of poverty, contemplation and mutual love, the sisters become what they are looking at in the cross of San Damiano, as Francis becomes what he sees in the vision of the crucified man on La Verna.

Thus, far from being otherworldly, or cutting one off from the world, contemplation turns one toward the world. Franciscan contemplation is "horizontally ecstatic." That is, it takes one out of oneself and into the other; contemplation de-centers, making one receptive to the revelation of the truth of the other. Again, the ecstasy is horizontal—the movement is out of oneself and toward the other as the effect of vision. Here, contemplation as a visual experience would underline the relationship between the contemplative

---

[52] E. Johnson, 1994: p. 13. Along the same lines, William Shannon describes contemplation in terms of awareness: "Awareness, which is central to contemplation, is a very different experience from thinking: it tends always to be unitive" (Shannon, 1993: p. 209). Patricia Hampl also places her experience of contemplation in the realm of the visual: "Prayer as focus is not a way of limiting what can be seen; it is a habit of attention brought to bear on all that is" (Hampl, 1992: p. 224).

[53] *Admonition* XIX:2; Armstrong 1982: p. 33.

and the other in terms of continuity, presence, similarity, immediacy, and even union between seer and seen.[54]

The primary Franciscan metaphor for contemplation is "footprint."[55] This is a distinct break with the Neoplatonic-Augustinian tradition which experiences contemplation as an ascent above, beyond and out of the world to God.[56] It is also different from the Benedictine ladder of humility described in Chapter 7 of Benedict's *Rule*, which takes the monk up the twelve steps that lead him out of the world to God. A significantly different "geography" of Franciscan experience emerges with the metaphor of footprint. Contemplation is not an ascent of a ladder but a looking down at and a following of footprints. It is this focus on Christ's footprints in this world that gives to Franciscan contemplation its own unique and particular dynamic. Different from both the monastic *lectio*, as well as the Ignatian composition of the senses, Franciscan contemplation is horizontally ecstatic. In this vein, Francis's comment on the beatitude "Blessed are the pure of heart, for they shall see God" (Matthew 5:8), is significant:

> The truly pure of heart are those who *look down upon* (*despicere*) the things of the earth and seek the things of heaven, and who never

---

[54] The traditional understanding of the visual experience from Plato through Augustine to Bonaventure is analyzed by David Chidester (1992). The visual is contrasted to the aural experience throughout, but see especially pp. 2-8. Nicholas Harvey speaks of the new relationship between self and world effected in contemplation: "to be contemplative is to be becoming fully alive in this world. ... The reality is that in putting us in touch with God contemplation brings a new birth in which everything is transformed. What was formerly a closed, oppressive universe now has open horizons" (Harvey, 1991: p. 155).

[55] It is interesting to note that Clare's self-designation in her *Testament* 37 (Armstrong 1993: p. 59) as *plantula sancti patris*, which is rendered into English by Armstrong as "the little plant of the holy father," could also be translated as "the footprint of the holy father." The sense of "footprint" carries a better Christological sense of the relationship between Francis and Clare, centered as they both were on the footprints of Jesus Christ.

[56] While Augustine's theology is deeply interested in "vestiges" of God in this world, the vestige functions primarily as the first rung of a ladder meant to be climbed upward toward God, while at the same time leaving the vestige behind and below as belonging to the earth.

cease to adore and behold the Lord God living and true with a pure
heart and soul [57]

If contemplation is understood as an activity that Francis engages in
as he goes about the world following the footsteps of Jesus Christ,
then this admonition suggests that in looking at the things of earth
we can adore God with a pure heart.

This further implies that contemplation is above all a relational
experience—it brings one out of oneself to creation, to other persons,
to the leper, to brothers and sisters, to the word of the gospel, to the
eucharist. In the seeing, one enters into the mystery and becomes
united with what one sees.

Thus, Franciscan contemplation describes the proper mode of
being human. This sense is embedded in the Franciscan tradition. It
has to do with the Franciscan understanding of obedience in terms
of being related as brother or sister. The Franciscan notion of person
derives from this insight—person is defined by relation, especially as
Bonaventure would develop this in his Trinitarian theology. Human
beings are personal, they exist only in and through relationships to
self, to another, others, and God. To be is to be in relation—horizontally ecstatic—out of oneself and toward the other. [58]

If the goal and purpose of ministry is to serve the other in imitation of Jesus Christ, then the Franciscan nuance is given by its contemplative identity—following in the footsteps of Christ means
contemplating the other, attending to the other so as to enter into the
other's experience and name grace.

---

[57] *Admonition* XVI:2; Armstrong, 1982: p. 32. Armstrong translates *despicere* in
this sentence as "despise," which carries a negative connotation regarding
the things of the earth. While certainly this negative reaction to the world
was part of the inherited, medieval world view, nevertheless, this sense
seems foreign to the meaning of Francis in this statement. Given the sense
of the things of the earth celebrated in his Canticle of Brother Sun, the
sense of Franciscan contemplation as developed in this paper would
suggest "to look down upon" as a more appropriate expression of Francis's
meaning. For a similar view consult Matura, 1994: pp. 4-14.

[58] Mary Catherine LaCugna names Bonaventure as a "notable exception" to
the Latin tradition which focuses more on substance and nature than
economy in theology. For the Greeks and Bonaventure, notes LaCugna,
"the heart of *theologia*, as also of *oikonomia*, is therefore relationship,
personhood, communion" (LaCugna, 1991: pp. 247-248).

Compassion

Franciscan contemplation is relational, it directs one out of one-self and toward the other in compassion. Contemplation is not primarily something which one does for oneself, its purpose is not primarily self-therapy. Rather, contemplation is a discipline whose practice develops the quality of receptivity, the ability to receive from others. While it engages human feelings, it channels their power for the purpose of authentically engaged encounter.

The purpose of contemplation, according to Clare, is for imitation: one looks upon the object one desires to imitate. Clare expresses her awareness of the need for coherence between the form of life—following in the footsteps of Jesus Christ—and the form of prayer—gazing, considering, and contemplating the poor and crucified Jesus Christ. The imitation is accomplished at the level of compassion. Clare exhorts Agnes,

> Place your mind before the mirror of eternity! Place your soul in the brilliance of glory. Place your heart in the figure of the divine substance! And transform your entire being into the image of [the Divinity] itself through contemplation. So that you too may feel what his friends feel as they taste the hidden sweetness that God himself has reserved from the beginning for those who love him.[59]

The language of Clare is highly sensual—to feel and taste the sweetness of God. This suggests an experience of personal union with God described as sweetness. Clare's experience of contemplation coincides with the experience of Francis when he embraced the leper and the bitterness was transformed for him into sweetness of body and soul. For Clare this sweetness of contemplation goes hand in hand with ordinary daily living. As Clare writes, the mother should find consolation from her burdens in her sisters "so that seeing the charity, humility, and unity they have toward one another, their mother might bear all the burdens of her office more easily, and, through their way of life, what is painful and bitter might be changed into sweetness."[60] Compassion as the fruit of contemplation is thus ministerial, and can be read as a synonym for ministry in the Franciscan tradition.

---

[59] *3EpAg* 12-14; Armstrong, 1993: p. 45.
[60] *TestCl* 69-70; Armstrong, 1993: p. 61.

4. Spirituality for Franciscan Ministry

Christian ministry has to do with communicating the gospel of Jesus Christ. Edward Schillebeeckx says:

> The real norm and justification for competent proclamation of the gospel message is the praxis of Jesus himself embodied in the life of the preacher. The Christian who is really competent to preach today is one who, in his or her faith, is able to enter into the *sequela Jesu* fully.[61]

The following of Jesus's life-praxis gives one the authority to proclaim the gospel. The praxis of Jesus is described as the way Jesus turned toward others. Schillebeeckx goes on:

> The competence to proclaim the gospel is only part of a more complete, all-embracing reality, expressed in Jesus's life and praxis and ratified in his death. That reality is his turning toward those around him, the foundation of which was the "compassion" he had on the crowds (Matthew 9:36).[62]

What Schillebeeckx describes here is the Franciscan *sequela Jesu*, the Franciscan following in the footsteps of Jesus Christ. As Jesus turned toward those around him, so Francis and Clare in contemplation and compassion incarnate the praxis of Jesus as they follow him in their world by turning to those around them.

What follows is the implication for the Franciscan practice of contemplation in "horizontal ecstasy" and compassion in terms of ministry. Franciscan ministry is not primarily the response to ecclesial need determined hierarchically. Rather, Franciscan ministry happens when Franciscans follow in the footsteps of Jesus Christ. It is not so much what Franciscans do, but more importantly, how they are doing it, the style, the grace of their engagement with the world. If God is named in action toward the other as Schillebeeckx contends, then "how" Franciscans do ministry, how they turn toward others in contemplation and compassion, is much more important than the words used to describe it.

Elizabeth Johnson suggests that a new form of religious life is emerging, indeed, is already a reality in the church. She comments:

---

[61] Schillebeeckx, 1983: p. 37.
[62] Schillebeeckx, 1983: p. 35.

This vision of a holistic contemplative, prophetic shape to religious life in the future, glimpsed in the literature, is already a living, growing reality in some cases. It also stands in contrast to the over-all shape of religious life in the present, which has become domesticated by too close an identification with the law, structure, and spirituality of the institutional church.[63]

Our own Franciscan origins are characterized by tension between the Franciscan movement and the institutional church in terms of the shape that Franciscan religious life was taking within the church. What Johnson suggests is being born now has been part of the Franciscan tradition since its inception, albeit a forgotten part of the tradition today, perhaps because of its dangerous implications.

However, it would seem that one, if not *the*, major task of Franciscan pastoral leadership today would be its role in recovering the value and role of contemplation and compassion in Franciscan life and ministry. This is largely a formational issue, for both initial and ongoing formation. The early Franciscans, at least until September of 1220,[64] were formed by journeying with the friars as they moved about the world—they learned what it meant to be a Franciscan by working side by side with friars and sisters minor, and lay people in the world. They were not formed in the rarefied environment of a house of formation. And it is quite possible that the move into houses of formation went hand in hand with a domestication of the Franciscan charism by the hierarchical church. Separated from the lepers, how does one turn toward them? One might learn contemplation as a method of prayer in a house of formation, but how does one learn contemplation as a life style, a way of being?

Patricia Hampl's insight into the Franciscan tradition provides an appropriate summary of what this paper has attempted to explore. She states that the Franciscan vision was not

> pietistic or lost in interior moments untranslatable to the world. Francis ran first to find the lepers. He didn't run howling into the woods to help them. He simply went to join them, to *be* with them.

---

[63] E. Johnson, 1994: p. 15.

[64] On September 22, 1220, Pope Honorius III issued the bull *Cum secundum consilium* to the order, mandating the novitiate, or year of probation prior to profession. The papal bull was likely issued in the absence of Francis while he was in the Holy Land, and indicates one of the ways the ministers of the order attempted to regulate and regularize the movement along the lines of monastic tradition.

He wasn't a do-gooder, not a missionary in the convert-the-heathen sort of way. He was a joyous mystic who *needed* to suffer the great pain of his age, because not to suffer, especially to miss out on the suffering of the world, was not to live.[65]

The challenge for Franciscans in ministry today, is the challenge of how to be with people in their human adventures. The tradition of Franciscan contemplation and compassion supplies a valuable resource, essential to the survival of the Franciscan ministerial charism in the present moment.

5. Pastoral Implications

1. Contemplation for ministry in the Franciscan tradition is relational, engaging, and "horizontally ecstatic." This means that the ministry itself, the relation and engagement with others is contemplative and compassionate. Thus, the movement of contemplative ministry takes one toward the other, that is, one does not wait for people to come to be ministered to but rather one moves toward people wherever they are to be found. The early friars worked shoulder to shoulder with men and women in the workplace and that is where the ministry took place. Bringing the good news to the piazza and marketplace as well as to the countryside and fields was part of the novelty of the friars. Can we wait for people to come to us today?

2. This implies that the ministerial agenda is set, so to speak, by the people and their real needs. Programs, no matter how well thought out and prepared, are meaningless if they do not respond to felt needs. The discipline of contemplation and compassion in the Franciscan tradition both demands and fosters attentiveness to what is happening in the world, in people's lives as they unfold. Given the reality of suffering in the lives of women and men in the world, the papers of both William McConville ("Contemporary Ecclesiology and the Franciscan Tradition")[66] and Elizabeth Dreyer ("Blessed Are They Who Mourn: Tears, Compunction, and Forgiveness")[67] point to a reality that Franciscans cannot bypass to focus simplistically on an upbeat, naive, and painless approach to living. The ministerial word must express and articulate for others the real presence of the Word

---

[65] Hampl, 1992: p. 121.
[66] See p. 113.
[67] See p. 179.

in their life and experience. One can only hear this word through attentiveness to the other from their location. This is another way of saying, to paraphrase Tip O'Neil, that all ministry is local!

3. Life in Franciscan brotherhood and sisterhood must also be horizontally ecstatic. This would imply that fraternal/sororal life be outwardly directed and not self-absorbed. Contemplation and compassion go hand in hand and must remain in balance. This would seem to call for renewed understandings and expressions of concrete Franciscan living, allowing new possibilities for concrete patterns of life, e.g., living alone, or with lay people.

4. Institutional and corporate forms of Franciscan ministry appeared early on in our history, e.g., the leper hospice, the parish. Corporate ministries contain a visibility not possible in more individualized apostolates. Particularly in today's world, institutions that give corporate witness to the value of contemplation and compassion in ministry can have a powerful impact on society. This would be a particularly appropriate expression of a charism that is not individual and private, but demanding public and social expression.

5. The regular practice of theological reflection, especially the method developed by Leonardo Boff or Robert Kinast,[68] would be essential to sustaining this ministerial life of contemplation and compassion, especially on the corporate level. Especially helpful in fostering the approach to contemplation and compassion as developed in this paper are the work of William Callahan, "Noisy Contemplation," as well as that of Elizabeth Dreyer's *Earth Crammed with Heaven*.

---

[68] Boff, 1989: pp. 22-42; Kinast, 1993: pp. 1-26.

REFERENCES

Armstrong, Regis, and Ignatius Brady. *Francis and Clare: The Complete Works*. New York: Paulist, 1982. *Clare of Assisi: Early Documents*. Revised and Expanded. St. Bonaventure, New York: Franciscan Institute Publications, 1993.

Beguin, Pierre, *L'anonyme de Perouse: Un témoin de la fraternité franciscaine primitive confronte aux autres sources contemporaines*. Paris: Éditions Franciscaines, 1979.

Boff, Leonardo, *Faith on the Edge: Religion and Marginalized Existence*. San Francisco: Harper and Row, 1989.

Brooke, Rosalind, editor and translator, *Scripta Leonis, Rufini et Angeli Sociorum S. Francisci*. Oxford: Clarendon Press, 1970.

Bynum, Caroline Walker, *Fragmentation and Redemption: Essays on Gender and the Human Body in Medieval Religion*. New York: Zone Books, 1991.

Chidester, David, *Word and Life: Seeing, Hearing, and Religious Discourse*. Urbana: University of Illinois Press, 1992.

Corstanje, Auspicius van, *Francis: Bible of the Poor*. Chicago: Franciscan Herald Press, 1977.

Desbonnets, Théophile, "Legenda trium sociorum: édition critique." Archivum Franciscanum Historicum 67: pp. 38-144, 1974.

Habig, Marion, editor, *St. Francis of Assisi: Writings and Early Biographies; English Omnibus of the Sources for the Life of St. Francis*. Third Edition. Chicago: Franciscan Herald Press, 1973.

Hampl, Patricia, *Virgin Time: In Search of the Contemplative Life* . New York: Farrar, Straus, Giroux, 1992.

Harvey, Michael Peter, "Revelation and Contemplation." pp. 152-160 in New Blackfriars 72 (1991).

Jacopone da Todi, *The Lauds*. Translated by Serge and Elizabeth Hughes. New York: Paulist Press, 1982.

Johnson, Elizabeth, "Between the Times: Religious Life and the Postmodern Experience of God,"pp. 1-16 in Review for Religious 53, (1994).

Johnson, Timothy, "Visual Imagery and Contemplation in Clare of Assisi's 'Letters to Agnes of Prague,'" pp. 161-171 in Mystics Quarterly 19, (1993).

Khanh, Norbert Nguyen Van, *The Teacher of His Heart: Jesus Christ in the Thought and Writings of St. Francis* . Translated by Ed Hagman, O.F.M. Cap. St. Bonaventure, New York: Franciscan Institute Publications, 1994.

Kinast, Robert, *If Only You Recognized God's Gift: John's Gospel as an Illustration of Theological Reflection*. Grand Rapids: Eerdmans Publishing, 1993.

LaCugna, Mary Catherine, *God for Us: The Trinity and Christian Life*. San Francisco: Harper and Row, 1991.

Manselli, Raoul, "San Francesco dal dolore degli uomini al Cristo crocifisso." *Analecta T.O.R.* 16:197, 1983.

Matura, Thaddee, "The Heart Turned Toward the Lord," pp. 4-14 in The Cord 44 (1994).

Miccoli, Giovanni, *Francesco d'Assisi: Realtà e memoria di un'esperienza christiana*. Torino: Einaudi editore, 1991.

Moltmann, Jurgen, *The Way of Jesus Christ: Christology in Messianic Dimensions*. San Francisco: Harper and Row, 1990.

Schillebeeckx, Edward, "The Right of Every Christian to Speak in the Light of Evangelical Experience 'In the Midst of Brothers and Sisters,'" pp. 40-59 in *Preaching and the Non-Ordained: An Interdisciplinary Study* , edited by Nadine Foley. Collegeville: Liturgical Press, (1983).

Scholl, Edith, "The Sweetness of the Lord: *Dulcis* and *Suavis*." pp. 359-366 in Cistercian Studies 27, (1992).

Schreiter, Robert, *Reconciliation: Mission and Ministry in a Changing Social Order*. Maryknoll, New York: Orbis, 1992.

Shannon, William, "Contemplation, Contemplative Prayer," pp. 209-214 in *New Dictionary of Catholic Spirituality*, Michael Downey, editor. Collegeville: Liturgical Press, 1993.

10

"Blessed Are They Who Mourn": Tears, Compunction, and Forgiveness

Elizabeth A. Dreyer

1. The Contemporary Context

For those of us old enough to remember, the phrase "Love means never having to say you're sorry" produces a wry smile. For it takes but a moment of reflection to realize the profound *untruth* of this statement. Life without "I'm sorry" would be hell indeed. And yet in many ways the topics of "compunction" (sorrow for sin) and forgiveness seem alien and threatening to modern sensibilities. There are many reasons for this. The word "sin" has all but vanished from our vocabulary. And legal, social and business etiquettes work against admitting that one is wrong.[1]

In addition, compunction belongs to the world of feeling—a world that has been neglected and diminished in Western culture. Many of us are ill at ease with the affective dimension of our existence because of fear or ignorance. We become defensive and dismissive when the topic of emotions comes up. By moving quickly to abuse—sentimentality, "touchy-feely" encounters or irrational responses—some give themselves permission to reject feeling as a whole. This problem is further complicated by the kinds of feelings compunction demands. They are not positive feelings of love or joy, but rather of egoism and failure and guilt. Such emotions often dredge up years of guilt-induced "baggage" that can prevent us from experiencing genuine sorrow and remorse.

Sebastian Moore calls the topic of forgiveness the most spiritually ambitious of religious ideas because it links two ultimate extremes of human experience: the infinite, all-transcending whole and the experience of one's life as sordid, trivial, and self-seeking. Forgiveness is an act of God acting like God in the very heart of the small, mean world of the sinner. The touch of God's mercy invites us to become more, not less aware of our meanness, knowing that it is in this very place that God touches us.[2]

---

[1] Menninger, 1973.
[2] Moore, 1977: pp. 85-86.

Acknowledgment of wrongdoing ideally leads to sorrow and forgiveness. And the more genuine the sorrow, the less likely that we will be paralyzed at the world's offenses or consumed with self-loathing at our own. In the Our Father, we ask for forgiveness *as we forgive others*. Reconciliation is indeed a community affair, without which the freedom to create our future is jeopardized. In a New Yorker Comment entitled "Getting Over," the author reflects on forgiveness in light of conflicts in ex-Yugoslavia, the Soviet empire, South Africa, Northern Ireland, Central America, Sri Lanka, India, Palestine, and Crown Heights, New York. The author notes that in *The Human Condition*, philosopher Hannah Arendt sees forgiveness as essential to human freedom. "Only through this constant mutual release from what they do can men remain free agents, only by constant willingness to change their minds and start again can they be trusted with so great a power as that to begin something new."[3] The article goes on:

> And yet the forgiveness she [Arendt] sees as the ground for that hope is not a simple forgetting. If anything, it is a highly charged and continuously recharged form of remembering that cannot be done in isolation.... True forgiveness is achieved in community: it is something people do for each other and with each other—and, at a certain point, for free. It is history working itself out as grace, and it can be accomplished only in truth.[4]

In significant ways, our future as a global community depends on the kind of remembering that leads to genuine compunction and forgiveness.

In the religious sphere one wonders whether Christians find "compunction" a morbid theme, or—at best—a curiosity of a remote past. Too often the churches are the last to admit to their own sinfulness. They focus on the mote in the other's eye, and miss the beam in their own. Roman Catholicism is not exempt from this criticism. In singular ways, this tradition has militated against its ministers and people coming to terms with their weaknesses and sinfulness.[5] A church that sees itself too closely identified with the kingdom opens itself to triumphalism and blindness. Today we raise questions about ethical accountability and our failure to nourish hearts of

---

[3] Arendt, 1958: p. 240.
[4] The New Yorker, 4/5/93.
[5] See William McConville's essay in this volume, p. 113.

flesh that are sensitive to the daily betrayal of God's love. Recent convictions of child abuse demand that we confront the destructive forces at work in our church. Can we seize this moment as an invitation to honest self-reflection, to return to a tradition that teaches so eloquently about sorrow and weeping for our sins?

There are other signs pointing us in the direction of compunction. In liturgical settings across the United States the ritual of ashes on Ash Wednesday is growing in many Christian denominations.[6] In the literary world we hear unexpected talk about sin. In her "spiritual geography" *Dakota*, writer Kathleen Norris finds herself asking about the meaning of sin. She says:

> Comprehensible, sensible sin is one of the unexpected gifts I've found in the monastic tradition. The fourth-century monks began to answer a question for me that the human potential movement of the late twentieth century never seemed to address: if I'm O.K. and you're O.K., and our friends are O.K., why is the world definitely not O.K.?[7]

Only when Norris begins to see the world's ills mirrored in her own behavior, does she understand sin as a useful tool for confronting the dark side of the human condition. She views fourth-century monks in the desert not as self-righteous moralists, worried about the behavior of others, but as persons "acutely aware of their own weaknesses, who tried to see their situation clearly without the distortions of pride, ambition or anger." Such insight invites us to speak about compunction in desert monasticism, in the medieval Franciscan tradition and in our own time, hoping that such a "word" will somehow yield real fruit as we live our lives and exercise our ministries in a world that stands in great need of compunction and reconciliation.

2. The Desert Tradition

The *Sayings* of these fourth-century monks, often referred to as "abbas" and "ammas," are perhaps the best traditional resource for learning about compunction. Like the parables in the gospel, the *Sayings* make us uncomfortable. They do not reflect the kind of practical, everyday values by which most of us live. Characters in these stories pay the same wages for one hour and for eleven hours of

---

[6] Steinfels, Peter, "More Protestants Accept Smudges of Ash," The New York Times, 2/24/93.

[7] Norris, 1993: pp. 97-98.

182 *Elizabeth A. Dreyer*

work; they break rules; they practice extreme forms of asceticism and yet relish the beauty of a woman or the wonderful and various tastes of fresh fruit; they run after robbers in order to give them a stick they left behind. And in the midst of such "odd" behavior, the monks talk continually about compunction—intense mourning, weeping, and profound sorrow for their sins. The Greek term for this experience is *penthos*, often translated as "mourning" or "compunction." It is an affective movement of the heart, pierced with sorrow, groaning, turning anew toward God. One who possesses the disposition of compunction mourns for the loss of divine intimacy for self and others and the world. For the monks of the desert, compunction was a lifelong disposition. They mourned for present and past failures, for an unwillingness to notice and respond to the totally embracing and unconditional love of God.[8]

Among the striking paradoxes in this literature is an abundance of joy in the midst of barrels and barrels of tears. What, we ask, is the reality behind this language? Most of us can recall experiences of spiritual joy and appreciate their value. More challenging to comprehend are the role and positive value that the desert monks attached to tears, and their conviction that tears and joy are two faces of the same truth.

A. What Compunction Is Not

True compunction is neither self-pity nor ego-centered guilt. When our sin is "discovered" and we can no longer defend a self-image of perfection, we are likely to experience shame, anger, and despair. When ego has the upper hand, acknowledging sin produces not sorrow, but hopelessness with its attendant loss of life and creativity. Egoism can also support scrupulosity—fastidious adherence to every jot of the law. Self-preoccupation lies at the heart of pseudo-compunction.

Irenee Hausherr notes that in the desert, *penthos* was always in danger of giving way to sadness, its dangerous counterfeit. This happened when the paradox of joyful sadness was forgotten. Abba Isaiah says:

> Brother, mount a vigilant guard against the spirit which brings sadness to a man. This sets off numerous diabolical mechanisms which

---

[8] Hausherr, 1982: p. 24.

will not stop until your strength is sapped. Sadness according to God, on the other hand, is a joy, the joy of seeing yourself in God's will.... Sadness according to God does not weigh on the soul, but says to it, "Do not be afraid! Up! Return!" God knows that man is weak and strengthens him.[9]

This warning points to the importance of discernment. When is sadness godly and when is it egocentric? *Penthos* is not melancholia. It does not lead to apathy or indifference. It does not deaden the spirit, but leads to a renewed life characterized by conviction, dedication, and above all, hope and joy.

The sadness of compunction is not the same as sorrow over the tragedies of human life, such as the loss of a loved one. But one experience can help us understand the other. Gregory of Nyssa says, "If we have understood human mourning, let us go from the better known to the less, to discover what is the blessed mourning which is followed by consolation."[10] Today we are likely to see much closer connections between human love, sorrow, forgiveness and our relationship with God than in the past. Our experience of compunction will be tied much more closely to our daily, lived experience of failure to love neighbor and God.

Compunction is not doing penance. Nor does it nurture extreme ascetical practices. A brother told Abba Poemen of his sins and said he wanted to do penance for three years. The response was that three years was too much. When the brother suggested two years of penance and then only forty days, Abba Poemen had the same response. He said that if one repents with one's whole heart and intends to sin no more, three days is plenty. Genuine compunction protects against the pride and self-righteousness that can accompany penitential practices. In fact, the one cannot exist in the presence of the other. Compunction, by its very nature, wipes out arrogant dispositions and the need to make constant reparation.

B. What Compunction Is

Mourning was important in the desert above all because the Scriptures commanded it. It was the duty of every Christian. The Scriptures are the source of the mourning-joy paradox. "Blessed are those who mourn for they will be comforted," we read in Matthew

---

[9] Hausherr, 1982: p. 141.
[10] Gregory of Nyssa, *De beatitudine*, 3.

5:4. This saying harks back to Psalm 126:5: "May those who sow in tears reap with shouts of joy" and the well-known Isaiah pericope:

> The Spirit of the Lord GOD is upon me, because the Lord has anointed me to bring good news to the oppressed, to bind up the brokenhearted, to proclaim liberty to the captives, and release to the prisoners; to proclaim the year of the Lord's favor, and the day of vengeance of our God; to comfort all who mourn; to grant to those who mourn in Zion—to give them a garland instead of ashes, the oil of gladness instead of mourning, the mantle of praise instead of a faint spirit (Isaiah 61.1-3. Cf. Luke 4.18-19).

We are not likely to see the Beatitudes as commands in such a literal way. But the Scriptures do point to the importance of sorrow for sin and the ways in which God treasures this disposition.

In the desert, tears and repentance were also closely associated with eschatology. Compunction was a response to God's judgment and mercy. Repentance was demanded and mercy promised. The book of Revelation promises "God will wipe away every tear from their eyes" (Revelation 7:17) and "Death will be no more; mourning and crying and pain will be no more, for the first things have passed away" (Revelation 21:4). But the joy and consolation of the second beatitude were not to be known only at the end of history. They were to be experienced in the present as the "ineffable sweetness of tears."

This feeling of sorrow or mourning is described with metaphors such as the gift of tears and the pierced heart and is expressed through wailing, groans, and lamentation. But rather than closing us in on ourselves, the gift of tears opens us to the hope that accompanies forgiveness. Dante's *The Divine Comedy* offers us insight into authentic tears by describing their opposite. In his journey through hell, Dante encounters the sorcerers whose heads are twisted to the back and whose endless tears are the result of the misuse of their eyes. They who tried to look too far ahead, usurping God's prerogatives, can now only look backward.[11] This form of tears, in which the sinner is prevented from any forward look, may be seen as the antithesis of *penthos*, which tends toward hope and the coming of the kingdom. The sadness at the loss of right relationship and intimacy with God is also attended by feelings of consolation and gratitude. For the desert monks, those who weep are the happy ones. The

---

[11] Dante, *Inferno*, XX.

unhappy are those with dry eyes and a cold heart.[12] Without gratitude, compunction becomes despair, and gratitude without compunction turns into presumption.

A sign of compunction's earthly dimension was its orientation toward love of neighbor. Compunction nurtures dispositions of forgiveness without which community life cannot thrive. As we have noted, human relationships can help us understand compunction. Many of us have been blessed with the experience of being loved in a profoundly gratuitous and freeing way. Such an experience can open a door onto the meaning of God's love. One's response to unqualified love is awe, astonishment, sometimes utter disbelief and rejection. One knows that one has done nothing to deserve this love. Teresa of Avila speaks of it as a drenching spring rain.[13] Her response is both utter gratitude and increased sorrow and desolation at her persistent indifference.

This intense sorrow for sin is experienced not only on behalf of oneself, but also for others—for loved ones, neighbors and even enemies. Today more than ever, we are aware of the human connections linking us across the globe. Awareness of love's betrayal leads to acknowledgment of the myriad ways in which we participate in the sins of the world. We too bear the burden of the violent and murderous behavior that results in abuse, starvation, torture, rape of the planet, war, and degradation in our world.

Compunction allows us to watch the evening news and weep. In identifying with the sin of the world, we are freed from projecting this evil onto others in hate, and from becoming paralyzed and silent. Compunction allows us to pray anew the simple prayers of the liturgy, "Lord, have mercy" and "Lamb of God, you take away the sins of the world: have mercy on us."

Arising from this heartfelt sorrow is an awareness that we need and want to be forgiven. Genuine compunction does not leave us in despair or embarrassed about our hardness of heart, but rather turns us toward God, confident that we will receive mercy and forgiveness seventy times seven. A pierced heart leads to repentance and conversion. "Though your sins are like scarlet, they shall be like snow" (Isaiah 1:18).

---

[12] Hausherr, 1982: p. vii.
[13] Teresa of Avila, *Interior Castle* VII.2.4; *Autobiography*, Ch. 11.

In the end, compunction, like unconditional love, is pure gift. Sometimes it comes unexpectedly with no effort; sometimes it eludes us even after sincere and lengthy entreaty. We are invited to pray without ceasing for, and open ourselves to, this gift of a heart of flesh (Ezekiel 36:26). Receiving this grace can be a moment when the truth about God and ourselves strikes us and makes a new life possible. In the enthusiasm of ties reestablished, we die to pettiness, self-centeredness, and inner addictions. We regain a perspective in which we see clearly the transitory nature of life and thus its preciousness.

The paradox of compunction is visible in the desert distinction between two types of tears. The first involves searing tears of sorrow for sin, tears that burn and purify the soul. A second type consoles and refreshes the soul, leaving in its wake a cheerful countenance (Proverbs 15:13). Tears of sorrow mix with tears of joy as one realizes the contrast between what is deserved and what is received.[14] Always, at the heart of authentic compunction lies the incomparable sweetness that will bear fruit in the "grace of tears." Intimacy with God is restored, renewed and deepened. Joy and peace emerge out of the very heart of mourning. Tears lead to peace and to deeper insight into the mysteries of God.

3. The Franciscan Tradition

A. Francis and Clare

For most people, the Franciscan tradition evokes images of joy, not tears. Francis is remembered as one who was gentle, simple, possessed of a highly developed sense of beauty and companionship with nature. Because Francis and his immediate successors did not speak of "compunction" in the explicit fashion of the desert, one might be tempted to think that this tradition, so central to early monasticism, was no longer relevant and important in the Middle Ages. But closer examination of Franciscan spirituality reveals several key elements of compunction—tears, poverty, penance, humility, pardon for sin, peace, joy, and the emphasis on community life.

Both Clare and Francis teach us about sorrow for sin in our relationships with God and with others. Clare speaks of the importance of reconciliation among the Poor Ladies when there has been an

---

[14] Hausherr, 1982: p. 138.

offense. They are not only to seek forgiveness from the offended sister, but they are to ask the one whom they have offended to intercede with God for divine forgiveness as well.[15] And Francis counsels the brothers to attend to the mote in their own eye. "And as the Lord says, they should not take notice of the little defects of others. Rather they should reflect much more on their own [sins] in the bitterness of their soul."[16]

The sources tell us that Clare's prayer was often suffused with tears. The author of the *Legend* presents an image of Clare as another Mary Magdalene, weeping and kissing the feet of Jesus.[17] And in her sleep, an angel of darkness comes to Clare to deter her from weeping, threatening that it will cause her to go blind or to dissolve her brain.[18] Clare wept when a sister was sad or tempted [19] and when Clare wept at prayer, her tears moved other sisters to tears of sorrow as well.[20] Clare wept with the suffering Christ and even wept as she taught the novices to do the same.[21]

In the generation following Francis and Clare, Bonaventure captured in a more systematic way the spiritual charism of the Order. What does he tell us about compunction?

B. Bonaventure[22]

I examine Bonaventure's treatment of compunction under five headings: compunction and prayer; poverty; the way of repentance; humility; and joy.

---

[15] *RegCl*9:6-10.

[16] *RegNB* XI.11-12. See Helen Rolfson's essay on Franciscan fraternity and sorority, p. 97.

[17] Renewed attention to Mary Magdalene points to another strain in our current interest in penitence. See *Mary Magdalen and Many Others* by Carla Ricci. Minneapolis: Fortress, 1994; *Mary Magdalen: Myth and Metaphor* by Susan Haskins. San Francisco: HarperCollins, 1993; *the Life of Saint Mary Magdalene and of her Sister Saint Martha: A Medieval Biography* by Rabanus Maurus 784?-856, translated by David Mycoff. Kalamazoo: Cistercian Publications, 1989; *Les perles, ou les larmes de la Sainte Magdeleine* by Cesar de Nostredame. University of Exeter, 1986.

[18] *LegCl*19.

[19] *LegCl*38

[20] *Proc*1:7; 3:7; 6:4; 10:3.

[21] *LegCl*30.

[22] Three types of texts are helpful: *The Soul's Journey Into God* [SJ]; a selection of sermons *Rooted in Faith* [RF] and *Disciple and the Master* [DM]; and *The Life of St. Francis* [LM].

1. Compunction and prayer

The penchant of the scholastics to see all of reality through a Trinitarian prism, and their conviction about the hierarchical nature of reality, distinguishes them dramatically from the desert hermits. In medieval spiritual literature, one is very conscious that the spiritual life happens in stages. While Bonaventure does not regard these stages as discrete units through which one proceeds in a strict, linear fashion, compunction is clearly a hallmark of the early, preparatory stages of the mystical journey.

In the prologue to *The Soul's Journey into God*, Bonaventure recalls Francis as a man of peace and desire. Desires are fanned by "an outcry of prayer that makes us call aloud in the groaning of our heart (Psalm 38:8-9) and by the flash of insight."[23] Along with intellectual vision, affective dispositions are highlighted. Bonaventure is a true academician, but ultimately his heart lies with Bernard of Clairvaux rather than with Aristotle. The final goal of theology is to increase love, not knowledge. Reading needs unction; speculation needs devotion; investigation needs wonder; observation, joy; work, piety; knowledge, love; understanding, humility; and effort, grace.[24] Bonaventure tells us that Francis "strove with constant sighs of sorrow to root out vice and sin" from his heart, and admonishes us to follow him in drenching the couch nightly with weeping.[25]

It is logical to place compunction at the beginning of the spiritual journey. If one is not aware of and sorry for sin, a major reason for undertaking the journey seems lacking. Yet, in other ways, compunction belongs to more mature stages. It is only when one attains a certain level of experience and security in one's relationship with God that one sees the horror of sin and is willing to face the "terror of admitting what one is doing to earn his self-esteem."[26] The experience of sin's ugliness and its forgiveness are inextricably connected with love.

The term "compunction" in Bonaventure's *Life of St. Francis* most often refers to the initial effect of Francis's word on his hearers.[27] Francis's preaching was characterized by a fervor that "struck," "pierced," "stirred," and "moved" the hearts of his listeners. By point-

---

[23] *SJ* 55.
[24] *SJ* 55.
[25] *DM* 63; *LM* 10:4.
[26] Becker 1973: p. 6.
[27] *LM* 3:3; 4:7; 4:9; 6:2; 12:7

ing to the effectiveness of Francis's preaching, Bonaventure empha-
sizes the importance of the evangelical task of preaching the word in
such a way as to move hearers to repentance.[28] "Compunction" is the
initial movement of the heart—along with a desire to follow Christ's
way of perfection—that first motivates persons to follow the path to
which Francis invites them. The range of those so moved is broad—
from troubadours to simple peasants, to popes and cardinals. In one
instance it is Francis's heart that is struck with compunction (*com-
punctus corde*) when he sees a poor man on the road. He says, "This
man's need puts us to shame, because we have chosen poverty as our
wealth; and see, it shines more clearly in him."[29]

In a sermon on Luke 19:46—"My house shall be a house of
prayer," Bonaventure mentions three things necessary for prayer.
The first is getting ready; the second is attentiveness; and the third is
passionate joy.[30] Bonaventure uses the metaphor of "being scrubbed
clean" to describe the repentance of the first stage of prayer. One
must be scrubbed clean from stubborn pride, from sensual amuse-
ment, and from frenzied activity. It is in the second stage of "scrub-
bing" that he uses the language of tears. He cites 1 Samuel, Judith,
and the Psalms. Hannah and Judith purified themselves with tears
and weeping (1 Samuel 1:10; Judith 9:1), and the psalmist is worn out
groaning every night, drenching his pillow and soaking his bed with
tears (Psalm 6:6). Bonaventure often recalls how Francis wept daily
and so weakened his eyes by tears that he lost his sight.[31]

One concludes from this material that, for Bonaventure, compunction is a gift that deeply affects one's heart with sorrow, a gift
that is the first of greater gifts to follow. For most baptized
Christians, the primary locus of reception of the gift of compunction
is within the warp and woof of daily life. It is here that we can be
attentive to the splendor of God's love. And it is here that we often
fail to appreciate and respond to that love, missing the numerous
invitations to compunction that daily life offers. Every time we
become conscious of, and grieve over our self-preoccupation and
lack of generous response to God's love and the love of others, we
are invited to yet another new beginning on the journey of life
toward God.

---

[28] *LM* 3:7.
[29] *LM* 7:6.
[30] *RF* 8.
[31] *DM* 69, 122, 138; *LM* 5:8.

2. Poverty

In part because Bonaventure had to defend poverty against its adversaries, it becomes for him a comprehensive theological category. Humans are doubly poor. They are poor in their very being because their existence depends on God's love. They are morally poor because in spite of God's infinite goodness they turn away from God, rejecting the uprightness and clear vision of salvation in favor of being bent over and blind. Like the prodigal son of Luke's gospel, humans are sinners, unworthy of God's goodness and gifts. But admitting our poverty gives rise to humility. Next to God, we are nothing, but in the spirit of Francis, Bonaventure encourages sinners to pray for forgiveness because God is a God of mercy. The subtitle of chapter one in *The Soul's Journey into God* puts the reader in mind of desert poverty: "Here begins the reflection of the poor man in the desert." Francis, imitating Christ, was a "type" of this poor beggar, standing before God with nothing.[32] Bonaventure goes on to describe entreaty for God's help as a sigh from the valley of tears.[33]

In a sermon on gratitude (1 Corinthians 1:4-5), Bonaventure says we need to acknowledge that to the extent we are separated from God, we are poor.[34] Our lives are filled with failure, foolishness, blindness, and nakedness. It is Christ who provides the remedy. Repentant sinners are gifted with compassion; the blind who pray are offered wisdom; the naked receive grace; the foolish receive glory. For Bonaventure, our poverty takes on dramatic proportions because it is seen in contrast to the generosity and riches of Christ.

Poverty—Francis's mother, bride, and lady—was a centerpiece of the Franciscan Order.[35] It is the sight of a poor man that causes Francis's own heart to be filled with compunction.[36] Experiencing our poverty is the first step toward a contrite heart. Whether it be moral, intellectual, spiritual, or physical poverty, we all stand poor before God. Are there specific ways in which we experience ourselves as "poor ones" in the desert? Examples include our inability to simplify our consuming ways; to heal intractable problems in relationships; to protect ourselves against illness and death; to abandon petty personal concerns. There is little hope that our hearts will be

---

[32] *LM* 7.
[33] *SJ* 53.
[34] *RF* 4.
[35] *LM* 7:6.
[36] *LM* 7:6.

pierced unless we become aware of our own and the world's poverty. Only when we stand together in solidarity as "the poor ones in the desert," will we be moved to address the ills of our world.

3. The way of repentance

Francis was part of a wider penitential movement in thirteenth-century Europe that was a response to perceptions of greed, arrogance, and high living in church and society. In *The Life of St. Francis*, Bonaventure begins with a portrait of Francis as poor and lowly, following in the footsteps of John the Baptist, preparing in the desert a way of highest poverty, and preaching repentance by word and example.[37] Francis's ministry was "to call men to weep and mourn, to shave their heads, and to put on sackcloth (Isaiah 22:12), and to mark with a Tau the foreheads of men who moan and grieve" (Ezekiel 9:4).[38] In the initial stages of his conversion, Francis sought out "solitary places, well suited for sorrow" where he prayed with unutterable groanings.[39] Like Clare, the image of Christ's passion was so imprinted on his mind that the very thought of the cross led him to weep and sigh. After this experience, he followed a way of poverty, humility, and intimacy with God.

Magdalene is also a model of repentance for Bonaventure.[40] As Mary of Nazareth epitomizes integrity, Magdalene is the soul of repentance. Bonaventure underlines the affective dimensions of her compunction: "Indeed, she seems to have loved Christ more than any of the others." Magdalene's love cleanses the pores of sin because she is not embarrassed by the intensity of her love. She is compared to the bride in the Song of Songs 3:2 who goes out to seek him whom her heart loves. And because of her immense love, she is forgiven much, thus becoming a model of repentance for all time.

The way of repentance is intended to have a purifying effect. In a sermon on Lamentations 1:13—"He has sent a fire from on high down into my bones"—Bonaventure explores the image of fire [41], describing it as grace (the zeal of God, hatred for sin), guilt (passion,

---

[37] *LM* Prol: 1; 3:7; 3:10.
[38] *LM* Prol: 2.
[39] *LM* 1:5. See Michael Cusato's treatment in this volume of "doing penance" as seeing the world through the eyes of the poor, p. 125.
[40] *RF* 53; *DM* 114.
[41] *RF* 24.

greed and anger enkindled by the devil), and repentance (purifying substance to be endured because it will strengthen us). The fire of guilt can only be quenched with the water of tears (Psalms 6:6 and 42:1). While the fire of our present problems can be beneficial if we endure them with patience, the fire of eternal damnation can be escaped by no one and is to be dreaded. The antidote to eternal fire is humility.

The context of twentieth-century North America is strikingly different from that of thirteenth-century Italy, yet are there not parallels to be drawn? Do not the newspapers present to us daily accounts of events around the world that should cause us to repent? How can we nurture a sense of personal and corporate responsibility for the ills of the world? And what are the distinctive contours of our way of repentance? Few of us will shave our heads or take to the streets in sackcloth and ashes, but who is prevented from fasting, weeping, meditating on the cross, or most importantly accepting gracefully the stripping, purifying asceticism of everyday life? In her book *A Feminist Ethic of Risk*, Sharon Welch echoes this sentiment. "Faced with humiliation, with the devastation of racism, with ecological destruction, with sexism, it is healthy to notice that something is wrong; it is healthy to grieve and rage over the violation of life."[42]

4. Humility

Humility is a fourth element of compunction reflected in the Franciscan tradition. Following in Christ's footsteps, Francis is seen as an exemplar of humility.[43] Bonaventure says, "St. Francis was a servant of God humble in his reverence for him, more humble still in caring for his neighbor and most humble of all in despising himself. I admire the humility of Francis more than all his other virtues."[44]

In a sermon on the verse from Matthew's gospel, "Learn from me, for I am gentle and humble of heart (Matthew 11:29), Bonaventure examines humility in his usual threefold way: 1) the fruits that make it so attractive; 2) the manner in which it is acquired; 3) the means by which it is maintained.[45] His first point is an important one that we often forget. That is, humility can only be acquired through meditation

---

[42] Welch, 1990: p. 36.
[43] *LM* 6.
[44] *DM* 107.
[45] *DM* 73f.

on the goodness and the judgments of God. Too often, we think of our sinfulness and our human frailty exclusively within the horizon of human existence, and shrink from it. The point of humility is not to dump on or belittle ourselves. Rather, humility is simply the truth of our condition *over against* the infinitely generous and unconditional love of God. Unless we gaze on this goodness, the truth about ourselves will never become evident and exhortations to compunction will fall on deaf ears. Only when we keep God's love before us—symbolized by Christ on the cross—will we open ourselves to this gift.

These days we rarely hear sermons that warn of "hell, fire, and brimstone." In fact, we are intent on distancing ourselves from the jealous and angry God who left Christians cowering in fear. But in the tradition, compunction flowed from fear of divine judgment as well as from love. Are there helpful ways for modern persons to think about God's anger? Surely God is angry at the pointless suffering and starvation around the world that is the fruit of greed and revenge. Surely God is angry at the ways in which we damage this beautiful planet. Surely God is angry at the myriad ways in which we belittle and ignore each other because of racism, sexism, classism, ageism. And surely each one of us is responsible in ways both subtle and blatant for these destructive forces. Should not the thought of God's anger at the obliteration of what God so lovingly created make us humble—piercing our hearts with genuine remorse and sorrow?

Humility also involves a just assessment of self. The truth demands admission of sinfulness and of the transient nature of human life. Ash Wednesday ashes remind us that we come from dust and return to dust. When we keep before us the truth that our lives are but a moment in the path of time we are less likely to sweat the small stuff. As Bonaventure reminds us, "Today you are alive, tomorrow you may be dead; healthy and strong today, sick and weak tomorrow, today a rich man, tomorrow perhaps a beggar; wise today, possibly you will become foolish tomorrow."[46]

It does not follow that we think less of, or denigrate, the lives we are given. Rather, the daily material and spiritual aspects of existence become even more precious, deepening our sorrow whenever we prove ungrateful or indifferent. Feeling truly wretched, poor, blind, and naked are genuine and valuable feelings that result from our growing love affair with the world and with the God who created it.

---

[46] *DM* 77.

Bonaventure points to the affective dimension of Francis's response to God's love: "Like a glowing coal, he seemed totally absorbed in the flame of divine love. Whenever he heard of the love of God, he was at once excited, moved and inflamed as if an inner chord of his heart had been plucked by the plectrum of the external voice."[47] Francis's intense love affair with God is the backdrop of his awareness of sin, his humility and his compunction.

Finally, humility involves respect for others. Bonaventure captured Francis' "persona" as one who had a deferential demeanor toward all other persons, toward animals and all of creation.[48] If we see ourselves rightly, it is unlikely that we will see ourselves as better than, and privileged over, others. Humility nurtures a profound reverence for all of creation, and to the extent that our love for the world grows, to that extent are we devastated when we, or others, act to destroy it.

According to Bonaventure, one maintains humility by having sorrow for one's sins; by being silent about one's virtues; by hard work and discipline; and by despising honors.[49] How can we understand Bonaventure's reiteration of Francis' advice to strive to be considered worthless by others? How do we free ourselves from a pseudo-humility that is a cover for self-preoccupation, insecurity, or self-hate? One cannot command humility. It is a gift for which we pray, a gift that emerges when we see truly the awesome beauty and goodness of God, others, world, and self.

5. Joy

For the desert fathers and mothers, and particularly for Francis, compunction is unintelligible without joy. In his *Life of St. Francis*, Bonaventure rarely speaks of one without the other, often in the same sentence. Of Francis at the Greccio crib: "The man of God stands before the crib, filled with affection, bathed in tears and overflowing with joy."[50] Francis, the man who wept daily,[51] enjoyed sweet smells, tastes, sounds and consolation.[52] Prostrate before the cruci-

---

[47] *LM* 9:1.
[48] *LM* 8:6; 12:3. See Thomas Shannon's discussion in this volume of the dignity of the human person in the Franciscan tradition, p. 59.
[49] *DM* 79.
[50] *LM* 10:7.
[51] DM 122, 138; LM 5:8; 8:1
[52] LM 5:11; 10:6.

fied, Francis was filled with consolation.[53] When his father was pursuing him in anger, Francis begged for deliverance with a flood of tears which produced an experience of excessive joy.[54] One day, while weeping for his sins (Isaiah 38:15), Francis experienced the joy of the Holy Spirit's forgiveness.[55] Every affront and condescending gesture was received with joy.[56] At the early chapter at the Portiuncula, the brothers "overflowed with spiritual joy."[57] At Francis's death, the larks were filled with joy, and Francis's sons both wept and rejoiced.[58] And above all, Francis was filled with joy whenever he contemplated the love of God.[59]

God's choice to make the humble his friends is also cause for joy.[60] Humble persons keep the commandments and attribute nothing of God's glory to themselves. Bonaventure cites Bernard: "You are indeed a faithful servant of the Lord when nothing of the Lord's abundant glory, which does not come from you but is channeled through you, remains clinging to your hands."[61] The result of putting oneself at the service of others in humility is to experience the joy of friendship with God and to be invited to "go up higher" (Luke 14:10).[62]

A pierced and humble heart also brings peace.[63] In the thirteenth century, as in the twentieth, the cry for peace was not rhetorical, but came directly out of the experience of chaos in church and society. As one who wept daily for his sins, Francis was able to offer genuine peace to every group to whom he spoke. He was known as a man of peace. The oft-repeated goal of the spiritual life was peace. From the beginning, Francis "wished to call all the faithful of the world to repentance and to bring them to birth in Christ the Lord. 'Go,' said the gentle father to his sons, 'proclaim peace to men and preach repentance for the forgiveness of sins'" (Mark 1:4)[64] This command was received by the brothers with joy. Peace and its accompanying joy run like a thread through all Franciscan literature.

---

[53] LM 2:1.
[54] LM 2:2.
[55] LM 3:6
[56] LM 3:8; 6;1; 6:5.
[57] LM 4:10.
[58] LM 14:6; 15:3.
[59] LM 9:1.
[60] DM 131.
[61] Bonaventure, *Sermon on the Song of Songs*, 13.3.
[62] DM 129.
[63] LM 4:9.
[64] LM 3:7

196 Elizabeth A. Dreyer

4. Implications for Ministry

Words like "penance," "compunction," and "repentance" are alien to modern sensibilities. There are good reasons for this. They have been used to oppress rather than liberate Christians and to this extent are well left behind. There is a further complication. Today sorrow for sin gets caught up in guilt feelings that move us to suppress any thought about sin. Left on our own, we shy away from feelings of falling short and being a sinner. But we need to be vigilant so as not to lose sight of the reality to which they point. Perhaps a term like "conversion" conveys better in our time what the tradition meant by *penthos*. And while talk about "tears" may make us uncomfortable, they will always be part of the human condition and of our biblical and spiritual traditions. They remain a symbol of sorrow that needs to be plumbed in every age.

Recent events make this an apt time for us to reflect on repentance and forgiveness. The daily newspapers inform us of genocide, religious and political warfare, acts of terrorism, the return of capital punishment. We live in a culture of "rights" that produces "victims" who seem uninterested in questions of personal and social responsibility. I suggest that our willingness and ability to face up to our own sin can help us both to be accountable and to respond to the world's ills with hearts of compassion and forgiveness.

In addition, our image of ourselves as a church above reproach has been shattered once again. We are challenged to confront our abusive, exclusive, arrogant and irresponsible behaviors. In his essay in this volume,[65] William McConville suggests that we develop an "ecclesiadicy"—discourse about the church that attends to its sinful and tragic dimensions. How do we respond to those who have been victimized by our actions? How do we embrace the sinner? True conversion is a community affair that leads to forgiveness of self and others. We recall Hannah Arendt's reminder that forgiveness is "something people do for each other and with each other—and at a certain point, for free."[66] Are we confident that grace will allow us to face our sinfulness in a way that leads not to depression and despair but to joy and hope?

---

[65] See p. 113.
[66] Arendt, 1958: p. 240.

How do we go about a creative retrieval of the sorrow for sin that is at the heart of conversion? I suggest five areas.

1. Image of God

The ways in which we image God affect our sense of sin. We no longer appeal to an angry, vengeful God in order to evoke feelings of compunction. Yet should we not be fearful of the consequences of arrogant, indifferent, secretive, irresponsible and addictive behaviors? Can we encourage one another to flee these destructive tendencies, to mourn their presence in our lives?

In our time, we are more likely to lament our failings by reflecting on God's loving gaze at the world; on God's generous desire to offer to us God's very self; on God's justice that demands the fullness of life for all. Are we convinced that God's love will not be impeded by our sin? The fourteenth-century anchoress Julian of Norwich sees the horror of sin, but in the end hears God's word that "all will be well."[67] She meets a God who in the end does not judge but consoles. The pain of the Passion turns to consolation. The closer we draw to the ever-loving and ever-forgiving God, the more we see the horror of sin and weep.

Perhaps the most important practical aspect of our image of God as merciful and forgiving is our role as mediators. The mercy of God does not drop down from heaven as a *"deus ex machina."* It remains invisible until human beings embody it in the history of our daily lives. The power of Christ operates not only as a vertical bridge between us and God but as a horizonal bridge between human beings. It is our ability to imitate the forgiveness of God that helps to secure the presence of God in the midst of a sinful and warring world. And it is doubtful that persons who are strangers to the depths of their own sin will function as authentic and effective mediators of God's loving mercy to the world.

2. Self-knowledge

History may label the twentieth century the "age of psychology." One of the benefits of the growth in psychological knowledge is our increased awareness of the geography of our psyches. Books on psy-

---

[67] Julian of Norwich, 1978: Chs. 13:27; 13:36.

chology—from Sigmund Freud to M. Scott Peck—have become a cottage industry. Millions of Americans are conversant with the basic language and processes of self-knowledge and self-help.

The Christian spiritual tradition also points consistently to the importance of self-knowledge. Those embarking on the spiritual journey are invited to "get the picture straight" at the beginning. This means that we are *both* sinners *and* made in the image and likeness of God. It is our glory that we are made in God's image, and our truth that we are both creatures and sinners. Conversion hinges on our ability and willingness to live in this truth. In their wisdom, the saints caution us against living in illusion and self-deception about ourselves, our families, our institutions and our countries.[68]

A brother asked Anthony, "What should I do about my sins?" He replied, "Whoever seeks deliverance from sins will find it in tears and weeping, and whoever wishes to advance in building up virtue will do so through weeping and tears."[69] Maximus the Confessor interrogates his readers who feel that they are in good standing with divine justice.

> What our Lord said against the Pharisees I take as directed to us, the Pharisees of today, we who have received such a great grace and who are worse than they. We too, do we not impose on others' shoulders burdens difficult to bear, without touching them withour fingers? We, too, do we not perform our works to be seen by men? We, too, do we not love the first places in assemblies?...Who then would not weep over us, since we have such dispositions? Who would not deplore a captivity such as ours?[70]

Such honest questioning can lead to a transformation of our identity as ministers. We no longer place ourselves above those we serve in order to judge or correct, but we walk with them humbly, knowing that we too are mired in the depths of egoism and hypocrisy. One can witness to conversion best when we experience our own need for sorrow and forgiveness.

Tears come only when we face the narrow, petty dimensions of our existence in the light of what God intends for us. Irenaeus reminds us that we were not created for weeping but so that God

---

[68] For an excellent treatment of this topic, see Columba Stewart's "Radical Honesty About the Self: The Practice of the Desert Fathers," Sobornost 12/1/1990, 239-250.
[69] *Lives of the Fathers*, 7.38
[70] Hausherr, 1982: p. 166.

might have someone in whom to place great gifts.[71] We are meant to pass through mourning into joy.

3. Recovery of Religious Feeling

Compunction belongs in an eminent way to the world of religious feeling. It follows that we will become more likely candidates for conversion when we notice, respect and develop our emotions. The Middle Ages in general, and the Franciscan tradition in particular offer valuable examples of a more personal, affective spirituality. And the saints knew well that feelings can be developed in good or bad directions, offering guidelines in the process of discernment. In this century, with the help of psychology, we have begun to attend more carefully to the emotions. Theological, psychological and ethical literature abounds that can help us to understand, accept and celebrate the affective as well as the cognitive aspects of our lives.[72] But the obstacles remain significant.

Some persons ev ade their feelings by allowing them to atrophy. For some this behavior is a defense set up in the interest of self-image or self-preservation. For others it is the result of cultural pressures that make us fear and repress our feelings rather than accept and appreciate them. Knowing and expressing feelings in appropriate ways makes us vulnerable, but it also opens us to solidarity and friendship. One can hardly imagine a good minister who is unable or unwilling to be in touch with and express to others this sacred aspect of human existence.

This rehabilitation of feeling is related to our re-appraisal of bodiliness. Feminist theology has called attention to the sacredness of the body, its sexuality, rhythms and expressions. In our culture the physical expression of tears is more acceptable for women, and perhaps those women who understand this gift most deeply can be our guides. Elizabeth Johnson reminds us of the relational nature of weeping. We weep not only for our own sins but for the sins of the world that cause endless suffering for those we love. She suggests

---

[71] Irenaeus, *Against Heresies*, 4.25.
[72] See Don E. Saliers, *The Soul In Paraphrase* (New York: Seabury, 1980); Rita Nakashima Brock, *Journeys by Heart: A Christology of Erotic Power* (New York: Paulist, 1990); Elizabeth Dreyer, *Passionate Women: Two Medieval Mystics* (New York: Paulist Press, 1989).

that "women do more than a fair share of the crying in the world." With Jesus who weeps over Jerusalem, Rachel weeps over her children, and South American women weep for the "disappeared."[73] Physical tears symbolize the depth of religious mourning.

While the desert *Sayings* counsel against both excessive weeping to gain relief and the suppression of tears that sometimes led to illness and even death, there was skepticism about the sincerity of an affliction that was not accompanied by tears. Weeping is a deeply human activity. Gregory of Nyssa called tears "the blood in the wounds of the soul."[74] As it is natural for a wound to bleed, except among the bloodless, so it is natural for Christians to weep, except for those with hearts of stone. Tears bring about not only personal consolation, but the purification and peace of the world. Conversion that produces tears of affection cannot happen unless we *feel* deeply for ourselves and for our world. To cut ourselves off from feeling is to cut ourselves off from compassion for the world and from imitating a compassionate God.

4. Sacraments

Ritual is a powerful way to nurture religious feelings.[75] Unfortunately, this may be the arena of our greatest failure. Reflection on the traditional practice of the sacrament of penance makes one wonder whether "the multiplication of confessions has [not] had its part to play in the gradual dying out of compunction."[76] Frequent sacramental confession was not the practice of the early church. The emphasis was on the *virtue* rather than the *act* of repentance. Frequency can also generate a mindless list of peccadillos—an affront to genuine conversion.

A second common ritual is the confession of sin at the beginning of eucharistic liturgy.[77] For many worshipers these words and ritual gestures have become routinized and empty, no longer capable of moving us to the profound sense of loss and mourning that is at the heart of conversion. We are embarrassed to weep and gnash our teeth. Perhaps we can bring new life to this confession by connecting

---

[73] Johnson, 1992: p. 259.

[74] Gregory of Nyssa, *Funeral Oration for Placilla*.

[75] See John Burkhard's essay on sacraments and symbol in this volume, p. 79.

[76] Hausherr, 1982: p. 31.

[77] Michael Blastic's essay in this volume examines the connection between eucharist and contemplation in Francis's life. See p. 149.

it with events from the local community and the world. Every week we become aware of new expressions of violence and indifference to humans and the environment. By bringing these stark and sinful realities to worship, we can arouse in the community feelings of deep sorrow that will make true the words, "I confess to almighty God and to you, my brothers and sisters...."

Preaching can also nourish genuine conversion. The Catholic community's long-standing dissatisfaction with preaching has led us to reexamine the function of both faith and rhetoric in the act of preaching. In the early church, Origen is recognized as the first great preacher of compunction. In his nineteenth homily *On Jeremiah*, Origen developed the idea that preachers should use their eloquence to bring their hearers "to mourning, to weeping and to tears ... for only weeping leads to laughter."

We have seen how Francis moved people by his preaching. It aroused feelings of sorrow in his listeners. These early sources invite preachers today to reflect on their own fervor and commitment. As preachers, do we allow the word of God to pierce our hearts? And do our pierced hearts influence the ways in which we minister to others? In our preaching, do we permit the veil to be drawn back so that others may see the truth of a heart filled with compunction, and so be drawn to receive the gift themselves?

5. Love of the World

Finally, the monks of the desert and Francis and Bonaventure prompt us to a deeper love of the world.[78] As we look at ourselves and at our hungry, poor, abused, and war-torn world, do we weep? Are we appalled at the evil around us and at the evil lodged securely in our own hearts? Those with pierced hearts do not face the world nor judge it with a superior, unfeeling, holier-than-thou countenance. Our tears will be commensurate with our love. A loving, compassionate gaze at the world presumes a sense of equality, respect and solidarity with all creation. Genuine conversion is not possible unless we lovingly identify with the world. We stand in and of the world, both image of God and sinner.[79]

---

[78] Zachary Hayes offers a nondualistic way to understand the cosmos in his essay "Christology—Cosmology" in this volume. See p. 41.

[79] For an alternate approach to the issue of relationship with the world see Michael Cusato's essay in this volume, p. 125.

Genuine love will lead us to an appreciation of the gifted nature of tears and away from our penchant to use tears in self-interested and manipulative ways. The commercialization and trivialization of contrition and conversion on radio and TV talk shows are often an example of such manipulation. In contrast, genuine love for the world can motivate us to create a culture of care and responsibility toward all people, even our enemies. The anonymous author of the early thirteenth-century English text *Ancrene Riwle* recommends offering one's tears as a drink to one's enemy—perhaps to slake the thirst of hate or as a toast of compassion and forgiveness?

Our love for the world and God can grow into a disposition of reverence toward all of creation. And as our love and reverence deepens, so too our sense of horror at the daily irreverence in ourselves and in the world. Then the gift of tears, with its sting of remorse at the deep and existential realization that we are all sinners can become a healing balm, a witness to the infinite mercy and forgiveness of God. This way of life is filled with challenge and difficulty. Even genuine tears provide no "quick fix" for the ills of our world.

A ministry of love and service requires that we pray for the gifts of tears; face our own sin; admit that we have served badly and will do so again; invite others to create with us a culture of reverence and love for all peoples; hold one another's tears in our hands. An important function of leadership is to witness to reconciliation by identifying and dealing with conflict in honest and responsible ways. Conflict happens on many levels: family, community,[80] institution,[81] nations. We can watch for the unexamined ways in which we avoid or deny conflict and instead create structures in which to deal with it. Addressing conflict honestly can contribute to our growth in holiness—even when the outcome is less than satisfactory.

Theodore the Studite (d. 826) speaks to us from across the centuries with astonishing relevance. He places God's love for the world before us in stark and powerful language and challenges us to imitate it.

> We should pray and lament for the world. Why? Because the Son of God came to save the world and the world denies him. Tribes and nations deny him. Even those who bear his name deny him,

---

[80] See essays in this volume by Helen Rolfson, p. 97, and Joseph Chinnici, p. 205.

[81] See Mary Meany's essay in this volume, p. 227.

some through their twisted beliefs, some through their evil lives. What should he have done that he has not done? Although God, he became man; he humbled himself and became obedient to death, even death on a cross; he has given us his body to eat and his blood to drink; he has allowed himself to be called father, brother, leader, master, spouse, coheir, and so much more [mother, sister, nurse, lover]. And still he is denied, and still he bears it.... Let his true disciples lament the denials of their fellow-servants.... And so we too [with Paul], disciples legitimately born, should not be concerned just with ourselves, but also lament and pray for the whole world.[82]

Our tradition offers direction, but it is up to us creatively to become aware of, understand, ask for, and nurture the "gift of tears" for our time.

---

[82] Theodore the Studite, *Small Catechism*.

REFERENCES

Arendt, Hannah, *The Human Condition*. Chicago: University of Chicago Press, 1958.

Becker, Ernest, *The Denial of Death*. New York: Free Press, 1973.

Bonaventure, *Rooted in Faith: Homilies to a Contemporary World*, translated by Marigwen Schumacher. Chicago: Franciscan Herald Press, 1974.

————, *The Disciple and the Master: Sermons on St. Francis*, translated by Eric Doyle. Chicago: Franciscan Herald Press, 1983.

Hausherr, Irénée, *Penthos: The Doctrine of Compunction in The Christian East*, translated by Anselm Hufstader. Kalamazoo, Michigan: Cistercian Publications, 1982.

Johnson, Elizabeth, *She Who Is: The Mystery of God in Feminist Theological Discourse*. New York: Crossroad, 1992.

Menninger, Karl, *Whatever Became of Sin?* New York: Hawthorn Books, 1973.

Moore, Sebastian, *The Crucified Is No Stranger*. London: Dartman, Longman & Todd, 1977.

Norris, Kathleen, *Dakota: A Spiritual Geography*. New York: Ticknor & Fields, 1993.

Welch, Sharon, *A Feminist Ethic of Risk*. Minneapolis: Fortress Press, 1990.

11

Conflict and Power:
The Retrieval of Franciscan Spirituality for the Contemporary Pastoral Leader

Joseph P. Chinnici, O.F.M.

"Today," St. Bernard writes in his *Commentary on the Song of Songs*, "the text we are to study is the book of our own experience. You must therefore turn your intention inward, each one must take note of his own particular awareness of the things I am about to discuss."[1] In asking his listeners to bridge the gulf separating the biblical text from their own personal experience, Bernard is trying to make real the way of salvation for the daily life of his own monks. His spirituality presupposes a union between God, the self, and the world of people and things. He believes this is the way outlined in the gospels—a learning which is acquired not through speculation or theory but through reflection and practice.

This reliance on experience as the premier teacher is certainly the tradition handed on to Bernard and other medieval thinkers by their own heritage. In modern times Étienne Gilson has referred to it as "Christian socratism":

> To know whence we came, where we stand, and whither we go is to know what we were, what we are, and what we are to be; in short it is to know ourselves. The first thing to be done then, by whoever would walk in the ways of charity, is to learn to know himself; and that is the true science, the only one the Cistercian needs, the one that in his case should supply for all the dialectical quibbles of Plato and all the sophisms of Aristotle.[2]

Locating various biblical texts on self-knowledge at the center of their spiritual quest (e.g., Deuteronomy 15:9; Psalm 118:59; Ecclesiasticus 2:1-2), masters such as Basil, Augustine, and the desert

---

[1] *Commentary on the Song of Songs*, 3.1.
[2] Gilson, 1940: p. 69.

fathers and mothers bequeathed to the Middle Ages a whole series of disciplines designed to facilitate the discovery of God through the pondering of one's own self.[3] We catch a glimpse of this same inheritance and its practices in the *Testaments* of Francis and Clare, and, following the same method, it is from such a parallel place in our own experience that I would like to begin a discussion of the meaning of pastoral leadership, its conflicts and possibilities within the contemporary Franciscan world in the United States. This essay will thus attempt 1) to name some dimensions of our present experience of leadership; 2) to relate this experience to a critical retrieval of our spiritual tradition; and 3) to conclude with some few comments on future directions.

1. Our Contemporary Experience

It would be impossible to encompass in any essay the full experience of the contemporary pastoral leader in the church today. There are simply too many situations and too many personalities in the current attempts at evangelization, from the grass-roots personal and face-to-face level to the more administrative personnel and planning concerns of those holding official and sometimes more removed positions of authority. However, given the context of American culture and the current ideal of "pastoral leadership" in the church there seems to exist in almost all situations an experience of the leader as living in the borderland between charism and institution, community and bureaucracy, individual rights and the demands of the common good, the Franciscan ideals of poverty and personalism and the corporate realities of efficiency and business.

In the Franciscan world this contemporary dilemma came to full articulation in July 1990 at the "Meeting of the Ministers, V," a gathering of the leadership of Franciscan men's orders in the United States. In preparation for that meeting each provincial was sent a questionnaire. Twenty-three ministers responded to the inquiry: seven from the O.F.M. jurisdiction; six from the Conventuals; seven from the Capuchins; two from the Third Order Regular; and one from the Society of the Atonement. The questionnaire covered four pages and asked the minister about his personal experiences, his working relationship with his council, and the critical issues and

---

[3] Bazelaire, 1953; Stewart, 1990.

friar expectations which he faced in his office. In response to Question 5, "How do you perceive your role as minister?," one particularly representative provincial replied:

> Basically to act as a "link" between the traditions of the order (enshrining charism, nature, spirit, and purpose of the order) and the present situation of friars of the province in church and world. Hence basic responsibilities are: to promote unity, spiritual and human development and mission of the friars of the province—and these "interdependently"! Hence: to provide real "spiritual direction" according to church teaching and order directives to the province as a whole and to each community; to promote the holiness of the friars, especially through initial and ongoing formation; to organize the life of communities, distribute offices to friars within the province and with reference to local churches. All this requires: reflection, participation, information, discussion, decision, and the observance, throughout, of the principle of subsidiarity.[4]

Given the terms of this definition of task and self-identity, what surfaced most in the experience of the ministers were the tensions and contradictions under which they live and work, their personal awareness and feeling for the conflicts which seem to be part and parcel of a Franciscan living within contemporary American culture. Thus, in answer to questions about the positive and negative elements within the culture, the participants listed the following as almost twin poles of experience:

Positive and Negative Aspects of American Culture	
What is best in American culture?	*What is of most concern?*
Freedom and pluralism.	Self-absorption.
The peace movement.	Militarism.
Openness, communication.	Polarization.
Respect for the person.	Individualism.
Search for matters spiritual.	Rampant materialism.
Ethnic mix.	Lack of common interest.
Generosity.	Addictive consumerism.
Organization, practical mind.	Energy for success.
Willingness to help.	Irresponsibility.

---

[4] The responses for the O.F.M. Conference are in the possession of this author. The committee on preparation was composed of Francis Anthony Lonsway, O.F.M.Conv., Edmund Walker, O.F.M.Cap., Richard Eldredge, T.O.R., Peter Taran, S.A., David Eckelkamp, O.F.M., and myself. Although all of us participated, Francis Lonsway designed the questionnaire.

When approached about the expectations which the friars place upon them, the provincials again listed dual realities:

What Friars Expect of Provincials	
Gentleness and compassion.	Confrontation, strength.
Fraternal service, affirmation.	Management, planning.
Animator.	Decision-maker.
Servant and brother.	A major superior.

As two respondents summarized: "Too many differing expectations"; "There probably are as many perceptions as there are friars."

As the material began to mount from these questionnaires, a certain self-experience for the contemporary pastoral leader emerged. The ministers were indicating that cultural and religious polarities existed within themselves, indeed cut deeply through their own hearts. The tensions grouped themselves internally in terms of image and externally in terms of personal and corporate functions:

1. *Self-image*: The ministers described themselves as "mothers" *and* "fathers," spiritual leaders *and* administrators, servants *and* decision-makers, counselors *and* planners.

2. *Corporate functions*: As corporate managers within American culture, ministers work with property, management, business, investments, and personnel, all of which require them to order, negotiate, discipline, challenge, transfer, remove, dismiss, and intervene. As embodying the moral values of the fraternity in themselves, the ministers are to listen, lead, inspire, visit, create vision, and exemplify a particular and spiritual concern for each person.

Significantly, the questionnaires indicated that the stresses and strains of living in a borderland of conflicting expectations was taking its toll on religious self-identity. Given the social context, these pastoral leaders seemed to be experiencing intellectual and emotional turmoil giving rise to feelings of confusion, fear, anger, inadequacy, apathy, and violation. Since most of the leaders had been raised in an environment that defined the religious life as a "state of perfection" marked by moral exactness, clear roles, separation from the world, and sharply delineated expectations, they could not help but ask the questions: What does it mean to be a Franciscan leader today? How can the demands of office be reconciled with the inherited self-definition of a minister? Are leadership and religious vocation antithetical? Is it possible for a Franciscan *servant* to exercise *power*? Conflict and power began to be linked with feelings of guilt and sin.

Traditional answers based on clear-cut ascetical and institutional interpretations of the *Rule* and Francis's own biography hardly seemed adequate to carry the freight of experience.[5] As a result of these questions, the conference designers presented a series of workshops which attempted to address the underlying issues. Such topics as "Social and Psychological Narcissism," "Contemplative Prayer," "Discernment of Spirits," "Creating New Leaders," and "Strategies of Group Solidarity" gave evidence of the interplay between culture and the shifting religious experience of the Franciscan leader.

Since the questionnaire was circulated in 1990, these social tensions and personal reactions have only increased with the debate in the American church over the pastoral for women, the increased awareness of the abuse of children by clergy, and the continued inability of ecclesiastical leadership to make creative institutional adjustments to the changing profile of the people of God.[6] Recently, social historians have indicated the broader cultural dimensions of these conflicts and now refer to a common state of "culture wars" or a "culture of victimization."[7] The situation is exacerbated by the internal Franciscan argument over the place of the evangelical life in the church.[8] What is needed, it seems, is a spirituality for a conflictual world, a vision of the religious tradition that is able to assimilate and creatively structure the experience of the pastoral leader towards his or her religious identity. It is in this context that the question arises for the Franciscan: Does our tradition have any resources to offer to the pastoral leader who lives from within the experience of conflict?

2. The Critical Retrieval of our Spiritual Tradition

Fortunately for Franciscans, a major sea change has taken place in medieval scholarship that allows both for a critical retrieval of the tradition and the construction of a bridge between the religious experience of Francis and Clare and that of our own times. The work of Cajetan Esser (1978) on Francis and Ignacio Omaechevarria (1970)

---

[5] Esser, 1977: I, 2.
[6] National Conference of Catholic Bishops, 1992; Chinnici, 1994.
[7] Hunter, 1992; Schlesinger, 1992; Sykes, 1992; May, 1972.
[8] Aschenbrenner, 1986; Chinnici, 1987.

on Clare have defined this generation of Franciscans as the first to have at their disposal scholarly editions of the founders' writings.[9] In addition, a host of American and European historians have begun to redefine the interpretative structures of the early medieval religious experience.[10] Particularly significant is the research influencing our understanding of the deeper religious roots and presuppositions of Francis and Clare in the desert tradition of early monasticism and in the pastoral vision of Gregory the Great.[11] Keeping pace with experience, scholarship seems to be providing a new perspective on the sources which would allow contemporary Franciscans to recover *their own identity* within their own *tradition*.

When this scholarship is applied to our modern dilemma of conflicting expectations and the intellectual and emotional loss of moorings involved in pastoral leadership, many areas of concern arise. This essay will examine two of them: 1) What was the basic grammar or structure of the personal experience and pastoral project of Francis? 2) How did Francis and Clare experience the relationship between sanctity, office, and power in the church? Although a thorough exploration of these areas is not possible, perhaps the following indications may be of some help in our situation.

Conflict and the Structure of Pastoral Experience

Throughout his life, Francis experienced considerable tension, even conflict, between the eremitical and apostolic dimensions of his life. The encounter with John of Saint Paul when Francis first went to Rome indicates that he located his own personal religious experience and project on the margins of the dominant social and ecclesiastical options for holiness.[12] The discernment of this evangelical option continued in his consultation with Sylvester and Clare[13] and embodied itself in the inherent tension between brothers who were "prayers, preachers, laborers," or, more juridically, in *The Rule for*

---

[9] Armstrong, 1982, 1988.

[10] Bynum, 1987; Erickson, 1976; LeGoff, 1988; Moore, 1987; Vauchez, 1993; Kselman, 1991.

[11] Brown, 1978; Burton-Christie, 1993; Gould, 1993; Pennington, 1976; Rousseau, 1971; Dagens, 1977; Straw, 1988; Catry, 1973; Markus, 1985.

[12] *1 Cel*:33.

[13] *SP* 16; *LM* 12.1.

Hermitages and *The Later Rule*.[14] Although he reflects later developments in the order, Bonaventure also gives eloquent testimony to a
personal dilemma between the traditional ideal of sanctity (the her-
mit devoted to prayer) and the work of a pastoral preacher that
Francis never resolved: "He discussed this problem with the friars
over a number of days, but he could not make up his mind which
course of action he should choose as being more pleasing to Christ.
The spirit of prophecy had enabled him to penetrate the deepest
secrets, but he was unable to solve his own difficulty satisfactorily."[15]
It is significant that, according to Celano, Francis experienced the
stigmata in the context of this same troubling issue.[16] In other words,
his lifelong project of identification with Christ, come to bodily
expression on La Verna, was located in the conflictual cultural matrix
established both socially and personally between the apostolic
necessity of preaching and the desire to be one with God.[17]

In addition to the basic biographical tradition, Francis's own
writings give witness to the fundamental conflicts at the heart of his
spiritual quest. A good example can be taken from the opening
words of the *Testament*:

> And when I left them, that which seemed bitter to me was changed
> into sweetness of soul and body; and afterward, I lingered a little
> and left the world.[18]

Historians correctly see the phrase "left the world" as technical-
ly implying entrance into a religious and penitential form of life.[19]
But it is also significant to analyze Francis's own understanding of
the word "world." For him, it implies breaking interiorly and exteri-
orly from the world of the merchant. This "world" is the world of his
father, the world he carries around in his own flesh and the world
which he must engage continually in the course of preaching
penance and shaping a "rule and life," his pastoral project. In other
words, he lives daily with the conflicts of the "world."

The word "world" occurs in several key passages in the writings
of Francis and is linked with the phrase "care and anxiety."

---

[14] *RegNB* 17.5.
[15] *LM* 13.1-3.
[16] *1 Cel* 91.
[17] Sorrell, 1988: III.
[18] *Test* 3.
[19] Esser, 1970: pp. 204-208; Desbonnets, 1988: p. 12.

1. ...and bodily serve the *world* by the desires of the flesh, the *cares and anxieties* of this *world*, and the preoccupations of this life.[20]

2. The Lord commands us in the gospel: Watch, be on your guard against all malice and greed. Guard yourselves against the preoccupations of this *world* and the *cares* of this life.[21]

3. At the same time I admonish and exhort the brothers in the Lord Jesus Christ that they beware of all pride, vainglory, envy, avarice, *cares and worries* of this *world*, detraction and complaint.[22]

In the context of Francis's social experience, "world" meant the "world of the merchant," a world that had deeply entered into his own heart. As the studies of Lester Little (1975) and Jacques LeGoff (1978) have argued, this world of the merchant, symbolically represented by money, was intimately related to the destruction of traditional relationships through lying, manipulation, avarice, and the use of others for one's own reward.

Given this economic and social context, it would have been natural for Francis to focus on those Latin Vulgate texts that connect "world" and "care and anxiety" with the "lure of riches" and "inordinate desires." Thus, Matthew 13:22, which is commented upon by Francis in the *Earlier Rule* (22.12-17): "That which fell among thorns are those who hear the word of God, yet anxiety and the worries of this world and the lure of riches and other inordinate desires come in to choke the word and they remain without fruit." Also, when the *Earlier Rule* discusses "begging alms" and how the friars are to react in the common situation of dealing with other people in the midst of suffering famine, Francis refers to Luke 21:34: "Be on your guard so that your hearts are not weighed down wilth dissipation and drunkenness and the worries of this life...."[23] The *Testament* interprets how Francis and the brothers are to react when encountering in the course of their pastoral project "pitiful priests of this world,"[24] presumably those trapped in the "lure of riches" and other "inordinate desires." The *exemplum* for the type of behavior to be avoided is given is the *Second Letter to the Faithful*, which describes the death of the merchant, a member of those who "bodily serve the world by the desires

---

[20] *EpFid* II.65.
[21] *RegNB* 8.1-2.
[22] *RegB* 10.7.
[23] *RegNB* 9.14.
[24] *Test* 7.

of the flesh, the cares and anxieties of this world and the preoccupations of this life."[25]

The remedy to the "cares and anxieties" of this world is the
virtue of poverty, living "without anything of one's own." Thus
Francis admonishes his followers, "Holy poverty destroys the desire
of riches and avarice and the cares of this world."[26] The *Admonitions*
and other writings indicate that the practice of this virtue, closely
connected with the free exchange of love between God and people in
society, was a continual struggle for Francis and his companions. The
experience of conflict associated with the dispositions and world of
the merchant touched all those things which Francis associated with
his pastoral project: the office of service in the order[27]; relationships
between brothers[28]; dealings with seculars in the course of pastoral
care, work, preaching, greeting violent situations with peace, and
begging[29]; posture towards the representatives of the church[30]; and
prayer.[31] Instead of the "cares and anxieties of this world," Francis's
project became, as he indicates in the *Form of Life* for Clare, the discovery of an experience of God issuing in a "loving care and special
solicitude" between people.[32] In the biblical world of the medieval
such a project could hardly have been divorced from that described
by the apostle Paul in 2 Corinthians 11:23-29, and summarized in the
phrase "my anxiety for all the churches" (v. 28).[33]

All of this biographical and personal material indicates that the
basic structure of Francis's personal religious project and experience,
the "what to do shown him by the Lord,"[34] was one of "leaving the
world" only so as to encounter it and to struggle with the exterior
values and interiorized dispositions of the culture of the merchant.
The grace of God led him into conflict. This struggle occurred, as the

---

[25] *II EpFid* 65.
[26] *SalVirt* 7.
[27] *Adm* IV.
[28] *Adm* XI.
[29] *Adm* XV, XVII, XVIII, XX.
[30] *Adm* XXVI.
[31] *RegNB* 22.
[32] Vs. 2.
[33] For an interesting commentary on the phrase "care and solicitude" see
Aelred of Rievaulx, *Spiritual Friendship*, translated by Mary Eugenia Laker,
S.S.N.D., Kalamazoo, Michigan: Cistercian Publications, 1977, 2. pp. 49-54.
[34] *Test* 14.

sources indicate, both when he was with others and when he was alone. His vocation was to embrace on an anthropological level the socially irreconcilable eremitical and apostolic alternatives. Such a project placed his spiritual quest on the margins of the inherited avenues to holiness. Although Francis continually tried to short-circuit the battle, this conflict was an inherent component of his relationship to God, his spiritual self-definition and, in his evangelical life, the only avenue to transformation into Christ.[35] In a very definite sense, this structure to his experience placed him squarely within the spiritual inheritance of Gregory the Great, and it is in reflecting briefly on that heritage that the contemporary significance of Francis's experience for pastoral leadership can be more deeply discovered.

The Inheritance of Gregory the Great

Recently historians have analyzed the structure of Gregory the Great's spirituality to consist of a system of contraries running through the earthly pilgrim's experience of life. Departing from the Augustinian dichotomies between the secular and sacred, Gregory imaged both church and believers as people who had "absorbed earthly power" into their being; the line did not exist between church and "world" but between the true and the false Christians, those feigned brothers "who conform outwardly with the faith of her truly humble sons, but from whose sins she now suffers."[36] In Gregory's world the boundaries are fluid, the visible and invisible intertwined. His religious experience is thus one of alternation between interiority and exteriority, spirituality and carnality, beauty and frailty, permanence and change, grace and sin—all dimensions of a single life. The very nature of these conflicts is under the providence of God, and thus body and soul are united in a relationship of complemen-

---

[35] The tension between the eremitical and apostolic ideals also permeated the life and spirituality of Clare and could be analyzed through an examination of her notions of enclosure and martyrdom, and in her relationship to the city of Assisi. See Marco Bartoli, *Clare of Assisi*, translated by Sister Frances Teresa, O.S.C., Cambridge: The University Press, 1993.

[36] Markus, 1985: p. 93; Dagens, 1977: II, p.1.

tarity and interdependence, like two poles of a magnet, or two athletes each of whose struggle makes the other more developed.[37] In a telling passage, anticipating both the conflict and the resolution of Francis himself, Gregory writes:

> So, there are those, who, endowed, as we have said, with great gifts, in their eagerness for the pursuit of contemplation only, decline to be of service to the neighbor by preaching; they love to withdraw in quietude and desire to be alone for meditation. Now, if they are judged strictly on their conduct, they are certainly guilty in proportion to the public service which they were able to afford. Indeed, what disposition of mind is revealed in him, who could perform conspicuous public benefit on coming to his task, but prefers his own privacy to the benefit of others, seeing that the Only-Begotten of the Supreme Father came forth from his Father into our midst, that he might benefit many.[38]

In this framework, Carole Straw argues, Gregory's saint is an ambassador between two worlds, a just penitent who constantly struggles to integrate contemplation with action, humility with authority, charism with obedience, contemplation with action, control with adaptation, office with the personal guidance of the Holy Spirit. The life of pastoral care is undertaken as a sacrifice of obedience in the following of Christ. The sins it occasions make opportunity for growth in fear and love, the twin poles of contemplation. For Gregory,

> Life is a trial whose moments of perfection are continually overthrown by sin, yet such imperfection is accommodated as a lesson of humility, so making one even more virtuous. If contemplation cannot be absolute, it may be possessed in degrees, and one may make progress. If sin is inevitable, even virtue cannot be performed without repentance of one's sins, and this ensures the acceptability of one's offering. All life mixes failures and success, light and darkness.[39]

Life in the Spirit here becomes a series of advances and reversals, a mix of adversity and success, a school of sorrow and joy, a battlefield between the impossible mix of vice and virtue, a constant growth marked by purification and penance.

---

[37] Straw, 1988.
[38] Gregory, 1950: p. 31.
[39] Straw, 1988: p. 231.

Gregory the Great's influence permeated the monastic Middle Ages and influenced Francis and Clare.[40] When Francis's experience and writings are examined from the perspective of this spiritual tradition, a similar structure of alternation and conflict leading to a deeper following of Christ appears. His writings are filled with the interplay of simultaneously existing opposites: bitterness and sweetness, inner and outer, spirit and letter, freedom and obedience, work and prayer, virtue and vice, sin and grace, rule and service, gratitude and penance. Nowhere is this clearer than in the description of the human person in Chapter 23 of the *Earlier Rule*: "He has given and gives to each one of us [our] whole body, [our] whole soul, and [our] whole life. He created and redeemed us, and will save us by his mercy alone. He did and does every good thing for us [who are] miserable and wretched, rotten and foul-smelling, ungrateful and evil."[41]

Straw in her study of Gregory the Great has labeled this tradition of the coinherence of opposites as the pursuit of "perfection within imperfection." Its paradoxical structure opens the door to a deeply incarnational spirituality, one well suited to Francis's own reaction to the Catharist heresy of his day.[42] From the perspective of the contemporary pastoral leader, this shapes the spiritual quest like a cylinder, not a line, like a drama, not a syllogism. The Gregorian framework provides a spiritual center for an increasingly conflictual religious and secular culture in search of *peace, tranquility, and justice*. It allows the Creator to move in the coexistence of contraries and to work through their interaction towards a goal yet to be realized. Franciscan identity can be rediscovered for a pastoral leader living in a conflictual world.

---

[40] Leclercq, 1961; Casey, 1988. The French editors of the writings of Francis and Clare also find evidence of Gregory's impact on them. See Marie-France Becker, Jean-Francois Godet, Thaddée Matura, éditeurs, *Claire d'Assise, Écrits*, Paris: Éditions du Cerf, 1985, p. 210; Théophile Desbonnets, Jean-François Godet, Thaddée Matura, Damien Vorreux, éditeurs, *François d'Assise, Écrits*, Paris: Éditions du Cerf, 1981, p. 359. It is significant, I think, that Bonaventure cites Gregory in his treatise on pastoral leadership, *St. Bonaventure: Opuscula, Second Series, The Works of Saint Bonaventure*, translated by José de Vinck, Paterson, New Jersey: St. Anthony Guild Press, 1966, p. 276.

[41] *RegNB*: 23.8; *Test.*: 1-3; *Adm.*: III, IV, VII, XVII, XX, XXVII.

[42] Esser, 1976: p. 2.

Power, Sanctity, and Office in the Church

Analyzed from a certain perspective, the writings of Francis and Clare indicate that they lived at a time when the functions of leadership—and its symbols of *office, power, authority*—had become separated from sanctity and the operations of the Holy Spirit (symbolized by the "gospel"). Certainly the ecclesiological problem of authority posed by the lay movements was partially predicated upon people's disgust with the lives and operations of the clergy and the incompatibility between lay and clerical culture.[43] In many instances this "moral revolt" over the exercise and practice of authority—the split between office, word, and example—occasioned the rise of heretical movements such as the Humiliati, Cathari, and Waldensians.[44] How Francis and Clare grappled with this ecclesial context indicates a great deal about the place of power and authority in their religious experience.

In a fashion similar to the conflict between his apostolic and eremitical vocations, Francis also experienced the ecclesiastical problem of the "hypocrisy of power" as cutting through his own heart. Rather than short-circuiting the contraries, his pastoral project became, then, the uniting of office and gospel witness. The *Anonymous of Perugia* (37b) captured the heart of his endeavor: "Likewise, Saint Francis used to give admonitions, reprimands and prescription, as he thought best, having first consulted the Lord. But everything that he put into words for them, he first demonstrated in action with tender affection." This short passage associates images and actions traditionally connected with office and power with the gospel values of prayer, interiority, and example. The *Admonitions* consistently interpret the gospel from within the experience of contraries, thus indicating that such an association was a continual project for the brothers, a component part of their evangelical way of life. Several examples can be cited:

1. Commenting on Luke 14:33, "He who does not renounce everything he possesses, cannot be my disciple," Francis insists on both renunciation and self-possession: "But if the prelate should

---

[43] Erickson, 1976: III; Fortini, 1981: I; Manselli, 1988: I; Vauchez, 1993.
[44] Wakefield, 1991; Bolton, 1972; Gonnet, 1980.

command something contrary to his conscience, although [the subject] does not obey him, still he should not abandon him."[45]

2. Commenting on Matthew 20:28, "I did not come to be served but to serve," Francis both acknowledges "those who are placed over others" (*praelatus*) and pushes them towards the disposition of washing the feet of the brothers (John 13:5).[46]

3. Commenting on 2 Corinthians 3:6, "The letter kills but the Spirit gives life," Francis applies the passage to those engaged in preaching, challenging them to unite word and example.[47]

Combinations like these occur throughout Francis's own writings and are deeply embedded in his relationship with his brothers and sisters. Although he himself called no one "father" or "master," a position certainly implying authority and precedence, he certainly accepted the reality of the title from his sons and daughters and tried to unite its social implications of ruling with the values of the softer title of "mother."[48] The combination of the titles "brother," "servant," and "minister," in the *Rule* 10.1 indicate the same experience. Nowhere is the underlying dynamic surfaced more clearly than in *A Letter to the Entire Order*, in which Francis refers to Brother A, who is also general minister, and "lord"; to all ministers, priests, and custodians, who are "brothers"; to "brothers who are priests." Clearly, what is being presented is a new image of authority, not the rejection of power but its proper interface with the gospel.

Clare furnishes an even better example of the pastoral project to create unity between power, office, and sanctity. She refers to herself as "mother"—a title implying compassion, tenderness, nurture, and protection. Yet she also possesses an office, that of being "abbess," a title that implies management, competency, self-discipline, assertiveness, independence, authority. As abbess and mother, Clare receives obedience, grants permissions, assigns manual work, admonishes, punishes, imposes penances, corrects and instructs, writes a rule, argues with the pope, consoles, cries, encourages, serves, and listens.[49] The struggle to create an image of the proper use of power was part and parcel of her evangelical self-identity.

---

[45] *Adm* III.
[46] *Adm* IV.
[47] *Adm* VII.
[48] *LP* 17, 23, 65; *1 Cel* 116-117; *TestCl*; *EpLeo*.
[49] See *Test* 19-20, 24; *Letter to Agnes* 4.33; *IVLCl* 33; *RCl*; *Rule* 1.5, 4.4, 5.6, 8.3, 9,1,12; *Process of Canonization* 8.3. 4.4, 5.6, 8.3, 9,1,12; *CP* 8.3.

Recent studies indicate that this project of Francis and Clare to unite the inner and outer, word and example, power and weakness, authority and service, prelate and subject, priest and brother belongs well within the context of the spiritual inheritance of the early Middle Ages. Peter Brown (1978) and Philip Rousseau (1971) have pioneered ground-breaking studies on the social and ecclesial significance of the ascetic ideal of the early monks. Most important, Graham Gould (1993) argues that many of the ascetical disciplines of the desert monks were designed to bridge the troubling gap between the necessity of acting as an "abba" and the duty of surrender of one's own will. Such a tension led to an emphasis on teaching by example, personal self-disclosure, solidarity in the experience of temptation, long-suffering, silence, and a constant grappling with issues of anger, scandal, and judgment. In an age of social dislocation when power and authority were being abused, Gregory the Great followed in this same tradition. He wished to unite status with merit, and office with humility, charity to others, and obedience to God. The dilemma is presented well in the opening pages of the *Dialogues* (I.1):

> The contact with worldly men and their affairs, which is a necessary part of my duties as bishop, has left my soul defiled with earthly activities. I am so distracted with external occupations in my concern for the people that even when my spirit resumes its striving after the interior life it always does so with less vigor. Then, as I compare what I have lost with what I must now endure, the contrast only makes my present lot more burdensome.

The solution for Gregory, as it would be later for Francis and Clare, lay in union with the redemptive power and suffering of Christ; 1 Peter 2:21 and the image of the Good Shepherd provided key texts: "This, in fact, is what you were called to do, because Christ suffered for you and left an example for you to follow in his steps."[50] Last, it should be noted that at the time of Francis and Clare, the spirituality of the canons regular made teaching by word and example a centerpiece of reforming efforts, and Caroline Walker Bynum argues persuasively for the combination of values represented by the terms *father, teacher, lord, mother* in the Cistercian sources for that period.[51] Clearly, today's Franciscan pastoral leader has a long tradition that

---

[50] Straw, 1988: p. 159; Lapsanski, 1976: III; Esser, 1963: II.1.
[51] Bynum, 1979.

sees the unity between holiness, office, and power as a significant dimension of the evangelical project in the church and world.

3. Concluding Remarks

In this essay, I have tried very briefly to indicate some lines along which contemporary Franciscans could develop a spirituality for pastoral leadership in a conflictual and confusing situation. It is my hope that through these and other examples we can begin more easily to relate our own experience with the rich tradition of our predecessors. Having been a participant in this seminar on leadership, it is clear to me that many of the situations in which pastoral workers find themselves are indeed deeply conflictual. The remarks of William McConville on "ecclesiadicy" have indicated how pertinent a theology of the tragic might be to our contemporary experience of church. Helen Rolfson has focused on the oftentimes conflictual relationships between men and women. Tears and compassion as essential components of religious experience and ministry point towards a rereading of our own spiritual tradition beyond the categories associated with the "perfect society" or the perfectionist hagiography of Christendom.

Certainly, a major task of reconstruction has begun, but it has only just begun. In conclusion, I would like simply to indicate a few of the future directions for research and application, which will themselves evolve as our experience unfolds.

1. Given the major advances in early medieval scholarship represented by the research of Brown, Straw, and Bynum, to name a few, it seems that our understanding of the early sources needs to be reimagined so as to incorporate a more relational and creative view of the evangelical life. This would include both a better analysis of how the project of Francis and Clare developed because of the continuous interaction between society, the church, and their gospel ideal of holiness, and a deeper understanding of the mutual relationship between the sisters and brothers and how the relationship itself was a constituent part of their project. To approach the sources from the perspective of their social meaning and context would help to form a bridge between contemporary Franciscan experience and the tradition itself. It would remove our pedagogies of formation from the heights of abstraction, so often associated with the older more scholastic ascetical manuals, and make contemporary

Franciscans the living carriers of the tradition's meaning. To accomplish this task we would need to establish training centers and programs for formators, as the Society of Jesus has done for many years, and make explicit our task of reinterpreting Franciscan spirituality into a contemporary culture.

2. Clearly, a deeper Christological focus needs to be developed in order to fully comprehend the radical nature of Francis and Clare's incarnationalism, so much so that the interplay between fragility, sin, limitation, and grace enter into the very self-definition of the pastoral leader and his or her task in society and church. This incarnationalism must be systematic and rooted in a deep praxis of fraternal life and personal and communal prayer. In our own approach, we need to move our communal discussions off of the classical issues of the practice of poverty and tensions with institutionalization to the deeper arena of "how is our life making credible in the contemporary world the experience of God's love for us in Christ?" While other, more institutional charisms by the power and force of their presence in society are more compatible with a typology of Christendom and might offer attractive public alternatives, our own witness will be focused on the simple dignity of all creatures made in the image of Christ. This Christological center will be more readily compatible with our own people's experience, in so many situations, of *minoritas*.

3. In our pedagogies of formation, the Franciscan ascetical tradition needs to be reexamined through the lens of the desert fathers and mothers and the spirituality of Gregory the Great. Once this tradition is interfaced with the sociology, political dynamics, economics, and history of the early movement, then the charism comes alive in its original meaning. Such a re-study would have major implications for how we talk about and practice prayer, the vows, and fraternity/sorority.

REFERENCES

Anonymous of Perugia, "Anonymous of Perugia," in New Round Table 36 (1983).

Armstrong, Regis J., and Ignatius C. Brady, editors, *Francis and Clare: The Complete Works*. New York: Paulist, 1982.

Armstrong, Regis J., editor, *Clare of Assisi: Early Documents*. New York: Paulist, 1986.

Aschenbrenner, George A., "Active and Monastic: Two Apostolic Lifestyles," pp. 653d-668 in Review for Religious (September-October) (1986).

Bazelaire, Louis de, "Connaissance de soi," in *Dictionnaire de Spiritualité*, II, Paris, 1953.

Bernard of Clairvaux, *Song of Songs I*, translated by Kilian Walsh, O.C.S.O., in *The Works of Bernard of Clairvaux*, II, Kalamazoo, Michigan: Cistercian Publications, 1979.

Bolton, Brenda, "Innocent III's Treatment of the Humiliati," pp. 73-82 in *Popular Belief and Practice*, edited by G. J. Cuming and Derek Baker. Cambridge: University Press, 1972.

Brown, Peter, *The Making of Late Antiquity*. Cambridge, Massachusetts: Harvard University Press, 1978.

Burton-Christie, Douglas, *The Word in the Desert, Scripture, and the Quest for Holiness in Early Christian Monasticism*. Oxford: Oxford University Press, 1993.

Bynum, Caroline Walker, *Docere Verbo et Exemplo: An Aspect of Twelfth-Century Spirituality*. Atlanta: Scholars Press, 1979.

——, *Jesus as Mother: Studies in the Spirituality of the High Middle Ages*. Berkeley, California: University of California Press, 1982.

——, *Holy Feast and Holy Fast: The Religious Significance of Food to Medieval Women*. Berkeley: University of California Press, 1987.

Casey, Michael, *Athirst for God: Spiritual Desire in Bernard of Clairvaux's Sermons on the Song of Songs*. Kalamazoo, Michigan: Cistercian Publications, 1988.

Catry, Patrick, "Amour du monde et amour de dieu chez Saint Grégoire le grand," pp. 253-275 in Studia Monastica 15 (1972).

Chinnici, Joseph, "Evangelical and Apostolic Tensions," in *Our Franciscan Charism Today*. New Jersey: Fame, 1987.

————, "One Pastoral Response to Abuse," pp. 4-8 in America 170, (January 15-22) (1994).

Dagens, Claude, *Saint Grégoire le grand, culture et experience chretiennes*. Paris: Études augustiniennes, 1977.

Desbonnets, Théophile, *From Intuition to Institution: the Franciscans*, translated by Paul Duggan and Jerry du Charme. Chicago: Franciscan Herald Press, 1988.

Erickson, Carolly, *The Medieval Vision: Essays in History and Perception*. New York: Oxford University Press, 1987.

Esser, Cajetan, *Repair My House*, translated by Micael D. Meilach. Chicago: Franciscan Herald Press, 1963.

————, *Origins of the Franciscan Order*, translated by Aedan Daly and Irina Lynch. Chicago: Franciscan Herald Press, 1970.

————, "Francisco de Asis y los cataros de su tiempo," pp. 145-172 in Selecciones de Franciscanismo V (1976).

————, *Rule and Testament of St. Francis: Conferences to the Modern Followers of Francis*. Chicago: Franciscan Herald Press, 1977.

————, *Opuscula Sancti Patris Assisiensis*. Grottaferrata: 1978.

Fortini, Arnaldo, *Francis of Assisi*, translated by Helen Moak. New York: Crossroad, 1981.

Gilson, Étienne, *The Mystical Theology of Saint Bernard*, translated by A.H.C. Downes. London: Sheed and Ward, 1940.

Gould, Graham, *The Desert Fathers on Monastic Community*. Oxford: Clarendon Press, 1993.

Gonnet, Giovanni, "La Donna Presso i Movimenti Pauperistico-Evangelici," pp.103-129 in *Movimento Religioso Femminile e Franciscanismo nel Secolo XIII* Atti del VII Covegno Internazionale Assisi, 11-13 Ottobre 1979, Assisi. (1980).

Gregory the Great, *Pastoral Care*, translated and annotated by Henry Davis. Westminster, London: The Newman Press, 1950.

————, *Dialogues*, translated by Odo John Zimmerman. New York: Fathers of the Church Inc., 1959.

Hunter, James D., *Culture Wars: The Struggle to Control the Family, Art, Education, Law, & Politics in America*. New York: Basic Books, 1992.

Kselman, Thomas, editor, *Belief in History: Innovative Approaches to European and American Religion*. Notre Dame: University of Notre Dame Press, 1991.

Lapsanski, Duane, *The First Franciscans and the Gospel*. Chicago: Franciscan Herald Press, 1976.

Leclercq, Jean, *The Love of Learning and the Desire for God: A Study of Monastic Culture*. New York: Fordham University Press, 1961.

LeGoff, Jacques, *The Medieval Imagination*, translated by Arthur Goldhammer. Chicago: University of Chicago Press, 1988.

Little, Lester K., "Evangelical Poverty, The New Money Economy and Violence," pp. 11-16 in *Poverty in the Middle Ages*, edited by David Flood. Werl/Westf: Dietrich-Coelde-Verlag, 1975.

Manselli, Raoul, *St. Francis of Assisi*, translated by Paul Duggan. Chicago: Franciscan Herald Press, 1988.

Markus, R. A., "The Sacred and the Secular: From Augustine to Gregory the Great," pp. 85-96 in Journal of Theological Studies 36 (1985).

May, Rollo, *Power and Innocence: A Search for Sources of Violence*. New York: Norton, 1972.

Moore, R. I., *The Formation of A Persecuting Society*. Oxford: Basil Blackwell, 1987.

National Conference of Catholic Bishops, "One in Christ Jesus," Origins 22 (December 31)(1992).

————, "Document on Women's Concerns Debated," Origins 22 (December 3)(1992).

————, "Future of Religous Orders in the United States, Origins 22 (September 24)(1992).

Omaechevarria, Ignacio, editor, *Escritos de Santa Clara y documentos contemporaneos*. Madrid, 1970.

Pennington, M. Basil, editor, *One Yet Two: Monastic Tradition, East and West*. Kalamazoo, Michigan: Cistercian Publications, 1976.

Rousseau, Philip, "The Spiritual Authority of the 'Monk-Bishop': Eastern Elements in Some Western Hagiography of the ?Fourth and Fifth Centuries," pp. 381-419 in Journal of Theological Studies 22 (1971).

Schlesinger, Arthur M., Jr., *The Disuniting of America: Reflections on a Multicultural Society*. New York: Norton, 1992.

Sorrell, Roger D., *St. Francis of Assisi and Nature, Tradition and Innovation in Western Christian Attitudes Towards the Environment*. Oxford: Oxford University Press. 1988.

Stewart, Columba, "Radical honesty about self: the practice of the desert fathers," pp. 25-39 in Sobornost 12/1, pp. 143-156 in Sobornost 12/2 (1990).

Straw, Carole, *Gregory the Great: Perfection in Imperfection*. Berkeley: University of California Press, 1988.

Sykes, Charles J., *A Nation of Victims: The Decay of the American Character*. New York: St. Martin's Press, 1992.

Vauchez, André, *The Laity in the Middle Ages: Religious Beliefs and Devotional Practices*, translated by Margery J. Schneider. Notre Dame: University of Notre Dame Press, 1993.

Wakefield, Walter L., and Austin P. Evans, editors, *Heresies of the High Middle Ages*. New York: Columbia University Press, 1991.

12
The Franciscan Tradition:
Strangers and Pilgrims

Mary Meany

While this essay originates in my experience at Siena College, it has become clear to me that there are themes in that experience which resonate in the larger world of Holy Name Province, indeed, in the larger world of Franciscan ministry. At Siena I have come to value the Franciscan tradition in ways that may be useful as we all move "Toward 2000." On the one hand, Siena College may stand as a microcosmic example of collaborative ministry, as a microcosm of friars working out their identity as ministers in situations where they are not in control, in milieus which they once owned, from which they have not withdrawn their corporate presence, but in which they now occupy a very different place. On the other hand, Siena may be a case study of ways the resources of the Franciscan tradition can shape these milieus, can enrich and enliven a diverse community, can challenge its members to conversion and proclamation.

On the one hand, I am going to argue that involvement in a liberal arts college is a valuable ministry; on the other hand, I am going to argue that there are resources within the Franciscan tradition that are valuable for college life. Exploring those resources in the context of a liberal arts college may lead to reflection on other ways those resources may be explored, how they work in other areas. This tradition is rich, lively, and valuable; it must be embodied in the presence of those who live the rule, who commit themselves to the fullness of the Franciscan tradition as the founders envisioned it.[1]

At Siena I have been inspired and required to think seriously about what it means to be "strangers and pilgrims, ... who during the day give themselves over to the active life of the apostolate..., at night return to their hermitage or withdraw into solitude...."[2] This quotation has become almost a mantra for me, giving me a perspec-

---

[1] The question of whether the Franciscan tradition is a unique resource, whether a college whose identity is Franciscan differs from a college whose identity is Jesuit or humanistic is not, I think, the significant question. Siena's Franciscan tradition is a given; the significant question is what that *tradition* means, can and should mean, for our *identity* as a liberal arts college in the Franciscan tradition.

[2] "Letter of Jacques de Vitry, 1220," *Omnibus*, p. 1608. *RegB*, ch. 6.

tive on my life at this college. As strangers and pilgrims, members of a college in the Franciscan tradition carry on a process of reconciliation and challenge in the larger society. Their active apostolate is the creation of an academic community shaped by respect for the individual and accountability to the community. The soul of a college, the principle that gives a college its life as a college, is learning, which is both an active apostolate and a contemplative life. Bonaventure's description of Francis's dividing his time between working for his neighbor's benefit and seeking places of solitude "where he could spend his time more freely with the Lord and cleanse himself of any dust that might have adhered to him from his involvement with men"[3] holds a lesson for all of us, but perhaps particularly for those of us who say the pursuit of learning is our job. Reflection, being still, is a necessity if we are to continue learning.

Franciscan Spirituality and the Intellectual Life

But what makes the Franciscan tradition valuable for a college is not only the balance of active and contemplative life. It is precisely because the Franciscan tradition is a spirituality, a way of viewing the world and living in the world that takes human knowledge and experience seriously, takes the world seriously, while knowing that neither the human nor the worldly reality is just what it seems, because it is a spirituality, it is a valuable resource for a college. We might use Zachary Hayes's language about theology in his essay "Franciscan Tradition as a Wisdom Tradition," to describe the intellectual project of a college in the Franciscan tradition: it uses methods that are inquisitive and argumentative in order to seek understanding. That is characteristic of any liberal arts college, but the Franciscan liberal arts college makes room for the importance of wisdom in intellectual life. The academic community itself, then, pursues wisdom. To paraphrase Hayes: The framework of learning in this college involves both intellect and will, both knowledge and love. Let me underline that this is not a statement now about philosophy and theology, but about liberal education. Because we are talking about a liberal arts college, we must also say that the endeavor of seeking wisdom means learning to articulate that wisdom. Conversation in a liberal arts college is carried on in an academic voice that should be clear, literate in the sources of the tradition, free of jargon. It will require careful reading and listening and a real con-

---

[3] *LM*, ch. 13.

cern to communicate; it will require a critical encounter with contemporary culture and a careful analysis clearly spoken. Bonaventure serves as a model here, but so might Bernardine of Siena.

This view of liberal education does not presuppose that every learning enterprise in the college will be illuminated by faith, but it allows room for faith as an integral part of learning. The Franciscan identity of Siena requires men and women of faith who are, in the description of the papal constitution, *Ex corde ecclesiae*, committed to professional excellence "within the framework of a coherent world vision, to [integrate] professional competence and Christian wisdom." In words often used at Siena, the friars are "living reminders" of a spirituality, a way of understanding the world.[4]

The Siena Context

Siena is a liberal arts college founded by the friars of Holy Name Province in 1938. It is now chartered as a private, independent college, but its self-identity is described in the phrase, "a liberal arts college in the Franciscan tradition." The historical unfolding of this transition has been long and complex, rich and painful, but the college has now come to a particularly challenging moment in its history. At this moment, Siena is keenly aware that its vitality, its ability to read and respond to the signs of the times, to meet the needs of its particular students and to empower them to be responsible citizens must be rooted in fidelity to its own tradition. Simultaneously it is aware that as a college it must articulate what that tradition means beyond the presence of the friars, and the memories and customs of senior college members and alumni.

At the same time that Siena is clarifying its sense of its identity, the Holy Name Province in its Refounding Project is clarifying its corporate sense of mission. These two processes can intersect.

The reality is that the Franciscan tradition lives because of the presence in the world of those men and women who live the rule. At Siena, that means that the corporate presence of Holy Name Province is essential if the college is to continue to be a Franciscan presence in the world. Without the friars' public commitment to the college, Siena's Franciscan tradition will become nothing more than a memory or a vague sense

---

[4] See Zachary Hayes, "Reflections on a Franciscan University" for a clear description of the academic and intellectual implications of the Franciscan tradition. His paper was originally delivered at St. Bonaventure University, but is not as specific to that institution as this essay is to Siena.

that it is important to be nice to everyone. It is the friars who live the tradition fully; whatever their personal strengths and weaknesses may be, they are "living reminders" that this tradition is a way of understanding the world as well as a way of living in the world.

As I have had the chance to participate in Holy Name Province's "Refounding through Ministry," I have come to think that the questions which Siena struggles with are questions for Franciscan leadership wherever the friars choose to engage in ministry where they are not in control, to engage in radically collaborative ministry. Although a minority of friars will choose to work in higher education, I have come to think that a liberal arts college like Siena can be a Franciscan presence in the world and that it can be important for Franciscans in other ministries. At first, I focused on the Franciscan tradition as a resource for the college; lately I have come to think of the Franciscan experience in a liberal arts college as a resource for Franciscan pastoral leadership. The Refounding rubric "Partners in Ministry" may seem inadequate for friars who are not sure it expresses their Franciscan life completely, but it does encourage a dialogue which begins in a shared sense of ministry and becomes increasingly reflective and contemplative. The same description applies to the college's ongoing conversations about its Franciscan identity: the process of conversation has been a process of opening up the "conversation circle" and of deepening our understanding of the Franciscan tradition as a way of looking at, criticizing, and appreciating the world we live in. "Good works must follow knowledge," as we read in "Admonition VII." This is often used to denigrate the importance of knowledge. Francis, however, is making a different point here, as he is when he quotes the *Rule* to Anthony, "It pleases me that you teach sacred theology to the brothers as long as ... you 'do not extinguish the Spirit of prayer and devotion.'" The message here is not that knowledge is useless or evil, but that it is incomplete if it does not move one to love and act.[5]

Academe is often accused of being insular and elitist, of depending on the economic and social structures that have allowed it to emerge as a set of "ivory towers." A college with a Franciscan identity, however, cannot be content with internal conversations that

---

[5] Elizabeth Dreyer, "Reclaiming Affectivity in the Liberal Arts Curriculum: Medieval Franciscan Sources," *Liberal Education: Crisis and Franciscan Response*. Papers delivered at Siena College, March 19, 1988. Zachary Hayes makes this point specifically in the context of theology in "Franciscan Tradition as a Wisdom Tradition." See p. 27.

benefit only the participants. While empowering more individuals to participate in college life, it must also remember its mission to empower them to participate in the wider civic life. These men and women should understand the world, should act in the world to transform the world in ways that reflect what I have been calling a Franciscan spirituality. They could learn this other places than in college, but what a college setting requires is learning to speak, to articulate that world view in a thoughtful, intelligible manner. There is a parallel here to Francis's advice in the *Earlier Rule* of how the brothers are to live spiritually among the unbelievers: to give evidence by their life that they are Christians, and then to speak out.[6] Good works, prayer, and devotion must flow from knowledge.

The college can provide a space for contemplation and proclamation of the good news—for considering what the world is, what life should be. This collaborative community committed to learning and to proclaiming what human Christian life should be is the ideal Franciscan college. The Franciscan tradition means pursuing wisdom; means devotion to service; means creating a community in which individuals respect each other and commit themselves to the common good. A college in the Franciscan tradition carries these ideals into the wider world as a challenge, as a call to conversion, to restructuring.

William McConville has described the liberal arts college as a mediating institution, analogous to the church: institutions which bring individuals into the common culture while providing a critique of the culture.[7] That notion of the mediating nature of the liberal arts college, of its simultaneously reconciliatory and critical mission is basic to Franciscan identity. The presence of the friars is significant because they challenge the societal structures and values which alienate and marginalize, which belittle individuals, and because they inherit a tradition of accountability. Franciscan community respects the individual and expects the individual to contribute to the community.

Robert Schreiter contrasts reconciliation with alienation or the condition of being strangers to each other.[8] But the perspective McConville suggests may provide a better angle on the importance of the Franciscan

---

[6] *RegNB*.
[7] McConville, "Franciscan Tradition, the Liberal Arts College, and Society."
[8] Robert Schreiter, 1992: pp. 52-56.

tradition for a liberal arts college. Francis, that man of peace, who preached peace to the Crusaders and the Muslims, to Assisi and Perugia, who wore himself out in the work of reconciliation, rejected his inherited place in the social structures which divided the world into *maiores* and *minores*.[9] Reconciliation among individuals may require alienation from social and political structures.[10] What is valuable in Schreiter's approach, however, is the reminder that what is needed is not a set of strategies or techniques for solving the problems which have brought us to the present cultural and social crisis, but a spirituality, a way of looking at the world, of being in the world.

A college supported by Holy Name Province should make the fruits of that reflection available to the members of the province, as it should also draw on the resources of the province in carrying forward that process of reflection in a complex environment. If Siena is to be a college with a Franciscan identity, it needs the corporate support of the province. If it has that support, it can offer the province an opportunity to be present in the world in a special way. Siena can introduce young men to the friars at a time when these men are making decisions about their lives. Siena can introduce men and women who will marry, work in the world, have families, to a Franciscan world view and can do this in the context of a supportive community.

The Challenge of Diversity

As the college turns its attention increasingly to creating a more diverse college community, new populations will have the opportunity to engage the Franciscan tradition. At the same time, maintaining that tradition will become increasingly complicated. The complications sustaining a clear sense of tradition in a diverse community occupy more and more of the college's attention on the practical level: How do we find ways to pray together that are inclusive but not vapid? How do we establish student life policies which reflect respect for individuals and accountability for the common good? which reflect Catholic moral teaching when there is no consensus about the meaning of that teaching? And on the theoretical level: How do we affirm the Franciscan tradition in its Catholic, integral reality in dialogue with the experiences,

---

[9] Leonardo Boff, *St. Francis: Model of Human Liberation*, demonstrates the radical meaning of Franciscan detachment.

[10] It might be useful to remember that the friars came into the system of higher education very much as outsiders. See William Short, O.F.M., "Shapers of the Tradition: Bonaventure and Scotus."

the traditions of non-Catholic, non-Christian members of the college? How do we make room for a variety of ways of entering into this tradition without losing sight of the fullness of the tradition?

Further, the college is increasingly a presence in the larger community, sponsoring special events, working with community groups, sending members out in volunteer programs and internships. Education no longer means just what goes on in a classroom (if it ever did!). This kind of interaction provides the opportunity to analyze and challenge the structures that shape and express American culture. Siena's location in New York's "Capital District" provides interesting opportunities for community outreach, both for cooperation in addressing urban problems[11] and in reaching out to create a community that reflects the pluralism of American society.[12]

The college is no longer a community with an assumed, shared culture, but it is a community whose *raison d'être* is its work, its ministry. In this situation, the presence of friars in the college, as administrators and staff, as campus ministers, as faculty becomes more important than ever. In whatever area they serve, the friars are expected to function as leaders in the college's attempt to understand and live the Franciscan tradition. On the other hand, entering this college is not escaping the world but joining it. I am always amazed when someone says, "I don't want to teach. I want to work with people." That is the essence of teaching, the essence of college life.

---

[11] Albany is, in some circles, infamous as the crossroads of drug traffic because I-90 and I-87 intersect here. Schenectady is a living example of a city that had a thriving economic base in General Electric, a thriving cultural base in the Italian-American community, and has now to face economic and cultural challenges. Troy is an old industrial stronghold that had a diverse religious and ethnic community. Drugs, violence, dislocation, unemployment, homelessness, failure of family support, and reliance on public welfare are realities throughout the region.

[12] The capital district can claim an old African-American community, Christian and Muslim, composed of descendants of free persons of color, of slaves, of Haitian and other Caribbean immigrants; a new Muslim community composed of several ethnic traditions, including African-American Muslims; a small but affluent Hindu community; a wide spectrum of Jewish congregations; a Christian community composed of high church Anglicans, new Evangelical groups, including a nationally important Presbyterian congregation, Eastern Orthodox communities, and a Roman Catholic community comprising Asians, African-Americans, Latinos, Irish, Italians, and Eastern Europeans.

Siena has drawn from all of these populations in recruiting students, faculty, and staff. It has worked with leaders from all of these communities in creating programs. It has sent volunteers and interns into all of these communities.

As the college has grown as a college, it has become increasingly diverse. The stories and customs that constitute part of the college's sense of its Franciscan tradition are no longer easily passed on and naturally assimilated by new members of the college. Diversity is a vague word; specifically, at Siena, it means that members of the college come from a variety of ethnic and racial and religious and social and economic backgrounds. Most specifically, it means that it is not possible to assume any common culture, much less any familiarity with or investment in Christianity or in the Franciscan tradition. It is in this context that this college has realized that it must focus on its Franciscan tradition. Diversity is also a quality that characterizes the Franciscan tradition. There are numerous anecdotes and proverbs about the difficulty of defining the Franciscan tradition, and it is not uncommon to be told that the very act of defining distorts the tradition. The difficulty seems to be intensified when the tradition is approached in the context of academic and intellectual life. In this context the echoes of Francis's concern that knowledge not interfere with love, that becoming learned not perpetuate the structure of *maiores-minores*, have sometimes been deafening. There are two sets of reasons, then, why it is necessary to focus on the resources within the Franciscan tradition: first, there is confusion about what the tradition can mean in a diverse college community, a confusion that, at least at first, is compounded by introducing the notion of spirituality; second, there is ambiguity about the appropriation of the spirituality rooted in the story of the *poverello*, the *idiota*, by an academic, intellectual community, a college. This college is a place where these problems can be articulated in a way which resonates beyond the college.

College and Community

Retrieval of the Franciscan tradition usually, and for good reason, begins with the historical commitment to building community by attending to the needs of individuals; this element receives explicit attention in virtually all discussions of Franciscan education.[13] A

---

[13] An example of the fruitfulness of the Franciscan respect for individuals is the model which Père Grégoire Girard, O.F.M. Conv., created in his reforms of the Swiss educational system in the nineteenth century. An essential element of this approach was the responsibility students assumed for each other's learning, a responsibility rooted in respect for each other, and a definition of teaching as service by senior members of the school to junior members.

further critical retrieval of the tradition, however, can identify themes or emphases within it that could—and should—shape not only the kind of communal experience specific to a college, that is, academic life, but also the intellectual life, the insight or perspective rooted in the riches of this tradition. The tradition determines ways to deal with personnel questions, questions of community life. It provides a way of knowing and being in the world, a way of reflecting on, of understanding life. Academic life is the rubric under which the questions of community are discussed in this essay. This usage is meant to underscore the reality that college community life is not the same as the life of other communities. The essence of a college is that it is a community whose life should be structured by the common endeavor to teach and to learn, better, by the common endeavor to learn together. Intellectual life is the rubric under which questions of knowing, of reflecting and understanding, are discussed. This usage is meant to underscore the importance of knowing, but the very definition of knowing will be shaped by the Franciscan tradition.

Consideration of collegial community life usually begins with the affirmation of the importance of respect for the individual and of the spirit of *fraternitas*. The ongoing discussion of collaborative ministry, however, opens up another dimension of collegial life that may be even more important as a way of understanding and living out the implications of the Franciscan tradition for creating and maintaining a respectful, supportive academic community. It is, in fact, service to the student population that holds the college together. That service intends to empower students to serve in, to participate in, the complex world of late-twentieth-century America. Understanding collaboration, working together, and defining work as ministry, can be the starting point for consideration of the resources this tradition provides for fostering a healthy, respectful community life.[14]

At Siena, collaborative ministry is the very structure of the community: it is work, ministry, which creates the community. What the college can contribute to the province is the clear sense that our work creates and defines our communal life and that colleagues bear equal responsibility for that work. What the college can learn from the

---

[14] This discussion obviously draws on observations of Holy Name Province's "Refounding through Ministry." See Anthony Carrozzo, "Refounding in the Franciscan Tradition." I am a member of Siena's Refounding Team.

friars is that this work is a ministry and that community life is in itself valuable.

Collaboration and the Work of a College

Collaboration, working together, is, in a sense, a natural model for college life. Unlike a community founded in a shared faith experience, a college is a community of staff, faculty, administrators engaged in a common project. The bond among college members, including students, is that they work together. The statement has two implications.

On the one hand, all members of the college are engaged in its work. This means that the contributions of each person who works in the college are necessary if the work is to go forward. College faculty have some tendency to focus on the centrality of what they do, and there is justification for that focus: the quality of the college, the quality of college life is the direct responsibility of the faculty. They are responsible for the curriculum, for the quality of teaching, for the admission of colleagues to tenure; they share responsibility for admitting and retaining students. While they are, in theory, accountable to the academic administration and to the president, in practice, their cooperation is essential to the effective exercise of administrative authority. They are able to ignore other elements in the college, but can always call attention to themselves. In large public universities their power may be constrained by the power of outside governing bodies that control funding, but in a small, liberal arts college, and certainly at Siena, the faculty is empowered in ways that no other element of the college is. Reflection on collaboration begins within the faculty.

Francis's definition of leadership as service is fundamental here, but another, and perhaps clearer, statement of collaborative leadership is described by Clare in Chapter Six of her *Rule*. Here Clare requires the abbess to call together the sisters once a week "to consult on whatever concerns the welfare and good of the monastery."

Three aspects of Clare's provision are worth thinking about. First, the process is regular, not at the whim of the abbess, not reserved for dealing with crises. Weekly, regularly, the community comes together in consultation. Second, the consultation is preceded by a common confession of faults and failures. It is not likely, not necessarily even desirable, that a general college or parish or other meeting will include a confession of faults. But what is useful here, what may be one of the most important ingredients in the Franciscan tradition of community is the humility required to acknowledge one's own faults and the docility necessary for benefiting from public discussion of college or institutional matters. Third, even the least of the community is to be listened to. The *Rule* says that this is because God speaks even to the least member. We might extrapolate from this and say that the perspective, what is seen by or shown to, each member of the college is significant in the life of the college, of the institution.

Still considering this point that all members of the college or community are engaged in a common work, and pursuing the importance of consultative governance, we still must take another step toward collaborative governance. Consultation can mean simply listening and that is not collaboration, working together, if it remains asymmetrical. What we may call Franciscan docility requires not only listening but explaining. And this requires a spirituality, not a strategy: a fundamental respect for the other. The model here is Francis's placing himself under obedience. But that requires also that the members of the community be willing to assume responsibility, to work toward a consensus. It is easier to live in a hierarchic organization than in a consensual, collaborative community. In a hierarchy, in a community structured as *maiores-minores*, there is always the possibility of winning, of getting one's own way. In a consensual, collaborative community there are no losers so there are no winners. This requires a radical rethinking, a conversion of the heart, a spirituality. It also means that everyone has to be responsible. Respect and responsibility are coupled.

Ministry and the Work of a College

The second point at which the Franciscan tradition can form the academic community is in the definition of work as ministry rather than as accomplishment.[15] From this perspective, the academic community exists for the students. The other members of the college bind themselves to this service. Every question is to be considered in the context of the welfare of the students. Here Francis's desire to be poorer than the poorest beggar may be a useful model. To be the servant of the servants, lesser than the *minores* was his desire. Within the academic community this model of service can be carried out in at

---

[15] This distinction is analogous to the distinctions Bonaventure makes about the purposes of learning. See Zachary Hayes, "Toward a Philosophy of Education in the Spirit of St. Bonaventure," pp. 31-33.

least two ways. First, there is the expenditure of energy in one's work. This can be done generously or grudgingly. Framed in those terms, it becomes impossible to argue that the man who drew others to himself by his sweetness can be a model for a complaining service. As Julien Green comments, he whose eyes ran with tears brought with him to others a sense of peace and joy.[16]

The second way in which Francis's example can be implemented, however, is the willingness to make judgments. When one is familiar with the fuzzy, popular image of Francis as a nice guy who loved birds and lepers, it comes as a surprise to read Francis's own writings where one learns that Francis was willing to, seemed compelled to, condemn certain behaviors and to admit that someone who engaged in these behaviors would suffer punishment. The description of the fate of the unrepentant miser in the *Letter to All the Faithful* is a clear statement of this mentality. But perhaps most significant is the requirement in the *Rule* that admonition and correction should be given "humbly and charitably."[17] What does this mean in the context of the academic community? in the context of service to students? Certainly, this statement precludes certain pedagogical methods based on intimidation, certain disciplinary methods based on condemnation and ridicule. Positively, it can be read as a requirement that members of the college offer support to those who are having difficulty meeting college standards.

In a time when colleges across the country are struggling with questions raised by increasing numbers of students who are unprepared for the kind of work college students twenty years ago could handle, students who, whatever their socioeconomic background, are educationally disadvantaged, the Franciscan commitment to the *minores* is a useful tradition. The educational world talks about remediation, implying that these students fall short. The Franciscan language of service among brothers and sisters expresses a different perspective. Here, again, it is possible for friars to be examples of fraternal community with the "poor." The image of going among the poor is useful: meeting the students where they are, respecting the learning, the experiences they come to college with, and bringing them into the community as participants, community members who contribute to the community, to the college community and then to the wider community. Like those of many colleges, Siena's mission

---

[16] Julien Green, 1991: p. 226.
[17] *RegB*, ch. 10.

statement says the college empowers its students. This is one, and perhaps one of the best, way to exercise the option for the poor in twentieth-century America.

The Franciscan Tradition and the Life of a College

There is some temptation to limit consideration of the Franciscan tradition as a resource for college life to consideration of community life, to identify the Franciscan quality of the college with the sense of community, here expressed as belonging to an academic community. But there are further resources within this tradition which can bridge the space between this emphasis on the college as a community and realizing that the college is a community of learners, a community whose business is living the life of the mind. A college in the Franciscan tradition does not, however, define intellectual life as the pursuit of one's own research for one's own sake, or for the sake of advancing discipline, of knowledge.[18] Intellectual life is a spirituality, a way of looking at and being in the world, and the Franciscan intellectual life is a way of understanding the relationship between the true and the good, of identifying the meaning of the world and of human life.[19] This is the tradition which is so fittingly described as "affective knowing," and this tradition is an intellectual tradition which is fittingly lived in an academic community. At this point, the two categories we have distinguished, academic and intellectual, come back together. The academic community is a community because its members are engaged in a life of learning, that is, in intellectual life. It is possible to speak of a community of learners or of a community of teaching and learning. In each case there is a mutuality. This is not a hierarchic academic structure in which experts impart information, but a community in which some members have engaged longer than others have.

There is a rhythm to Franciscan life, a point made most recently in *The Santa Croce Program*. Without forcing the metaphor unduly, it seems possible to trace a *triple way* that is peculiarly suited to academic life, a life lived in the city, in the desert, and on the mountain.

---

[18] Hayes, "Toward a Philosophy of Education...", pp. 33-35.

[19] Guy Bougerol, *Introduction to the Works of Bonaventure*, ch. 2, "The School of the Minors in Paris," provides a useful historical perspective on the importance of "judging Aristotle by Augustine" in the Franciscan intellectual tradition.

Engagement, detachment, contemplation, engagement, there is a patterned movement from place to place that characterized the friars' life from the beginning, and that is desirable in academic life

Life in the city, life "in the public square," refers to the active teaching and learning life. It involves two dimensions. First, there must be a commitment to academic excellence in the pursuit of truth. Anything less is a disservice to students and a betrayal of the trust society vests in academic institutions, a trust now often tarnished by the frequent failure of these institutions to involve students in the pursuit of excellence.

The second dimension of living the academic life in the city is constant attention to the pursuit of the good. Identifying assumptions, clarifying value judgments are part of this project. But pursuit of the good must begin from a vision of what is good, a vision that goes beyond the pragmatic, beyond self-interest, however broadly defined. In the attempt to understand, to see what is good, one comes back to the question of truth. American academic institutions have often not come back to that question, but have engaged in moralism, in activism. The Franciscan tradition of discernment and witness provides a corrective to activism and to escapism.

The academic dimension of college life is formed by the college's responsibility to engage in the pursuit of truth and goodness and to remind, to speak to, the larger society of this pursuit. It carries out this responsibility when its members speak and write for the larger community, but the most important way it carries out this responsibility is to prepare its members to become or to continue to develop as responsible citizens. Franciscan education at its best has always been engaged, has called itself "useful" as a preparation for living the Gospel life in the world, in the city. This tradition should shape a curriculum that pulls together the questions of truth and goodness, and a pedagogy that fosters active involvement and critical thought.

Academic life has, of course, its own temptations and pitfalls. There are resources within the Franciscan tradition that can speak to these difficulties. Intellectual life, the life of the mind, is the inner life of the college, and this life can be described as the life of the spirit. Both the desert and the mountain are important refuges from the city and its temptations.

The desert here stands as a figure for ascetic life, a life of discipline and detachment. For the academic there is always the temptation to think one knows the answer, is in control. On one level, that affects community life. On another level, it affects those essential activities of pursuing the true and the good. Put another way, humility is the only appropriate stance before Truth and Goodness, as it is the only appropriate stance before the other members of the community. The way of purgation may be described as learning to be humble, realizing that one is in service to the community. It is also learning that one pursues rather than masters Truth and Goodness. The mountain stands, to continue the pattern of the triple way, as a figure for reflection and contemplation, for enlightenment. The desert and the mountain, are, of course, not two different places, and enlightenment does not come without or before humility.

What resources within this tradition shape the contemplative moment? How does the intellectual life become a Franciscan spiritual life? The first, the fundamental connection is making the connection between Goodness and Truth and the presence of the Spirit in the world. This is an implication of the Franciscan perception, shared by Francis and Bonaventure and Scotus, each of whom contributes a different perspective, that God, the Holy Mystery, has entered the world and draws close to human beings. That the central human experience is becoming aware of that presence. Neither truth nor goodness are human constructs. The life of the spirit, the life of the mind, is a matter of encounter not of creation or mastery.

Bonaventure may be taken as the master of an intellectual life which is encounter, which is discovery of truth and goodness, of the intellectual life which is a spirituality. *Reductio artium ad theologiam*, the title of a small treatise written late in his life, may be taken as a motto for Bonaventure's approach to knowledge, to intellectual life: all knowledge leads to God because all knowledge comes from God. Bonaventure's use of analogy is "dynamic," it expresses the relationship of creation to creator; but it is also the means of returning to the creator.[20]

In his *Collations on the Six Days of Creation*, left unfinished at his death, Bonaventure expresses what one translator has called "the clear and even luminous expression of the existential presence of God among men through every manifestation of being."[21] The classic expression of Bonaventure's dynamic use of analogy is, however, the work commonly called the *Itinerarium, The Soul's Journey to God*,

---

[20] Bougerol, 1964: p. 77.
[21] de Vinck, "Foreword," p. ix.

called by Bonaventure "The Vision of the Little Poor Man in the Desert." The conjunction of those two titles brings together the themes of vision or understanding and pilgrimage and poverty, an evocative conjunction considered as a resource for intellectual life and as Franciscan spirituality.[22]

Conclusion

The Franciscan tradition is rich in resources that can be brought into the world through the channel of college life, and it is a tradition that can shape college life so that higher education is not an avenue into the mainstream of American life, but a challenge to the culture. The college, like the friars, lives in the city and frames its discourse by the needs of the city. Like the friars, it must look beyond those needs for a vision of Truth and Goodness. It must move outside the city, go to the desert and mountain. Francis, Bonaventure, Scotus, and modern writers like Ewert Cousins and Zachary Hayes among others have prompted some of these reflections. The opportunity of participating in the "Refounding through Ministry" program of Holy Name Province, and of knowing friars from that province has stimulated me to think seriously about the importance of the Franciscan life of Siena. Most of all, living in a college that prizes the riches of this tradition and struggles to see what it means in academic, and intellectual life, working with friars like Michael Cusato and William McConville, has stimulated my appreciation of the Franciscan tradition as a living intellectual vision and a source of community life. This college is a resource the province can draw on in two ways: it is a place for reflection on the Franciscan tradition in a living community; and it introduces men and women into that tradition.

The toughest question is not what are the resources within this tradition, but whether the college and the friars choose to appropriate this tradition in the context of college life. And if the answer to that is yes, how?

---

[22] Examples: The centrality of Christ in the Franciscan tradition can introduce the affirmation of the sacramentality of the world, which is created in Christ's image, of the goodness, not of humanity, but of each human, as well as providing the Christocentric basis for accepting the mandate to serve, even to serve in suffering, and to carry forward the task of transforming the world. Leonard Bowman, for example, in *A Retreat with St. Bonaventure* (Rockport, Massachusetts: Element, 1993) uses *Soul's Journey* and *The Tree of Life* as avenues into consideration of the God in the world, within us, and above us, and of entry into Christ's passion and death as the means of ascent to God.

For the college the question is whether we affirm this as a tradition which has more than historical and marketing value. Enhancing the Franciscan tradition at the college is the second goal in the strategic plan. Moreover, the trustees at their December 1993 meeting agreed that the self-study being undertaken in preparation for the visit of the accrediting agent should include specific reference not only to the generic, historical importance of the Franciscan tradition, but to the ways in which the college is working to implement that commitment. The Middle States accreditation team identified the Franciscan tradition as one of the college's major strengths precisely because it gives the college a "foundation and context for its philosophy of education, its commitment to its students, and its sense of community."[23]

There is a college Franciscan tradition committee which is charged with this responsibility. This committee, appointed by and accountable to the president, comprises members from virtually every unit of the college and deliberately focuses on what the Franciscan tradition means in the current sociological state of the college community, a community diverse in so many ways. The committee has faced and set aside the "slippery question" of uniqueness to deal with the historical reality that this is the tradition we acknowledge and intend to carry forward. Our charge is to articulate that tradition and to call attention to it in the everyday life of the college.

The formation of friars in the resources of this tradition in the context of academic and intellectual life would seem at least as vexed as the formation of college members. Is there a commitment in the province to maintaining a significant presence in its two institutions of higher learning? What does that mean? How are real decisions made on this question, specifically, in what way are the institutions involved in the decision? If there is such a commitment, how can the process of formation go forward? On the one hand, and this seems to be well recognized, members of a college must have the requisite professional expertise. But that expertise will not necessarily take place in an environment that fosters a Franciscan intellectual and academic spirituality. Nor will Franciscan formation necessarily include attention to the resources that are most useful for intellectual and academic life.

---

[23] "Report to ... Siena College," p. 6.

This essay addresses theoretical and practical questions in the specific context of one Franciscan college: What are the resources within the Franciscan tradition that can shape academic life because they enrich community life and intellectual life? What is the real advantage to the friars of undertaking this ministry? How does this ministry enhance their service in the world and in the church?

How can the college foster the presence of friars from Holy Name Province at the college, or more concretely, how can the college and the province arrive at a common understanding of personnel needs and opportunities? How can Holy Name Province, with fewer friars and many calls for their ministerial presence, sustain a corporate commitment to a ministry that often requires extensive, expensive preparation?

In the larger world of Holy Name Province, these questions may ask how the friars shape the life of a community in its active and contemplative dimensions as witnesses to the gospel, rather than as owners of the institution. For the college these questions ask how the college maintains fidelity to a tradition while shaping a vital identity and presence in the world. In both cases, these are questions that enrich the community in their asking.

REFERENCES

Bougerol, J. Guy, *Introduction to the Works of Bonaventure*, translated by Jose de Vinck. Paterson, New Jersey: St. Anthony Guild Press, 1964.

Bowman, Leonard, *A Retreat with St. Bonaventure*. Rockport, Massachusetts: Element Press, 1993.

Carrozzo, Anthony, *Refounding in the Franciscan Tradition*. Spirit and Life 5 (1994), *passim*.

de Vinck, Jose, "Foreword." *The Works of Bonaventure*, Vol. V. *Collations on the Six Days*. Paterson, New Jersey: St. Anthony Guild Press, 1970.

de Vitry, Jacques, "Letter 1." *St. Francis of Assisi: Omnibus of Sources*, edited by Marion Habig. Chicago: Franciscan Herald Press, 1983. p. 1608.

Dreyer, Elizabeth, "Reclaiming Affectivity in the Liberal Arts Curriculum: Medieval Franciscan Sources." *Liberal Education: Crisis and Franciscan Response*. Papers delivered at Siena College, March 19, 1988. Edited by James Dalton.

Green, Julien, *Frère François*. Paris: Editions du Seuil, édition illustré, 1991.

Hayes, Zachary, O.F.M., "Reflections on a Franciscan University." Spirit and Life, Vol. II, 1992, pp. 96-109.

————, "Toward a Philosophy of Education in the Spirit of Bonaventure," pp. 18-37 in Spirit and Life, 2, (1992).

McConville, William, O.F.M., "Franciscan Tradition, the Liberal Arts College and Society." *Liberal Education: Crisis and Franciscan Response*. Papers delivered at Siena College, March 19, 1988. Edited by James Dalton. Reprinted pp. 129-142 in Spirit and Life 2 (1992).

Schreiter, Robert. *Reconciliation: Mission and Ministry in a Changing Social Order*. Maryknoll, New York: Orbis Books, 1992.

Short, William, "Shapers of the Tradition: From Bonaventure to Scotus." pp. 45-58 in Spirit and Life 2 (1992).